# 1989
# GREEN
# COIN
# BOOK

# 1989 GREEN COIN BOOK

## Eighteenth Edition

A complete, illustrated catalog of U.S. coins
and bills and their cash premium values
from 1652 to the present
and
The complete coinage of Canada and Nowfoundland
from 1858 to date

### BY ROBERT FRIEDBERG
### EDITED BY ARTHUR L. AND IRA S. FRIEDBERG

Associate Editor: Arthur S. Goldenberg

Bell Publishing Company
New York

This 1989 edition is published by Bell Publishing Company, distributed by Crown Publishers, Inc., 225 Park Avenue South, New York, New York 10003 by arrangement with Mr. Arthur L. Friedberg and Mr. Ira S. Friedberg.

Originally published as *The Green Coin Book Appraising and Selling Your Coins*

Printed and Bound in the United States of America


ISBN 0-517-66980-3
h g f e d c b a

# CONTENTS

# A Note from the Publishers

The cash premium values in this book are published for the information and guidance of all concerned—for those who have coins for sale as well as for those who want a complete reference work on the market value of coins and currency.

**The valuations listed do not indicate retail prices, but instead, closely approximate how much established coin dealers will actually pay for any material needed in their stock. The valuations are based on the coins being in Good to Very Good condition, unless otherwise noted. Coins in better condition are worth more.**

The editors are professional coin dealers. Anyone interested in either buying or selling coins and paper money may contact them at the following address: The Coin & Currency Institute, Inc., P.O. Box 1057, Clifton, NJ 07014. When shipping coins, be sure to use insured or registered mail.

Since silver and gold have risen to their current levels, the values of many coins are based on their precious metal content. Most coin dealers are paying a premium over face value for any and all of these silver coins regardless of date or condition; in many cases, even uncirculated coins are not worth more than their melt value. For the purpose of this book, silver has been calculated at $7.50 per ounce, and gold at $425.00 per ounce. Therefore, all dimes, quarters and half dollars which are valued at $.45, $1.15 and $2.25 respectively, and many United States gold coins, fluctuate in relation to the commodity price of silver and gold and their actual premium value will vary accordingly.

Because of this, the cash premium values of Silver coins, dollars, Commemorative Half Dollars, Proof & Mint sets and gold coins are subject to fluctuation.

Do not clean or polish any coins! They will lose a great deal of their premium value if you do. Coins should be left in the same condition as when found, no matter how dark they may appear.

## The American Eagles

These coins were approved by Congress and first released by the mint in the fall of 1986. Although each coin bears a denomination, the uncirculated versions are bought and sold strictly on the basis of their gold or silver content and bullion prices at the time of the transaction. The proof versions were intended for collectors and were sold by the mint at a premium over bullion content.

### Type: Silver Eagle

| Denom | Date | Unc | Proof |
|---|---|---|---|
| 1 Dollar | 1986 | 10.00 | 20.00 |
| 1 Dollar | 1987 | 5.00 | 17.00 |

### Type: Gold Eagle

| | | | |
|---|---|---|---|
| 5 Dollars (1/10 oz) | 1986 | 35.00 | none |
| | 1987 | 35.00 | none |
| 10 Dollars (1/4 oz) | 1986 | 100.00 | none |
| | 1987 | 100.00 | none |
| 25 Dollars (1/2 oz) | 1986 | 200.00 | none |
| | 1987 | 200.00 | none |
| 50 Dollars (1 oz) | 1986 | 415.00 | 470.00 |
| | 1987 | 415.00 | 500.00 |

## *Preface*

At some time or another almost all of us acquire or come across some coins or old pieces of paper money which excite our curiosity or otherwise hold our interest. What is it about these coins that has thus captured our attention? It may have been the strangeness of denomination (a copper 2 Cent piece or a nickel 3 Cent piece or a silver Half Dime or a 3 Dollar gold piece); it may have been antiquity (a large Cent of 1794 or a Colonial Copper of 1694); or the surprise of discovering for yourself an untoward bit of information (that we once used a 15 Cent piece of paper money that was, and still is, legal tender); it may have been sheer, compelling intrinsic value (any gold coin) or immediate negotiable value (an old large size 5 Dollar bill); or it may have been the historical associations evoked by the coins (the Battle of Gettysburg, the exploits of Daniel Boone, the Landing of the Pilgrims, the discovery of America itself); or perhaps it was the glittering beauty of perfection (a set of current coins in brilliant proof condition, or a single older coin so finely preserved that it assumed the status of a gem in your mind).

No matter which quality it has been, or what circumstance introduced you to the coins, you have held them in your hand, you have scrutinized them (perhaps under a magnifying glass), you have conjured with them in your imagination, and after the first flush of recognition has passed and the pride of ownership has asserted itself, one question, one unknown factor still remains unanswered for you—how much are these coins worth? It is at this point that for you

**THE SEARCH FOR RARE COINS**

has begun, a pursuit, or pastime, if you will, indulged in passionately by millions of us for pleasure or for profit. That your coins are worth more than their face value, there is somehow no doubt in your mind. You have been conditioned to believe it, or at the least, to hope it, by the larger and larger amounts of rare coin publicity in recent years.

A boy, rummaging around among his grandmother's effects, finds an 1856 Flying Eagle Cent and sells it to a coin dealer for several hundred dollars; the story is picked up by a news association and is carried in the daily press from coast to coast—or the Treasury Department throws into circulation through the banking system several million silver dollars (as it did in the mid-1960's)—coins which had lain in the vaults for a generation, undisturbed, still in bright, newly minted condition and containing many dates considered rare. The story is headlined in a great eastern daily and almost at once the switchboard of a leading coin dealer is clogged with thousands of incoming phone calls—urgent inquiries from both buyers and sellers—or a banker leaves a map with his will, leading to a hoard of gold coins buried on his estate. The government seizes the coins, you read about it, you hear about it, and you wait to see if the heirs will ever get the coins. The story has a happy ending; they do. The government says that all gold coins may be freely bought and sold or otherwise traded in.

On the other hand, you may have heard some tales about coins that are not quite authentic. You cannot find a 1913 Liberty Head Nickel, because only five pieces were minted and all are accounted for in known collections; and the likelihood of finding an 1804 Silver Dollar or a 5 Dollar gold piece of 1822, or a Brasher Doubloon challenges the laws of probability; no U.S. coin has ever been called in because of a defect in the design; the Columbian Half Dollar of 1892 is *not* worth $10,000.00, as was once mistakenly reported.

The so-called fabulous coins do, of course, exist, but they are not easily to be found or had. The great rarities of U.S. coinage—the pieces that bring many hundreds of dollars—were recognized as rare and valuable almost immediately after striking and they have been jealously guarded ever since by the intelligent, well-informed and alert collectors in each generation. Therefore, if one does come across an 1827 Quarter, or an 1838-O Half-Dollar, or an 1804 Silver Dollar; if you should have a 3 Dollar gold piece of 1875 or a 4 Dollar gold piece of 1880 or a 5 Dollar gold piece of 1815, then it is most likely that these coins were originally purchased as rare collectors items for large sums of money, and have come from a highly regarded coin collection, rather than from the accumulated small change of bygone days.

But instead of a few dozen legendary pieces, we still have the main output of U.S. coinage for our field of activity, containing, as it does, multitudes of coins with cash premium values ranging from the modest to the substantial. It is the search for, and the recognition of these coins that is occupying so many millions of Americans today, for pleasure as a pastime or for business as a profession. It is for them and for you that this volume has been created, and in our attempt to make it the finest and most useful coin book of its kind in existence it has of necessity become

## A COMPLETE CATALOGUE OF U.S. COINS

from 1652 to date, including the pre-revolutionary Colonial coinage as well as the Pioneer gold coinage struck after the California gold rush at the various Territorial Mints.

We have thus accounted for all the "hard money" that has ever been issued in this country; but what of our paper money? The first U.S. Government notes were issued in 1861 and since then many rare and valuable notes have been produced, including some of quite recent years. These are just as much sought after and collected as are coins and for many years now currency for collectors has assumed an importance equal to that of coins.

We have therefore decided to present the subject of American monetary issues in its entirety and accordingly you will find in this book, as an adjunct to the coin listing, a companion catalogue of

## ALL TYPES AND SERIES OF U.S. PAPER MONEY

## ALL TYPES OF CONFEDERATE PAPER MONEY

from 1861 to the present day and including (a) the early large size notes, (b) the later or present size notes, (c) Fractional Currency issues—the 3, 5, 10, 15, 25 and 50 Cent notes which circulated as U.S. paper money in the 1860's and 1870's, and which are still legal tender, (d) Confederate Money from the 50 Cent note to the 1000 Dollar note.

The tabular arrangement used in cataloguing the paper money has been designed for efficient use and the information given is both concise and complete, so that even without illustrations, you will be able to locate and identify any note without any confusion.

The concluding section of this book is devoted to the coinage of our neighbors to the north, with whom we share such a long common border. As with the U.S. coinage, we have aimed for thorough coverage and in these pages you will also find a complete catalogue of

## THE COINS OF CANADA AND NEWFOUNDLAND

together with those of New Brunswick, Nova Scotia, Prince Edward Island and British Columbia. The Canadian series begins in 1858 when the first, true coins on the Dollar or Decimal standard were issued.

The inclusion of the Canadian series in this catalogue is not an afterthought but is rather dictated by the existing necessity for this information, since the Canadian issues rank next in popularity to U.S. coins. Canadian coins are now considered as important as our domestic coins, and in some sections of the country they form the major part of numismatic activity. A glance at the catalogue will reveal many coins with high premium values and an active interest in the coinage of British North America can prove to be a rewarding experience.

With the inclusion of the Canadian series in this volume the publishers believe this to be

## A UNIQUE BOOK

in the annals of numismatic literature, since never before has so much varied and useful information been offered in a single, low-priced, convenient book. For example, until now there has never been a listing in the same book of the premium values of paper money together with coins. The premium books of the past have rarely had listings with any completeness of both Colonial coins and Pioneer gold coins.

It is thus believed that by the proper reference to this book, one should be able to evaluate any coin of American origin, any type of U.S. or Confederate paper money and any coin in the British North American series.

It is important at this point to attempt an answer to the question

## WHAT MAKES A COIN VALUABLE?

a perplexing and sometimes vexing question. At the outset let it be said that mere age alone has nothing to do with establishing the value of a coin. Many persons mistakenly regard the figure 100 with especial reverence, thinking that the age of 100 years or more automatically confers a special value on a coin. This is simply not so, as an analysis of the coin valuations will reveal. For example, the 1794 Cent commands a premium of $30.00, but the 1914-D Cent brings $32.00. A bronze coin of ancient Greece from about 350 B.C. can be bought for about $20.00; a silver coin of Rome from about 200 A.D. for about $40.00; an English Shilling of Queen Elizabeth dated 1587 for about $15.00—and so on— yet a *1932-D Quarter—only 57 years old at the present writing has a premium value of $20.00.*

There are actually three factors which combine to determine the cash premium value of any coin, namely, rarity, demand and condition. The first of these

## RARITY

is the most important, since without rarity, the other two factors are only of minor significance. A coin becomes rare out of various circumstances; it may be struck in much fewer numbers than is normal for a contemporary coin of that type (witness the 1877 Cent, the 1931-S Cent, the 1885 Nickel, the 1916-D Dime, the 1901-S Quarter); or it may be a coin of a type struck in only one year (witness the 1793 Half-Cent, the 1796 Quarter, the 1808 Quarter Eagle, the 1907 Double Eagle with Roman numerals); or it may be a coin struck in relatively large numbers for the period but of which only a very few have survived (witness the 1802 Half-Dime, the 1873-CC Dime, the 1876-CC 20 Cent piece, the 1822 Half-Eagle); or it may be one of the fabled pieces of which so few were struck to begin with that it became a great rarity on the day of minting (witness the 1913 Liberty Head Nickel, the 1894-S Dime, the 1804 Silver dollar, the 1885 Trade dollar, any proof coin before 1858); or, as is also likely, the rarity may be determined by the condition of the coin. In these days when millions of collectors are competing for and buying up the choicest specimens, coins which may be very common in used or circulated condition have become quite rare in new or uncirculated condition (witness the entire series of 10, 25 and 50 cent pieces from 1892 to 1933, all Liberty Head nickels, most Indian Head cents, early Lincoln cents with mint marks, etc.). In fact almost any uncirculated coin before about 1930 is now considered scarce in one degree or another.

Assuming then that a given coin is of some rarity, another factor that determines its value is

## DEMAND

which is both judge and jury and your only true indicator of the coin's popularity in the numismatic market place. No matter how rare a coin may be, it cannot be easily sold for a price commensurate with its rarity, unless there is a demand for it by collectors. This demand manifests itself to the professional coin dealer through his customers. Repeated requests for a coin not in his stock automatically create a demand for that coin, and if he wishes to stay in business, he must sooner or later buy it. The ultimate demand is thus created by the ultimate consumer, the collector himself, but the large amounts of cash that support the numismatic market are furnished by the professional coin dealers, who thus perform an essential service for both seller and buyer.

It is obvious that all coins cannot be equally in demand at all times; that is why so many coins appear to have a value disproportionately high or low in relation to their rarity. As mentioned above, demand, and hence value, is created by the mass of collectors who are subject to all sorts of collecting impulses. Hence there are fashions, changes of taste and recurrent cycles in coin collecting, as there are in other cultural pursuits. One year Roosevelt Dimes may be the rage; the next year Franklin Half-Dollars; then it may be Proof Sets or Commemoratives or rolls of coins.

But out of all the welter of intense numismatic activity, one trend remains constant through the years—the lower the denomination of the coin, the greater the demand. Hence the King of American coins is the Cent. There are millions more who collect cents—Lincoln and Indian—than any other coins; many more who collect dimes than quarters; many more who collect silver dollars than 5 dollar gold pieces; and many more who collect 20 dollar gold pieces than 50 Dollar bills.

One example selected out of many will show how demand is uncompromising and inexorable in determining coin values. The 1914-D Lincoln cent with a coinage of 1,193,000 pieces has a listed premium value of $32.00, but the 1914-S Quarter with a much smaller coinage of 264,000 pieces lists at only $6.50; compare both with the Cent of 1814—a hundred years earlier—which has a coinage of 357,800 pieces and a listed value of $13.00. Obviously, the 1914-D Cent will tend to keep increasing in value, whereas the other two coins will tend to remain about as they are—unless there is a radical change in collecting habits.

An analysis of the material in this book will reveal much interesting and some surprising data about our coins and their values. Fortunately for numismatics, there are now so many collectors clamoring for all types of coins and there is so much nationwide interest in coin and currency collecting, that one will find a ready sale for almost any American coin, providing always, of course, that it is in suitable

## CONDITION

for collecting purposes, since condition, or the state of preservation, is the third factor that helps determine the value of a coin.

Regarded purely as objects of the past (a Greek urn, a Flemish tapestry, a Colt firearm), coins are desired by collectors in the finest condition in which they can be found, within a given price range. Some can afford the finest pieces, others only the average ones. Perhaps this love of new, beautiful coins goes back to our childhood. How pleased we were to be given a new, shiny coin in our change and how reluctant we were to spend it! The true collector among us did not spend it but put it away—if he could afford it—and when found again many years later, it would still be in new condition and by then it would have gained something else—numismatic value.

In this respect a new coin can be likened to a beautiful woman in the full bloom of her youth—lustrous, desirable and admired by all; but as she circulates through the days and years of her life, subtle changes occur in her appearance and after a certain length of time she bears little resemblance to the thing she once was; only her identity is the same; but if only she were the Sleeping Beauty of the fable, she would be found one hundred years later, still lustrous, desirable and admired by all. Coins have become the true sleeping beauties of our generation and there are many such waiting to be restored to life by the diligent prince charmings who will discover them in their "piggy" banks, attics, family souvenirs, bank vaults, or among long-forgotton, unused possessions.

The condition of a very rare coin is not so important a factor in value as it is of a more common coin. The rare piece would be valuable in its own right and the difference in value between the best and poorest condition would not be too great. Some series of coins tend to exist in choice condition, others in poor condition. For example, most gold coins exist in well preserved, brilliant condition and there is not much difference in value between an average used piece and a new one. (From about $2,000.00 to $10,000.00 for the 5 Dollar gold piece of 1795.) Early Large Cents, on the other hand, exist mostly in quite worn condition and new pieces are very rare indeed (from about $55.00 to $1,000.00 for the Large Cent of 1795). Among the more modern coins for example the

1927-S Quarter in average used condition has a premium listing of only $4.00 but a new or uncirculated specimen can easily be sold for $1500.00 because it is so very rare in this choice condition. Similarly, from used to new, the 1926-S Nickel ranges from $2.75 to about $400.00, the 1921 Half-Dollar from $22.50 to about $2,000.00; the 1927-D Dime from $1.00 to about $250.00. But the 1909-S-VDB Cent, which is a rare coin in any condition, has a narrow range of values, and a used piece brings about $125.00, a new piece about $350.00.

It is thus evident that condition is intimately tied to rarity and hence to demand, and it is these three factors operating together in various proportions that determine the price at which a coin can be sold at a given time in a given place.

The condition of a coin is usually denoted by a degree of fineness. (Please note that the numismatic meaning of the word "fine" is quite different from its literary meaning, as will be seen below.) The standard terms used in grading the condition of coins, their abbreviations, and what the terms mean are as follows:—

*PROOF or PR.* The ultimate condition of coins, since proof coins are struck purely for collectors and not for circulation. The greatest care is lavished in their production so that they will emerge as supreme examples of the art of coinage. A premium over face value has always been charged by the Mint for its proof coins. The coins are struck from scientifically polished dies and metal blanks, and the resultant proof coins are easily recognized by their unusual brilliance. They shine like no other coins you have ever seen, because the surface of a proof coin is like that of a spotless mirror. You can actually see yourself in one of these coins.

*UNCIRCULATED or UNC.* This denotes a coin in new or unused condition and Unc. coins are usually in the same brilliant condition as when they left the mint. That shiny coin you sometimes get from your bank is considered an Unc. coin if you are the first person to whom this coin has been paid out in the normal course of coin distribution from government mint to local bank via the Federal Reserve System. As soon as you have put your finger marks on the coin and let it jingle in your pocket with other coins for any length of time, it is no longer considered Unc. in the true sense of the word.

*EXTREMELY FINE or EF.* This denotes a coin which has been in circulation so little, that it shows only the slightest sign of wear or use. For the most part, an EF coin still retains the lustre or mint bloom of an

Unc. piece. Actually many EF coins are truly Unc. pieces which have been poorly handled through the years, so that they now show slight friction, minor abrasions or other unimportant blemishes.

*VERY FINE or VF.* A coin described as VF will generally have been in circulation a relatively short time. It will certainly show evidence of use such as loss of lustre, wear on the highest struck portions, and a proportionate amount of small surface markings which, however, do not detract from the over-all choiceness of true VF quality. Every detail of lettering and design that was originally impressed into the coin will be boldly visible. In general, a coin taken out of your change at random, that is from one to two years old, will tend to be in VF condition.

*FINE or F.* A fine coin has begun to show signs of more obvious circulation and can best be recognized by the letters and numerals appearing on it. By now they have become somewhat thick and blurry from the constant soft friction of circulation. All of the larger letters will be fully visible but the smaller ones may have begun to fade in a coin rated as fine. If the coin is silver, the reeding or milling on the edge will have begun to lose its character, and is approaching the point when it will vanish from the coin altogether, leaving it with a smooth edge. A truly fine coin makes an overall pleasing impression on the eye, as the amount of circulation is nicely and evenly distributed over its entire surface, but is still not severe enough to give the coin a shopworn appearance.

*VERY GOOD and GOOD or VG and G.* These two terms are all-embracing in scope because they accurately describe the condition of most of the millions of non-current coins now in existence. (By non-current we mean all types of coins except those presently being struck.) These terms are used singly as VG and G or sometimes together as G-VG. Coins in either of these two conditions (between which there is only a minor difference in value) are the general, run-of-the-mill, circu-lated coins found everywhere. They have spent long, faithful years in the service of ther country and they look it. The reason so very many of our older type coins are found in this condition is that there were few coin collectors in the old days. Consequently most coins got into circulation and stayed there for many years, passing routinely into the government melting pot or casually into a private holding.

G and VG coins present a well-worn appearance and are in a more advanced state of circulation than fine coins. Most of the larger letters will have shrunk somewhat from the creeping paralysis of circulation, moving from the outer edge of the coin to the center. The smaller lettering may have disappeared altogether, such as the word "Liberty" which appears on the head band of a Liberty-head coin or on an Indian Head Cent. But such coins are still recognizable for what they are; you can easily read the date, the denomination, the main legends and the mint mark, if any. Just as they are the most common, so are they the most widely collected, because they represent decent, collectible coins at moderate prices, the appeal thus being to the great mass of collectors.

**In this book, for example, the valuations are based on the coins being in G-VG condition, except as noted elsewhere in the catalogue proper.**

*FAIR and POOR.* These two terms (no standard abbreviations) are used for coins in the lowest possible condition. Such coins are so badly worn or have such defects, that they are barely recognizable and hence are called "space fillers." They will do in a collection simply because better ones cannot be found or may cost too much. Only very rare coins would command a premium in fair or good condition. Such coins might be a 1793 Half-Cent or Cent, a 1794 Dollar, or 1796 Half-cent, Quarter, or Half-Dollar, etc. Fair and poor coins present an appearance which some have described as miserable. Most of the design and lettering are gone and so little remains on the coin that sometimes only experienced numismatic deduction can properly attribute it.

Sometimes coins will be found that cannot properly be described by any of the above conditions because they have been mutilated in various ways or are false. **Such coins are of no numismatic value and command no premium.** If genuine, they are worth only their face amount, but if a hole has been drilled into any coin it has lost even its face value, since the government will not redeem such a coin. Some of these various mutilations, defects or deceptions are described as follows:—

*HOLED.* A coin with a hole drilled completely through it.

*PLUGGED HOLE.* A holed coin in which the hole has been filled in with some metal to reduce the ugliness of the coin.

*LOOPED.* A coin with a loop attached to the edge by solder, enabling it to be attached to a chain. This is most common in gold coins.

*LOOP REMOVED.* A coin from which a loop has been removed by breaking or sawing it off. The edge of the coin will usually reveal evidence of a former loop.

*GILDED.* Any coin which has been gold plated.

*NAMES and INITIALS.* These will sometimes be found scratched, engraved or stamped on coins. Only in the case of a great rarity would a coin thus mutilated command a premium.

*ELECTROTYPE.* A false coin made by making impressions of a genuine coin on a thin shell of the same metal. The Obv. and Rev. are on different shells, which are then joined after filling them with a cheap alloy to give them weight. A thin line running around the edge will usually identify an electrotype, as well as the fact that it will not have the true ring of a genuine coin.

*CAST.* A false coin made by making a cast from a genuine coin. Casts can generally be identified by a rough, mottled surface.

*ALTERED DATE.* A false coin made by changing the date on a genuine coin to another date of much greater rarity and value. Some altered date coins are very difficult to detect and hence dangerous, bearing in mind that the coin itself is genuine. A strong magnifier will generally discover this deception.

*MINT MARK ADDED OR REMOVED.* Similar in principle to altered date coins, but in this case, the mint mark, not the date, has been tampered with. A mint mark may be added to a coin or removed from it, in order to make it more valuable. As with altered date coins, a strong magnifier should be used on a suspected piece.

*POLISHED COINS.* Although not mutilated, coins which have been polished to a high shine by cleaning powders, polishing creams, or other abrasives lose a great deal of their premium value, even if in otherwise choice condition. Coins should be left in the same state of preservation as when found, and no attempt should be made to clean or polish them, no matter how dirty they may appear.

## TOKENS—CALIFORNIA GOLD PIECES

Sometimes copper or nickel pieces will be found which appear to be U.S. coins and yet cannot be located in this book, which is complete insofar as U.S. coinage is concerned. Such pieces will no doubt turn out to be privately struck tokens of the 19th century. Enormous amounts of these were made during the late 1830's and early 1860's. In both cases the tokens were issued to relieve shortages of small change and they actually circulated as 1 Cent pieces; the early pieces being the size of large Cents and called "Hard Times Tokens"; the later pieces being the size of small Cents and called "Civil War Cents." Such tokens generally have a cash premium value of from $1.00 to $2.00 each.

Other coins which appear to be U.S. pieces are the so-called California gold coins. Like the tokens described above, they are not really coins but private issues; in neither case were they struck under authority of the U.S. Government, nor did they emanate from any government mint.

These California gold pieces—also called charms—exist in denominations of ¼, ½ and 1 Dollar; they may be round or they may be octagonal in shape; they are quite tiny and very thin and they may, or may not, be of gold; some of them have been restruck in recent years.

They were first made in the middle of the 19th Century, ostensibly to augment the gold coins then in circulation out west. It is doubtful if they ever served that purpose, because their minute size and insubstantial weight must have made them impossible to handle with any assurance of safety.

Those pieces are considered to be the original issues which are struck in genuine gold and have the word, "Dollar" or "Dol" as part of the denomination. In this case they have a value ranging from about $25.00 to $50.00 Any other pieces are worth considerably less.

## APPRAISING AND SELLING YOUR COINS

If you have any U.S. coins or currency for sale or any Canadian coins, it would be prudent to acquaint yourself with the contents of this book, so that you can be better informed and be guided accordingly.

This book has been so prepared that by proper reference to the catalogue section as well as to this Preface and to the General Information which follows, you will be able to appraise your coins yourself and estimate their cash value with a fair degree of accuracy. The following points should be borne in mind when appraising and selling your coins:—

*PRICE.* **The cash premium values in this book reflect the approximate prices that established, professional coin dealers will pay for material. These values, which are averages, have been arrived at by a careful study of many years duration of market conditions and buying trends from coast to coast. Since the valuations are averages, the price actually offered may vary from the published values.**

*SUPPLY.* Sometimes a dealer will not wish to buy certain coins—even high-premium pieces—because he has an ample supply of them at the time of offer. In this respect he is like any other merchant who has to exercise a certain amount of inventory control to keep him from getting unhealthily overstocked in any one item.

*DEMAND.* On the other hand, if your coins are popular issues and continually in demand, the dealer will be tempted to buy them even though he has an ample stock. In this case, he is taking a calculated risk, based on his experiences and judgment, and he is gambling either that the demand will continue strong or that the coins will enhance in value.

*RARITY.* In general, the higher the premium value of the coin, the easier it will be to sell. A coin with a value very much above its face value, or very much above the average for that type, will tend to be a scarce coin in short supply and hence in demand.

*CONDITION.* The values in this book are based on the condition in which the coins are most frequently found, namely, good to very good, as has been proven by experience. If your coins are in much choicer condition they will command a higher price than listed; if in inferior condition either a lower price, or no premium at all, will prevail. In some cases, as will be noted in the catalogue, the valuations are for uncirculated or proof specimens. In the case of all gold coins the valuations are for specimens in choice, well preserved condition, ranging from extremely fine to uncirculated.

*CLEANING.* As noted earlier, coins should be left in the same condition as when found. No attmept should be made to alter their appearance by cleaning or polishing.

*COIN DEALERS.* Coins and currency should be offered to professional coin dealers established in a regular place of business. For a list of the coin dealers in any community, consult the local classified telephone directory under the heading "Coin Dealers," or those Sunday newspapers that have a Stamp and Coin section and carry the advertising of coin dealers. The material you have may be brought to them in person or it may be shipped in for their inspection and offer, or a list of it may be sent by mail to see if they are interested.

## MINT AND MINT MARKS—ABBREVIATIONS

The capital letters you will see after certain dates represent mint marks. They appear in this manner: 1853-O, 1878-S, 1890-CC, etc. The actual spot on the coin where the mint mark may be found is indicated clearly in the catalogue, before the listing of each type of coin. The letters and the mints they represent are as follows (please remember that coins struck at the Philadelphia mint do not have a mint mark except as noted below):—

C—Charlotte, N.C. On gold coins only from 1838-1861.

CC—Carson City, Nev. On gold and silver coins from 1870-1893.

D—Dahlonega, Ga. On gold coins only from 1838-1861.

D—Denver, Colo. On all coins from 1906-1964, 1968 to date.

O—New Orleans, La. On gold and silver coins from 1838-1909.

P—Philadelphia, Pa. On nickels from 1942-1945. On Anthony dollars from 1979 to date. On nickels, dimes, quarters and half dollars from 1980 to date.

S—San Francisco, Calif. On all coins from 1854-1955, 1968 to date.

W—West Point, N.Y. On the $10.00 1984 Olympic commemoratives, and the $5.00 1986 Statue of Liberty commemorative.

## CANADIAN ISSUES

H—Heaton Mint in Birmingham, England.

C—Ottawa Mint in Canada.

No mint mark—Before 1908, London and after 1908, Ottawa.

Abbreviations for the condition of coins are given under the heading "Condition" (see above). Other abbreviations used are:

OBV.—Obverse or the "head" side of a coin.

REV.—Reverse or the "tail" side of a coin.

ARR.—Arrows, as on certain silver coins from 1853-1855 and 1873-1874.

In the General Information, which follows, you will find important data on various coins.

## *GENERAL INFORMATION*

(Notes and comments on various coins, giving more specific or detailed information than is to be found in the catalogue proper.)

## COLONIAL AND STATE COINAGE

Many of these coins are so rare, that forgeries have been created. There are various types of these forgeries, such as electrotypes, casts and struck copies. The last type is especially difficult to recognize since the forged piece is struck from an actual die manufactured for that purpose. In general, any very rare Colonial coin in really first class condition should be suspected of being a forgery or other type of facsimile, and all such pieces should be authenticated.

*CAROLINA ELEPHANT TOKEN COINAGE.* A very rare variety has the spelling "Proprieters." Forgeries exist.

*CONNECTICUT.* Higley Token Coinage. Forgeries exist. There is also a unique variety in which a wheel appears on the Rev. In the State Coinage, there are very many minor varieties in the appearance of the bust and in the spelling of the legends.

*MARYLAND.* Forgeries exist of the Lord Baltimore Penny, which is a very rare coin. The head on the 3 Pence piece of Standish Barry is reputed to be that of Washington. This coin has the date as "July 4, 90."

*MASSACHUSETTS.* Forgeries exist of the NE coinage and of the Oak Tree and Pine Tree issues. In the State Coinage there is a rare variety of the 1787 Cent in which the eagle holds the bundle of arrows in the right talon, rather than in the left one.

*NEW ENGLAND COINAGE.* The Elephant Half Penny of 1694 is similar in design to the Carolina Half Penny of 1694. The New England piece, however, is extremely rare and forgeries exist.

*NEW HAMPSHIRE.* Forgeries are known of the 1776 Cent.

*NEW JERSEY.* The St. Patrick coins, sometimes attributed to New Jersey, will be found in Part Two, since they bear nothing on them to identify them with New Jersey. A scarce variety of the 1788 Cent shows the horse's head facing to the left.

*NEW YORK.* Forgeries exist of the Cents of Gov. Clinton, of the "Non VI..." type, of the Indian type and of the Excelsior type. A unique specimen is known of a New York Cent which shows the head of George III on one side and a standing Indian on the other. There are several varieties of the 1787 Cent with laureate male bust. These varieties are called "Nova Eboracs" (New Yorks). The bust may differ in size or the seated figure may face either to right or left.

*UNITED STATES OF AMERICA.* The 1792 coinage of the U.S. Mint has traditionally been catalogued with Colonial Coins, the whole forming the subject of Early American Coins. The 1792 coins were experimental and all are very rare and seldom met with, except for the Half Disme. Regular U.S. coinage began in 1793. (The illustration of the 1792 Cent with silver center does not show the silver center.)

On the other hand, the Fugio Cents of 1787 were the first coins issued under the authority of the United States Government and were reportedly struck at New Haven. These actually circulated and are far commoner than the 1792 issues.

*CONFEDERATIO COINAGE.* Forgeries exist of the 1785 Cent.

*THE CONTINENTAL DOLLAR.* On some varieties, the word is spelled as "Curency." Forgeries and imitations are known.

*NOVA CONSTELLATIO—IMMUNE COLUMBIA COINAGE.* The "U.S." that appears on the Rev. of the 1783-1786 Cents may be either in block letters or in a script monogram. On some varieties the word is spelled as "Constelatio." Forgeries are known of the 1785 Cents inscribed "Immune Columbia."

*THE TRIANGLE TOKEN.* This piece has sometimes been called a Kentucky Cent, only because "K" appears at the top of the triangle of 15 rosettes, each bearing an initial of one of the 15 states. Otherwise, this coin does not bear the name of a specific colony.

*GEORGE WASHINGTON COINS AND TOKENS.* Forgeries are known of most valuable pieces including the 1792 Half Dollars.

## UNITED STATES COINS

*HALF CENTS.* Various type forgeries are known of 1793 and 1796 and electrotype forgeries mainly of 1831, 1836, 1852, and 1840-1848 inclusive.

1797. A rare variety has lettering on the edge.

1808. A scarce variety shows the last 8 struck over a 7.

*LARGE CENTS.* 1793. All three major varieties of this date have been forged, mainly by electrotyping. "America" on the Chain type sometimes appears as "Ameri"; the wreath type has either lettering on the edge or vines and bars, and there is an extremely rare variety with a strawberry sprig under the head rather than a 3-leaf sprig.

1797. A scarce variety has a stemless wreath on the Rev.

1798. A scarce variety has the Rev. typical of 1796 Cents.

1799. This coin has been extensively forged by altering the date of another Large Cent of similar type to read 1799.

1801. A scarce variety has three errors in the design; there is but one stem to the wreath; the fraction appears as 1/000 and "United" as "IInited."

1804. This coin too has been forged by altering the date of another coin.

1815. Cents have been struck in every year from 1793 to date except 1815. In order to maintain an unbroken continuity of years, some collectors have altered other cents to read "1815." An 1815 Cent is therefore a fantasy created by self-delusion.

1839. A rare variety shows the 9 struck over a 6.

*FLYING EAGLE CENTS.* 1856. More forgeries must exist of this date than of any other U.S. coin. Most of these forgeries are altered dates, which are clearly visible under a strong magnifier; 1858 Cents have been used most often for this alteration, the last 8 being converted into a 6.

*INDIAN HEAD CENTS.* 1864-L. The L appears as a quite small letter at the end of the ribbon as it trails off the feather head dress on the Indian head.

*LINCOLN HEAD CENTS.* 1909-VDB. The VDB appears as three small letters at the extreme bottom of the Rev. They indicate the initials of the designer, Mr. Victor D. Brenner.

1914-D. This coin has recently been forged by alteration. A "D" has been added to a plain 1914 Cent or a D mint marked coin ending in a 4 has been changed to 1914.

*2 CENT PIECES.* 1864 Small Motto. This refers to "In God We Trust." The quickest way to distinguish the small letters in the motto from the large ones in the Large Motto type is to look at the letter D in God. In the Small Motto the D is quite rounded; in the large motto it is narrow and oval.

*BUFFALO NICKELS.* A scarce variety of 1918-D shows the 8 struck over a 7. The 3-legged buffalo of 1937-D shows the buffalo standing on only three legs, the result of a die defect obliterating the fourth leg.

*HALF DIMES.* 1796. A rare variety shows the 6 struck over the 5 of 1795.

1872-S. The mint mark may be either within or below the wreath.

*DIMES.* 1811. All coins are struck over 1809.

1823. All coins are struck over 1822.

1824. All coins are struck over 1822.

1873-CC. Only one specimen is known without arrows at the date.

1875. The S and CC mint marks may be either within or below the wreath.

1942/1. A scarce variety exists on which the 2 is struck over the 1 of 1941.

*QUARTERS.* 1822. A rare variety shows the 25c on the Rev. struck over 50c.

1823. All coins are struck over 1822.

1825. All coins are struck over other dates.

1828. A rare variety shows the 25c struck over 50c.

1842. A rare variety has a small date and exists in proof condition only.

1853/2. All coins are struck over 1852, and are without arrows. This coin has been forged by changing the last 8 of an 1858 into a 3.

1918-S/17. A scarce variety shows the 8 struck over the 7 of a 1917-S.

*HALF DOLLARS.* 1795. A rare variety shows a stem with three leaves, rather than two, on the upper part of the branch under each wing of the eagle.

1805-1836. Coins of these years are rich in varieties. There are overdates, small and large dates, small and large letters, etc.

1842-O. A rare variety exists with the date much smaller in size.

1846. A rare variety shows the 6 struck over another 6 at right angles to it.

1846-O. A scarce variety shows the date in much taller numerals.

1847. A rare variety shows the 7 struck over the 6 of an 1846.

1853-O without arrows or rays. This great rarity has been forged by altering the last 8 of an 1858-O to a 3.

1917. The mint marks may appear on the Obv. under the motto or on the Rev. to the left of "Half Dollar."

*SILVER DOLLARS.* 1797. A rare variety has the Rev. legend in smaller letters with a 9 × 7 arrangement of the stars on the Obv.

1895. This rare coin, which exists in proof condition only, has been forged by removing the mint marks on an 1895-O or 1895-S.

## UNITED STATES PROOF SETS

The prices of proof sets are subject to some very sudden changes, either upward or downward. This is caused by the private accumulation of large amounts of sets and the resultant speculation therein.

### U.S. SILVER COMMEMORATIVE COINS

*GRANT 1922\*.* This coin has been forged by adding a star to an ordinary Grant Half Dollar. All Grant coins with star should be authenticated.

*BOONE, 1934-1938.* The small 1934 appears on all issues beginning with 1935. It will be found to the right of the standing figure on the Rev.

## U.S. GOLD COMMEMORATIVE COINS

*LEWIS AND CLARK ISSUE.* The Gold Dollars of this issue tended to be used as jewelry. All specimens should be examined for evidence of loop removed or solder remains.

## UNITED STATES GOLD COINS

*1 DOLLAR.* A minor variety appears in the 1849 coinage. The wreath on the Rev. may form a full circle or an open circle.

*2½ DOLLARS.* 1802. All coins are struck over 1801.

1806. All coins are struck over 1804 or 1805.

1824. All coins are struck over 1821.

1826. All coins are struck over 1825.

1841. This coin has been forged by removing the mint marks from 1841-C or 1841-D coins.

1854-S. This coin has been forged by adding an S mint mark to an 1854 coin of the Philadelphia Mint.

1863. This coin exists in proof condition only, but forgeries have been made by removing the S from 1863-S coins.

*3 DOLLARS.* 1873 and 1878. These dates should always be looked at under a magnifier. Many persons have accidentally misread these dates because the 3 and the 8 tend to look similar at first glance.

*4 DOLLARS.* These pieces should always be authenticated as being of gold. Genuine specimens struck from these dies in minor metals as patterns, have sometimes been gold plated as a deception or as an act of self-delusion.

*5 DOLLARS.* 1795, 1797 and 1798. These three dates each exist in two distinct types; please see the catalogue for proper attribution.

1802. All coins are struck over 1801.

1803. All coins are struck over 1802.

1825. All coins are struck over 1821 or 1824.

1807 and 1834. These two dates each exist in two distinct types.

1854-S. This very rare coin should always be verified as not being an 1854 Philadelphia coin to which an S has later been added.

1887. This coin was struck only in proof condition but forgeries have been made by removing the S mint mark from an 1887-S.

1909-O. This coin should be carefully examined to verify that the mint mark is genuine, or if genuine, that the O is not being mis-read for a D, since these mint marks are usually quite weak.

*10 DOLLARS.* 1797. This date exists in two distinct types.

1858. Forgeries have been created by removing the mint marks from 1858-O or 1858-S coins.

1907, 1908. These dates exist in more than one distinct type.

*20 DOLLARS.* 1861 and 1861-S. Each of these two coins exists as a great rarity when the Rev. design is the Paquet type. This type can be identified by the much taller letters in the legend.

1907, 1908. These dates exist in more than one distinct type.

All rare coins of the Philadelphia Mint should be examined for evidence of removed mint marks.

Rare date issues of the period 1908-1932 are subject to sudden price changes, as large amounts tend to be found unexpectedly from time to time.

In recent years, counterfeit coins, struck in gold, have appeared in all denominations, rare as well as common dates.

## PIONEER GOLD COINS

The valuations are for coins in average VG-F condition. Really choice pieces are very rare and would command higher prices. If several varieties exist of a given coin, the valuation is for the commonest one.

*NORRIS, GRIEG & NORRIS.* A 5 Dollar piece has recently been discovered issued at Stockton rather than San Francisco.

*TEMPLETON REID.* The only known specimen of the 25 Dollar piece of 1849 was stolen in 1858 from the U.S. Mint collection and has never been recovered.

## UNITED STATES PAPER MONEY
## CONFEDERATE PAPER MONEY

**The valuations given for the large size notes and Fractional Currency are for specimens in presentable, used condition (fine to very fine) and not giving a dirty, shopworn appearance.** Notes which are torn, thin from use, very badly wrinkled or generally unattractive, would command a smaller premium than listed or none at all, since currency is collected mainly for the beauty and eye appeal inherent in well preserved specimens. Notes which are in new or unused condition would naturally be purchased at higher prices than listed.

**Small size or present day notes, on the other hand, are valued in new condition only.** Since the notes are recent and more readily available, they are not generally wanted in used condition.

Those who are interested in a fully illustrated book on U.S. paper money are referred to the standard work on this subject, "Paper Money of the United States" by Robert Friedberg. This complete and definitive volume illustrates front and back of every type of paper money ever issued from the 3 Cent note to the 10,000 Dollar note and from the first year of issue in 1861 to the present day. In addition, all varieties of seals and signatures are listed with collectors' valuations. "Paper Money of the United States" is available at almost any coin dealer or you may write for information to the publishers of this book.

There are many varieties of currency, formed by differences in the seals, signatures, series letters, etc., and in all cases, the valuations are for the commoner varieties.

## THE COINAGE OF BRITISH NORTH AMERICA

This series begins with the Canadian issues of 1858, which were the first true coins based on the Canadian Dollar consisting of 100 Cents. Prior to 1858, the coinage in use consisted of a miscellaneous variety of copper tokens based on the English Pound. There are hundreds of varieties of these Penny and Half Penny tokens, most of them of only small value (from about .10 to .50) and they are omitted from this book because they are not considered as coins.

Following the introduction of Canadian coins in 1858, the first coins of Newfoundland were issued in 1865, and of Nova Scotia and New Brunswick in 1861. The only issue of Prince Edward Island was a 1 Cent piece in 1871 and of British Columbia a 10 and 20 Dollar gold piece in 1862. These gold coins, however, were not placed in circulation because of opposition from England.

**As with the U.S. coins, the valuations for Canadian coins are based on G-VG condition except where otherwise stated.**

In 1936 a small dot was placed under the date on some of the 1, 10 and 25 Cent pieces struck in that year. 25 Cent pieces with the dot are somewhat scarce, but the 1 and 10 Cent pieces are very rare.

The maple leaf on part of the 1947 coinage of all denominations may be found as a quite small symbol to the immediate right of the date.

*CANADIAN COIN VARIETIES.* There are some variations from the normal among certain Canadian coins, making them of greater scarcity and value. The most important varieties follow.

1 Cent 1859. Struck over 1858.

1 Cent 1891. With a smaller date than normal.

1 Cent 1936. With dot below date.

5 Cents 1858. With a larger date than normal.

5 Cents 1900. With round O's in date rather than oval.

5 Cents 1902-H. With a smaller H mint mark than normal.

5 Cents 1921. Not a variety but very rare as a coin because most of the 2½ million struck were melted down rather than issued.

10 Cents 1893. With the top part of the 3 rounded rather than flat.

10 Cents 1913. With larger leaves on the Rev. than normal.

10 Cents 1936. With dot below date.

25 Cents 1936. WIth dot below the wreath under date.

50 Cents 1921. Like the 5 Cents 1921, not a variety but very rare as a coin because most were melted down.

50 Cents 1946. With part of the design extending into the 6.

50 Cents 1947. With maple leaf and a curved 7 pointing to the right, rather than a straight 7 pointing to the left.

1 Dollar 1947. With a pointed 7 rather than a blunt 7 in the date.

# Colonial and State Coinage

## (1652–1792)
### *PART ONE*

Coins and tokens issued by or for specific colonies or states. These pieces bear either a state name or a device that identifies the state. The valuations below are for coins in used or circulated condition. Bent and holed coins are worthless.

Collectors should be aware that many of the following pieces exist as casts and electrotypes. These are also worthless.

### CAROLINA ELEPHANT TOKEN COINAGE

*Elephant. Rev. "GOD PRESERVE CAROLINA AND THE LORDS PROPRIETORS 1694," Copper.*

Half Penny 1694 . . . . . . . . . . . . . . . . . . . . . . . . . . . . . . . . . . . . . . . . . . . . . . . . . . . . . . 550.00

### CONNECTICUT
### *Higley Token Coinage*

*Deer standing. Rev. Three axes. Copper.*

3 Pence 1737 . . . . . . . . . . . . . . . . . . . . . . . . . . . . . . . . . . . . . . . . . . . . . . . . . . . . . . .2,500.00

*Deer standing. Rev. One large axe. Copper.*

3 Pence. No date, 1739 . . . . . . . . . . . . . . . . . . . . . . . . . . . . . . . . . . . . . . . . **3,500.00**

## State Coinage

*Laureate bust facing right or left. Rev. Female seated. Copper.*

1 Cent 1785, 1786, 1787, 1788 . . . . . . . . . . . . . . . . . . . . . . . . . . . . . . . . . . .**18.00**

## KENTUCKY

### Myddelton Token Coinage

*Liberty stretching hand out to two children. Rev. Female seated with shield.*

1 Cent 1796. Struck in copper . . . . . . . . . . . . . . . . . . . . . . . . . . . . . . . . . . . **3,200.00**
1 Cent 1796. Struck in silver . . . . . . . . . . . . . . . . . . . . . . . . . . . . . . . . . . . . **2,500.00**

# MARYLAND

## *Cecil Calvert (Lord Baltimore) Coinage*

*Head of Lord Baltimore. Rev. Crowned shield and Roman numeral. Silver.*

1 Shilling. No date (1658) . . . . . . . . . . . . . . . . . . . . . . . . . . . . . . . . . . . . . . . . . **600.00**
6 Pence. No date (1658) . . . . . . . . . . . . . . . . . . . . . . . . . . . . . . . . . . . . . . . . . . .**500.00**
4 Pence. No date (1658) . . . . . . . . . . . . . . . . . . . . . . . . . . . . . . . . . . . . . . . . . . . **550.00**

*Head of Lord Baltimore. Rev. Two flags over crown. Copper.*

1 Penny (Denarium). No date (1658) . . . . . . . . . . . . . . . . . . . . . . . . . . . . . . . . . . **Very Rare**

## *Annapolis Token Coinage of John Chalmers*

*Clasped hands in wreath. Rev. Two birds and snake within circle. Silver.*

1 Shilling 1783 . . . . . . . . . . . . . . . . . . . . . . . . . . . . . . . . . . . . . . . . . . . . . . . . . . . . . **200.00**

*Clasped hands. Rev. Circle of rings. Silver.*

1 Shilling 1783 . . . . . . . . . . . . . . . . . . . . . . . . . . . . . . . . . . . . . . . . . . . . . . . . . . **Very Rare**

*Long cross. Rev. Wreath. Silver.*

6 Pence 1783 ................................................................ **350.00**

*Clasped hands. Rev. Plant in wreath. Silver.*

3 Pence 1783 ................................................................ **275.00**

## Baltimore Token Coinage of Standish Barry

*Large male head. Rev. Name and value. Silver.*

3 Pence 1790 ................................................................ **1,250.00**

# MASSACHUSETTS

## NE (New England) Coinage

*NE at top, the rest blank. Rev. Roman numeral for value at top,*
*the rest blank. Silver.*

1 Shilling. No date (1652) ................................................. **2,000.00**
6 Pence. No date (1652) ................................................... —
3 Pence. No date (1652) ................................................... —

## Willow Tree Coinage

*A willow tree. Rev. Date and Roman numeral for the value. Silver.*

| | |
|---|---:|
| 1 Shilling 1652 ........................................................ | **1,500.00** |
| 6 Pence 1652 ........................................................ | — |
| 3 Pence 1652 ........................................................ | — |

## Oak Tree Coinage

*An oak tree. Rev. Date and Roman numeral for the value. Silver.*

| | |
|---|---:|
| 1 Shilling 1652 ........................................................ | **150.00** |
| 6 Pence 1652 ........................................................ | **150.00** |
| 3 Pence 1652 ........................................................ | **125.00** |
| 2 Pence 1662 ........................................................ | **100.00** |

## Pine Tree Coinage

*A pine tree. Rev. Date and Roman numeral for the value. Silver.*

| | |
|---|---:|
| 1 Shilling 1652. Large size ........................................... | **125.00** |
| 1 Shilling 1652. Small size ........................................... | **110.00** |
| 6 Pence 1652 ........................................................ | **100.00** |
| 3 Pence 1652 ........................................................ | **90.00** |

## State Coinage

*Pine tree. Rev. Female seated on globe. Copper.*
1 Cent 1776 . . . . . . . . . . . . . . . . . . . . . . . . . . . . . . . . . . . . . . . . . . . . . . . . . . **Unique**

*Three heads in Janiform position. Rev. Female seated on globe. Copper.*
Half Penny 1776 . . . . . . . . . . . . . . . . . . . . . . . . . . . . . . . . . . . . . . . . . . . . . **Unique**

*Indian standing. Rev. Spread eagle. Copper.*
1 Cent 1787, 1788 . . . . . . . . . . . . . . . . . . . . . . . . . . . . . . . . . . . . . . . . . . . . . **15.00**
Half Cent 1787, 1788 . . . . . . . . . . . . . . . . . . . . . . . . . . . . . . . . . . . . . . . . . . **17.50**

## NEW ENGLAND COINAGE

### Elephant Token Coinage

*Elephant. Rev. "GOD PRESERVE NEW ENGLAND 1694." Copper.*
Half Penny 1694 . . . . . . . . . . . . . . . . . . . . . . . . . . . . . . . . . . . . . . . . . . . . . **Very Rare**

## *Lion Token Coinage*

*Two lions facing in opposite directions. Rev. "NEW ENGLAND." Copper.*
Token coin. No date (1675) ............................................... **700.00**

## NEW HAMPSHIRE

*Pine tree. Rev. Harp. Copper.*
1 Cent 1776 ............................................................ **3,500.00**

## *NEW JERSEY*

## NEW JERSEY

*Horse's head and plow with date below plow. Rev. Shield. Copper.*
1 Cent 1786, 1787, 1788 ............................................... **12.00**

*Horse's head and plow with date to right of plow. Rev. Shield. Copper.*
1 Cent 1786 . . . . . . . . . . . . . . . . . . . . . . . . . . . . . . . . . . . . . . . . . . . . . . . . . . . . . . . . . **20.00**

*Head of Washington. Rev. Spread eagle. Copper.*
1 Cent. No date (1786) . . . . . . . . . . . . . . . . . . . . . . . . . . . . . . . . . . . . . . . . . . . . . . . . ——

*Head of Washington. Rev. Shield. Copper.*
1 Cent. No date (1786) . . . . . . . . . . . . . . . . . . . . . . . . . . . . . . . . . . . . . . . . . . . . . . . . ——

*Liberty holding scales, "Immunis Columbia." Rev. Shield. Copper.*
1 Cent 1786 . . . . . . . . . . . . . . . . . . . . . . . . . . . . . . . . . . . . . . . . . . . . . . . . . . . . . . . ——

*Spread eagle. Rev. Shield. Copper.*
1 Cent 1786 . . . . . . . . . . . . . . . . . . . . . . . . . . . . . . . . . . . . . . . . . . . . . . . . . . . . . . . ——

## NEW YORK

### *State Copper Coinage*

*Bust of Gov. Clinton. Rev. Shield supported by two figures.*
1 Cent 1787 . . . . . . . . . . . . . . . . . . . . . . . . . . . . . . . . . . . . . . . . . . . . . . . . . . . . **2,000.00**

*Laureate male bust. Rev. Female seated to right or left.*

1 Cent 1787 . . . . . . . . . . . . . . . . . . . . . . . . . . . . . . . . . . . . . . . . . . . . . . . . . . . . . **25.00**

*Armored bust, "NON VI VIRTUTE VICI." Rev. Liberty holding scales.*

1 Cent 1786 . . . . . . . . . . . . . . . . . . . . . . . . . . . . . . . . . . . . . . . . . . . . . . . . . . . . **1,000.00**

*Liberty holding scales, "IMMUNIS COLUMBIA." Rev. Eagle.*

1 Cent 1787 . . . . . . . . . . . . . . . . . . . . . . . . . . . . . . . . . . . . . . . . . . . . . . . . . . . . . **100.00**

*Indian standing. Rev. Eagle on globe.*

1 Cent 1787 . . . . . . . . . . . . . . . . . . . . . . . . . . . . . . . . . . . . . . . . . . . . . . . . . . . **1,500.00**

*Indian standing. Rev. Shield supported by two figures.*

1 Cent 1787 . . . . . . . . . . . . . . . . . . . . . . . . . . . . . . . . . . . . . . . . . . . . . . . . . . . . **1,500.00**

*Shield supported by two figures. Rev. Eagle. The EXCELSIOR cent.*

1 Cent 1787 . . . . . . . . . . . . . . . . . . . . . . . . . . . . . . . . . . . . . . . . . . . . . . . . . . . . **300.00**

## *Miscellaneous Token Coinage*
## *New Yorke in America Token*

*Spread eagle. Rev. Two figures under palm tree.*

Brass token. No date (1700) . . . . . . . . . . . . . . . . . . . . . . . . . . . . . . . . . . . . . . . . **1,000.00**

## *The Mott Token*

*Large clock. Rev. Eagle. Copper.*
Token 1 Cent 1789 . . . . . . . . . . . . . . . . . . . . . . . . . . . . . . . . . . . . . . . . . . . . . . . . . . . . . **35.00**

## Talbot, Allum & Lee Token

*Liberty standing. Rev. Ship. Copper.*
1 Cent 1794, 1795 . . . . . . . . . . . . . . . . . . . . . . . . . . . . . . . . . . . . . . . . . . . . . . . . . **14.00**

## RHODE ISLAND

*Admiral Howe's flagship. Rev. Group of ships.*
Copper token 1778, 1779 . . . . . . . . . . . . . . . . . . . . . . . . . . . . . . . . . . . . . . . . . **250.00**

## UNITED STATES OF AMERICA

## FUGIO CENT COINAGE

*Sundial, radiate sun above, and "MIND YOUR BUSINESS" below.*
*Rev. Circular chain of thirteen links.*
1 Cent 1787 . . . . . . . . . . . . . . . . . . . . . . . . . . . . . . . . . . . . . . . . . . . . . . . . . . . . . **30.00**

**38**

## EARLY MINT ISSUES

*Liberty head. Rev. Flying eagle.*

1 Disme 1792. Silver ....................................................... ——
1 Disme 1792. Copper ..................................................... ——
Half Disme 1792. Silver ................................................... **700.00**

*Liberty head. Rev. Wreath. With silver center plug.*

1 Cent 1792 .............................................................. **Rare**

*Liberty head. Rev. Wreath. The so called Birch Cent, and much
larger than the above cent.*

1 Cent 1792 .............................................................. **Very Rare**

## U.S.A. BAR CENT

*Monogram of USA. Rev. Thirteen bars. Copper.*
1 Cent. No date (1785) ................................................. **175.00**

## VERMONT

*Hills over plow. Rev. Radiate eye. Copper.*
1 Cent 1785, 1786 ......................................................... **45.00**

*Male bust. Rev. Seated female, "IMMUNE COLUMBIA." Copper.*
1 Cent 1785 ............................................................. **600.00**

*Male bust to right or left. Rev. Seated female. Copper.*
1 Cent 1786, 1787, 1788 .................................................. **45.00**

## VIRGINIA

### *Gloucester Token Coinage*

*Building. Rev. Star. Brass.*
1 Shilling 1714 ......................................................... **Very Rare**

### *English Royal Coinage*

*Head of George III. Rev. Arms and date.*

1 Shilling 1774. Silver . . . . . . . . . . . . . . . . . . . . . . . . . . . . . . . . . . . . . . . . . . . **Very Rare**
1 Penny 1773. Copper . . . . . . . . . . . . . . . . . . . . . . . . . . . . . . . . . . . . . . . . . . . . **Rare**
Half penny 1773. Copper . . . . . . . . . . . . . . . . . . . . . . . . . . . . . . . . . . . . . . . . . 15.00

## *PART ONE*

Coins and tokens issued for general use in early America and not inscribed with the name of any specific colony or state.

## AUCTORI PLEBIS TOKEN COINAGE

*Male bust, "AUCTORI PLEBIS." Rev. Seated female. Copper.*

1 Cent 1787 . . . . . . . . . . . . . . . . . . . . . . . . . . . . . . . . . . . . . . . . . . . . . . . . . . . . . 20.00

## CONFEDERATIO COINAGE

*Figure at pedestal holding bow and arrow. Rev. Thirteen stars in radiate circle. Copper.*

1 Cent 1785 . . . . . . . . . . . . . . . . . . . . . . . . . . . . . . . . . . . . . . . . . . . . . . . . . . . . . **Rare**

## THE CONTINENTAL DOLLAR

*Sundial with radiate sun above. Rev. The names of the thirteen states
inscribed on the links of a circular chain. Many copies exist.*

1 Dollar 1776. Struck in pewter .......................................... **500.00**
1 Dollar 1776. Struck in brass ............................................ —
1 Dollar 1776. Struck in silver .................................................. ——

## GEORGE III—IMMUNE COLUMBIA COINAGE

*Head of George III. Rev. Liberty holding scales "IMMUNE COLUMBIA." Copper.*
1 Cent 1785 ..................................................................., **700.00**

## GEORGIUS TRIUMPHO TOKEN COINAGE

*Laureate male head. Rev. Liberty standing behind screen of thirteen bars. Copper.*
1 Cent token 1783 .......................................................... **20.00**

## NORTH AMERICAN TOKEN

*Seated female (Hibernia). Rev. Ship. Copper.*

Token coin 1781 . . . . . . . . . . . . . . . . . . . . . . . . . . . . . . . . . . . . . . . . . . . . . . **10.00**

## NOVA CONSTELLATIO—IMMUNE COLUMBIA COINAGE

*Radiate eye. Rev. "U.S." in wreath. Copper.*
*(The U.S. in either block or script letters)*

1 Cent 1783, 1785, 1786 . . . . . . . . . . . . . . . . . . . . . . . . . . . . . . . . . . . . . . . . **20.00**

*Radiate eye. Rev. Liberty holding scales, "IMMUNE COLUMBIA."*

1 Cent 1785. Copper . . . . . . . . . . . . . . . . . . . . . . . . . . . . . . . . . . . . . . . . . . . **Rare**
1 Cent 1785. Struck in silver . . . . . . . . . . . . . . . . . . . . . . . . . . . . . . . . . . . . . —

## PITT TOKEN COINAGE

*Bust of William Pitt. Rev. Ship and "AMERICA." Copper.*

Half penny 1766 . . . . . . . . . . . . . . . . . . . . . . . . . . . . . . . . . . . . . . . . . . . . . . . . **60.00**
1 Farthing 1766 . . . . . . . . . . . . . . . . . . . . . . . . . . . . . . . . . . . . . . . . . . . . . . . . **—**

## PLANTATION TOKEN COINAGE

*Horseman and titles of James II of England. Rev. Four shields. Pewter. (This token is sometimes attributed to Florida, but was used in many colonies.)*

1/24th Part Real 1688 . . . . . . . . . . . . . . . . . . . . . . . . . . . . . . . . . . . . . . . . . . . . **50.00**

## ST. PATRICK COINAGE OF MARK NEWBY

(Used Mainly in New Jersey)

*St. Patrick standing before throng. Rev. Crowned figure playing harp.*

Half Penny. No date (1678). Copper . . . . . . . . . . . . . . . . . . . . . . . . . . . . . . . . . . . . **65.00**

*St. Patrick holding cross, snakes in foreground. Rev. Crowned figure playing harp.*

1 Farthing. No date (1678). Copper . . . . . . . . . . . . . . . . . . . . . . . . . . . . . . . . . . . . **35.00**
1 Farthing. Same but struck in silver . . . . . . . . . . . . . . . . . . . . . . . . . . . . . . . . . . . **300.00**

## THE TRIANGLE TOKEN

*Hand holding scroll. Rev. Triangle formed by fifteen stars, each bearing
the initial of a state. K for Kentucky is at top. Copper.*

1 Cent. No date (1792) ...................................................... **25.00**

## VOCE POPULI—HIBERNIA COINAGE

*Male bust. Rev. Seated female and "HIBERNIA." Copper.*

Half Penny 1760 ........................................................... **10.00**
1 Farthing 1760 ........................................................... **40.00**

## WOOD'S COINAGE—HIBERNIA TYPE

*Head of George I. Rev. Seated female with harp. Copper.*

Half Penny 1722, 1723, 1724 ............................................. **15.00**
1 Farthing 1722, 1723, 1724 ............................................. **15.00**

## WOOD'S COINAGE—ROSA AMERICANA TYPE

*Head of George I. Rev. Rose. Copper.*

2 Pence 1722, 1723 or no date . . . . . . . . . . . . . . . . . . . . . . . . . . . . . . . . . . . . . . . **45.00**
1 Penny 1722, 1723 . . . . . . . . . . . . . . . . . . . . . . . . . . . . . . . . . . . . . . . . . . . . . . . **35.00**
Half Penny 1722, 1723 . . . . . . . . . . . . . . . . . . . . . . . . . . . . . . . . . . . . . . . . . . . . . **35.00**

## PART THREE

## GEORGE WASHINGTON COINS AND TOKENS

(All are copper except the Half Dollars of 1792)

*Obv: Military bust. "WASHINGTON & INDEPENDENCE."*
*Rev: Liberty seated. "UNITED STATES."*

1 Cent 1783 . . . . . . . . . . . . . . . . . . . . . . . . . . . . . . . . . . . . . . . . . . . . . . . . . . . . . . **15.00**

*Obv: Head. "WASHINGTON & INDEPENDENCE."*
*Rev: Liberty seated. "UNITED STATES."*

1 Cent 1783 . . . . . . . . . . . . . . . . . . . . . . . . . . . . . . . . . . . . . . . . . . . . . . . . . . . . . . **15.00**

*Obv: Head. "WASHINGTON & INDEPENDENCE."*
*Rev: Wreath. "UNITY STATES OF AMERICA."*

1 Cent 1783 . . . . . . . . . . . . . . . . . . . . . . . . . . . . . . . . . . . . . . . . . . . . . . . . . . . . . . **20.00**

*Obv: Military bust. "WASHINGTON."*
*Rev: Same bust. "ONE CENT."*

1 Cent. No date (1783) ........................................................ **25.00**

*Obv: Bust. "WASHINGTON PRESIDENT."*
*Rev: Large or small eagle. "ONE CENT."*

1 Cent 1791 ................................................................ **60.00**

*Obv: Bust. "WASHINGTON PRESIDENT."*
*Rev: Ship. "LIVERPOOL HALFPENNY."*

Half Penny 1791 ........................................................... **300.00**

*Obv: Bust. "WASHINGTON PRESIDENT."*
*Rev: Large spread eagle. No legend.*

1 Cent 1792 ............................................................ **Rare**

*Obv: Laureate Roman-type head to right. "WASHINGTON PRESIDENT."*
*Rev: Eagle. "CENT."*

1 Cent 1792 ............................................................ **Rare**

*Obv: Bust. "WASHINGTON PRESIDENT."*
*Rev: In ten lines, "GENERAL OF THE AMERICAN ARMIES 1775.*
*RESIGNED 1788. PRESIDENT OF THE UNITED STATES 1789."*

1 Cent 1792 ............................................................ **Rare**

*Obv: Bust. "GEO. WASHINGTON BORN VIRGINIA FEBRUARY 11, 1732."*
*Rev: In ten lines, "GENERAL OF THE AMERICAN ARMIES 1775.*
*RESIGNED 1788. PRESIDENT OF THE UNITED STATES 1789."*

1 Cent. No date (1792) ........................................... **650.00**

*Obv: Bust. "G. WASHINGTON PRESIDENT."*
*Rev: Small eagle, stars above. "UNITED STATES OF AMERICA."*

Half Dollar 1792. Struck in silver ........................................... ——
Half Dollar 1792. Struck in copper .......................................... ——
Half Dollar 1792. Struck in silver. Similar to above but Rev. has
    larger eagle and is without stars ...................................... ——

*Obv: Bust. "WASHINGTON PRESIDENT."*
*Rev: Ship. "HALFPENNY."*

Half Penny 1793 ............................................................... **25.00**

*Obv: Bust right. "GEORGE WASHINGTON."*
*Rev: Eagle over shield. "LIBERTY AND SECURITY 1795."*

1 Penny 1795 ................................................................. **200.00**
Half penny 1795 .............................................................. **50.00**

*Obv: Bust left. "GEORGE WASHINGTON."*
*Rev: Eagle over shield. "LIBERTY AND SECURITY."*

1 Penny. No date (1795) ....................................................... **75.00**

*Obv: Bust. "G. WASHINGTON FIRST FRIEND TO PEACE...."*
*Rev: Grate, legend around edge and "LONDON 1795."*
1 Cent 1795. The Grate Cent ............................................... **40.00**

*Obv: Bust. "GEORGE WASHINGTON."*
*Rev: Circle of fifteen stars. "SUCCESS TO THE UNITED STATES."*
Success Token. No date (1795). Large size .................................. **50.00**
Success Token. As above but small size .................................... **50.00**

*Obv: Bust. "GEORGIUS WASHINGTON."*
*Rev: Crowned harp. "NORTH WALES."*
Half Penny. No date (1795) ................................................ **50.00**

---

The valuations listed in this book closely approximate how much established coin dealers will pay for any material needed in their stock.

# United States Coins
## (Complete from 1793 to date)

### HALF CENTS

**Type: Liberty head with cap facing left.**

| Date | Amount Minted | Value | Date | Amount Minted | Value |
|------|---------------|-------|------|---------------|-------|
| 1793 | 31,900 | **700.00** | | | |

**Type: Liberty head with cap facing right.**

| Date | Amount Minted | Value | Date | Amount Minted | Value |
|------|---------------|-------|------|---------------|-------|
| 1794 | 81,600 | **100.00** | 1796 | 115,500 | **1,000.00** |
| 1795 | 25,600 | **80.00** | 1797 | 107,000 | **80.00** |

**Type: Draped bust of Liberty.**

| Date | Amount Minted | Value | Date | Amount Minted | Value |
|------|---------------|-------|------|---------------|-------|
| 1800 | 211,500 | **10.00** | 1805 | 814,500 | **10.00** |
| 1802 | 14,400 | **90.00** | 1806 | 356,000 | **10.00** |
| 1803 | 97,900 | **10.00** | 1807 | 476,000 | **10.00** |
| 1804 | 1 million | **10.00** | 1808 | 400,000 | **10.00** |

# Half Cents (continued)

**51**

## Type: *Liberty head in turban.*

| Date | Amount Minted | Value | Date | Amount Minted | Value |
|------|--------------|-------|------|--------------|-------|
| 1809 | 1¼ million | 9.00 | 1831 Proof Only | 2,200 | **4,000.00** |
| 1810 | 215,000 | 17.00 | 1832 | 154,000 | 9.00 |
| 1811 | 63,100 | 40.00 | 1833 | 120,000 | 9.00 |
| 1825 | 63,000 | 9.00 | 1834 | 141,000 | 9.00 |
| 1826 | 234,000 | 9.00 | 1835 | 398,000 | 9.00 |
| 1828 | 606,000 | 9.00 | 1836 Proof Only | —— | **2,750.00** |
| 1829 | 487,000 | 9.00 | | | |

## Type: *Liberty head with braided hair.*

| Date | Amount Minted | Value | Date | Amount Minted | Value |
|------|--------------|-------|------|--------------|-------|
| 1840 | | 1,500.00 | 1849 | 39,900 | 14.00 |
| 1841 | | 1,500.00 | 1850 | 39,800 | 13.00 |
| 1842 | | 1,500.00 | 1851 | 147,700 | 13.00 |
| 1843 | Only proofs were | 1,500.00 | 1852 | Proof only | 1,300.00 |
| 1844 | struck of these coins. | 1,500.00 | 1853 | 129,700 | 13.00 |
| 1845 | The exact quantities | 1,500.00 | 1854 | 55,400 | 13.00 |
| 1846 | minted are not known. | 1,500.00 | 1855 | 56,500 | 13.00 |
| 1847 | | 1,500.00 | 1856 | 40,400 | 13.00 |
| 1848 | | 1,500.00 | 1857 | 35,200 | 16.00 |
| 1849 | | 1,500.00 | | | |

*(The valuations in this book are based on the coins being in G-VG condition, unless otherwise noted.)*

# LARGE CENTS

## Type: Liberty head with close flowing hair; chain on Rev.

| Date | Amount Minted | Value | Date | Amount Minted | Value |
|------|---------------|-------|------|---------------|-------|
| 1793 | — | 950.00 | | (About 224,000 were coined of all types of 1793 cents) | |

## Type: Liberty head with loose flowing hair; wreath on Rev.

| | | | | | |
|------|---|---|------|------|---|
| 1793 | | 425.00 | | (See above) | |

## Type: Liberty head with cap.

| Date | Amount Minted | Value | Date | Amount Minted | Value |
|------|---------------|-------|------|---------------|-------|
| 1793 | (See above) | 600.00 | 1795 | 82,000 | 55.00 |
| 1794 | 918,500 | 30.00 | 1796 | Part of 974,700 | 65.00 |

## Type: Draped bust of Liberty.

| Date | Amount Minted | Value | Date | Amount Minted | Value |
|------|---------------|-------|------|---------------|-------|
| 1796 | Part of 974,700 | **35.00** | 1802 | 3½ million | **10.00** |
| 1797 | 897,500 | **16.00** | 1803 | 2½ million | **11.00** |
| 1798 | 979,700 | **15.00** | 1804 | 756,800 | **150.00** |
| 1799 | 904,600 | **300.00** | 1805 | 941,100 | **11.00** |
| 1800 | 2¾ million | **12.00** | 1806 | 348,000 | **15.00** |
| 1801 | 1⅓ million | **12.00** | 1807 | 727,200 | **11.00** |

## Type: Liberty head in turban.

| Date | Amount Minted | Value | Date | Amount Minted | Value |
|------|---------------|-------|------|---------------|-------|
| 1808 | 1 million | **13.00** | 1812 | 1 million | **13.00** |
| 1809 | 222,900 | **35.00** | 1813 | 418,000 | **17.50** |
| 1810 | 1½ million | **13.00** | 1814 | 357,800 | **13.00** |
| 1811 | 218,000 | **17.50** | | | |

## Type: Liberty head in coronet.

| Date | Amount Minted | Value | Date | Amount Minted | Value |
|------|---------------|-------|------|---------------|-------|
| 1816 | 2¾ million | **4.00** | 1818 | 3¼ million | **2.75** |
| 1817 | 4 million | **2.75** | 1819 | 2⅔ million | **2.75** |

| Date | Amount Minted | Value | Date | Amount Minted | Value |
|------|---------------|-------|------|---------------|-------|
| 1820 | 4½ million | 2.75 | 1830 | 1¾ million | 2.75 |
| 1821 | 389,000 | 8.00 | 1831 | 3⅓ million | 2.75 |
| 1822 | 2 million | 2.75 | 1832 | 2⅓ million | 2.75 |
| 1823 | 855,700 | 15.00 | 1833 | 2¾ million | 2.50 |
| 1824 | 1½ million | 2.75 | 1834 | 2 million | 2.75 |
| 1825 | 1½ million | 2.75 | 1835 | Part of 4 million | 2.50 |
| 1826 | 1½ million | 2.75 | 1836 | 2 million | 2.50 |
| 1827 | 2⅓ million | 2.75 | 1837 | 5½ million | 2.50 |
| 1828 | 2¼ million | 2.75 | 1838 | 6⅓ million | 2.50 |
| 1829 | 1½ million | 2.75 | 1839 | 3¼ million | 2.50 |

**Type: Liberty head with braided hair**

| Date | Amount Minted | Value | Date | Amount Minted | Value |
|------|---------------|-------|------|---------------|-------|
| 1840 | 2½ million | 2.50 | 1849 | 4¼ million | 2.50 |
| 1841 | 1½ million | 2.50 | 1850 | 4½ million | 2.50 |
| 1842 | 2⅓ million | 2.50 | 1851 | 10 million | 2.50 |
| 1843 | 2½ million | 2.50 | 1852 | 5 million | 2.50 |
| 1844 | 2½ million | 2.50 | 1853 | 6⅔ million | 2.50 |
| 1845 | 4 million | 2.50 | 1854 | 4¼ million | 2.50 |
| 1846 | 4 million | 2.50 | 1855 | 1½ million | 2.50 |
| 1847 | 6¼ million | 2.50 | 1856 | 2⅔ million | 2.50 |
| 1848 | 6½ million | 2.50 | 1857 | 333,500 | 15.00 |

## SMALL CENTS

**Type: Flying eagle—Copper-Nickel**

| Date | Amount Minted | Value | Date | Amount Minted | Value |
|------|---------------|-------|------|---------------|-------|
| 1856 | About 1000 | 700.00 | 1858 | 24⅔ million | 4.00 |
| 1857 | 17½ million | 4.00 | | | |

### Type: Indian head; without shield on Rev.—Copper-Nickel

| Date | Amount Minted | Value |
|------|--------------|-------|
| 1859 | 36⅓ million | **2.00** |

### Type: Indian head; with shield on Rev.—Copper-Nickel

| Date | Amount Minted | Value | Date | Amount Minted | Value |
|------|--------------|-------|------|--------------|-------|
| 1860 | 20½ million | **2.00** | 1863 | 49¾ million | **1.00** |
| 1861 | 10 million | **4.00** | 1864 | 13¾ million | **4.00** |
| 1862 | 28 million | **1.25** | | | |

*(The bronze Indian Head Cents which follow are of the same design as the Copper-Nickel Cents above)*

### Type: Indian head—Bronze

(The "S" mint mark of 1908 and 1909 is on the Rev., under the wreath)

| Date | Amount Minted | Value | Date | Amount Minted | Value |
|------|--------------|-------|------|--------------|-------|
| 1864 | 39¼ million | **1.50** | 1884 | 23¼ million | .85 |
| 1864-L | Part of above | **14.00** | 1885 | 11¾ million | **1.25** |
| 1865 | 35½ million | **1.50** | 1886 | 17⅔ million | **.60** |
| 1866 | 9¾ million | **9.00** | 1887 | 45¼ million | .35 |
| 1867 | 9¾ million | **9.00** | 1888 | 37½ million | .35 |
| 1868 | 10¼ million | **9.00** | 1889 | 48¾ million | .35 |
| 1869 | 6½ million | **12.00** | 1890 | 57¼ million | .35 |
| 1870 | 5¼ million | **9.00** | 1891 | 47 million | .35 |
| 1871 | 4 million | **12.00** | 1892 | 37⅔ million | .35 |
| 1872 | 4 million | **20.00** | 1893 | 46⅔ million | .35 |
| 1873 | 11⅔ million | **4.00** | 1894 | 16¾ million | .65 |
| 1874 | 14¼ million | **4.00** | 1895 | 38⅓ million | .25 |
| 1875 | 13½ million | **4.00** | 1896 | 39 million | .25 |
| 1876 | 8 million | **7.00** | 1897 | 50½ million | .25 |
| 1877 | 852,500 | **80.00** | 1898 | 49¾ million | .25 |
| 1878 | 5¾ million | **7.50** | 1899 | 53⅔ million | .25 |
| 1879 | 16¼ million | **1.25** | 1900 | 66¾ million | .20 |
| 1880 | 39 million | .70 | 1901 | 79⅔ million | .20 |
| 1881 | 39¼ million | .70 | 1902 | 87⅓ million | .20 |
| 1882 | 38½ million | .70 | 1903 | 85 million | .20 |
| 1883 | 45½ million | .70 | 1904 | 61⅓ million | .20 |

| Date | Amount Minted | Value | Date | Amount Minted | Value |
|---|---|---|---|---|---|
| 1905 | 80¾ million | .20 | 1908-S | 1 million | 8.00 |
| 1906 | 96 million | .20 | 1909 | 14⅓ million | .50 |
| 1907 | 108¼ million | .20 | 1909-S | 309,000 | 40.00 |
| 1908 | 32⅓ million | .20 | | | |

### Type: Lincoln head

(The mint mark is on the Obv., under the date)

| Date | Amount Minted | Value | Date | Amount Minted | Value |
|---|---|---|---|---|---|
| 1909-VDB | 28 million | .75 | 1919 | 392 million | .03 |
| 1909-S-VDB | 484,000 | 125.00 | 1919-D | 57¼ million | .07 |
| 1909 | 72¾ million | .15 | 1919-S | 139¾ million | .07 |
| 1909-S | 1¾ million | 20.00 | 1920 | 310¼ million | .03 |
| 1910 | 146¾ million | .05 | 1920-D | 49⅓ million | .05 |
| 1910-S | 6 million | 3.00 | 1920-S | 46¼ million | .05 |
| 1911 | 101¼ million | .05 | 1921 | 39¼ million | .05 |
| 1911-D | 12¾ million | 1.50 | 1921-S | 15⅓ million | .30 |
| 1911-S | 4 million | 5.00 | 1922-D | 7¼ million | 1.50 |
| 1912 | 68¼ million | .05 | 1922 | Plain Part of above | 70.00 |
| 1912-D | 10½ million | 1.50 | 1923 | 74¾ million | .03 |
| 1912-S | 4½ million | 4.50 | 1923-S | 8¾ million | .50 |
| 1913 | 76½ million | .05 | 1924 | 75¼ million | .03 |
| 1913-D | 15¾ million | .60 | 1924-D | 2½ million | 4.00 |
| 1913-S | 6 million | 2.50 | 1924-S | 11¾ million | .25 |
| 1914 | 75¼ million | .05 | 1925 | 140 million | .03 |
| 1914-D | 1¼ million | 32.00 | 1925-D | 22⅔ million | .05 |
| 1914-S | 4 million | 4.00 | 1925-S | 26½ million | .05 |
| 1915 | 29 million | .20 | 1926 | 157 million | .03 |
| 1915-D | 22 million | .15 | 1926-D | 28 million | .05 |
| 1915-S | 4¾ million | 3.00 | 1926-S | 4⅔ million | .75 |
| 1916 | 131¾ million | .03 | 1927 | 144½ million | .03 |
| 1916-D | 36 million | .07 | 1927-D | 27¼ million | .05 |
| 1916-S | 22½ million | .15 | 1927-S | 14⅓ million | .15 |
| 1917 | 196½ million | .03 | 1928 | 134 million | .03 |
| 1917-D | 55 million | .05 | 1928-D | 31¼ million | .05 |
| 1917-S | 32⅔ million | .05 | 1928-S | 17⅓ million | .10 |
| 1918 | 288 million | .02 | 1929 | 185⅓ million | .03 |
| 1918-D | 47¾ million | .07 | 1929-D | 41¾ million | .03 |
| 1918-S | 34¾ million | .07 | 1929-S | 50 million | .03 |

| Date | Amount Minted | Value | Date | Amount Minted | Value |
|------|---------------|-------|------|---------------|-------|
| 1930 | 157½ million | .03 | 1945 | 1 billion | .02 |
| 1930-D | 40 million | .03 | 1945-D | 226⅓ million | .02 |
| 1930-S | 24⅓ million | .04 | 1945-S | 181¾ million | .02 |
| 1931 | 19½ million | .10 | 1946 | 991¾ million | .02 |
| 1931-S | 866,000 | 15.00 | 1946-D | 315¾ million | .02 |
| 1932 | 9 million | .40 | 1946-S | 198 million | .02 |
| 1932-D | 10½ million | .20 | 1947 | 190½ million | .02 |
| 1933 | 14½ million | .15 | 1947-D | 194¾ million | .02 |
| 1933-D | 6¼ million | .80 | 1947-S | 99 million | .02 |
| 1934 | 219 million | .02 | 1948 | 317⅔ million | .02 |
| 1934-D | 28½ million | .05 | 1948-D | 172⅔ million | .02 |
| 1935 | 245½ million | .02 | 1948-S | 81¾ million | .02 |
| 1935-D | 47 million | .03 | 1949 | 217½ million | .02 |
| 1935-S | 38¾ million | .03 | 1949-D | 154⅓ million | .02 |
| 1936 | 309⅔ million | .02 | 1949-S | 64⅓ million | .02 |
| 1935-D | 40⅔ million | .03 | 1950 | 272¾ million | .02 |
| 1936-S | 29 million | .04 | 1950-D | 335 million | .02 |
| 1937 | 309¼ million | .02 | 1950-S | 118½ million | .02 |
| 1937-D | 50½ million | .03 | 1951 | 294⅔ million | .02 |
| 1937-S | 34½ million | .04 | 1951-D | 625½ million | .02 |
| 1938 | 156¾ milliion | .02 | 1951-S | 101 million | .02 |
| 1938-D | 20 million | .05 | 1952 | 187 million | .02 |
| 1938-S | 15¼ million | .12 | 1952-D | 746 million | .02 |
| 1939 | 316½ million | .02 | 1952-S | 137¾ million | .02 |
| 1939-D | 15¼ million | .12 | 1953 | 257 million | .02 |
| 1939-S | 52 million | .03 | 1953-D | 700½ million | .02 |
| 1940 | 586¾ million | .02 | 1953-S | 182 million | .02 |
| 1940-D | 81½ million | .02 | 1954 | 72 million | .02 |
| 1940-S | 113 million | .02 | 1954-D | 251½ million | .02 |
| 1941 | 887 million | .02 | 1954-S | 96¼ million | .02 |
| 1941-D | 128¾ million | .02 | 1955 | 331 million | .02 |
| 1941-S | 92½ million | .02 | 1955 | double die. (Very Fine) | 200.00 |
| 1942 | 657¾ million | .02 | 1955-D | 563⅓ million | .02 |
| 1942-D | 206¾ million | .02 | 1955-S | 44⅔ million | .10 |
| 1942-S | 85⅔ million | .02 | 1956 | 421 million | .02 |
| 1943 | 684⅔ million | .02 | 1956-D | 1 billion | .02 |
| 1943-D | 217¾ million | .02 | 1957 | 282½ million | .02 |
| 1943-S | 191⅔ million | .03 | 1957-D | 1 billion | .02 |
| 1944 | 1½ billion | .02 | 1958 | 252½ million | .02 |
| 1944-D | 430⅔ million | .02 | 1958–D | 801 million | .02 |
| 1944-S | 232¾ million | .02 | | | |

*(The valuations in this book are based on the coins being in G-VG condition, unless otherwise noted.)*

58

**Type: Lincoln head with the Lincoln Memorial on the reverse**

| Date | Amount Minted | Value | Date | Amount Minted | Value |
|---|---|---|---|---|---|
| 1959 | 609¾ million | .01 | 1976 | 4½ billion | .01 |
| 1959-D | 1¼ billion | .01 | 1976-D | 4¼ billion | .01 |
| 1960 | 586½ million | .01 | 1976-S | proof only 4 million | 1.00 |
| 1960 | Small Date (unc) | 1.00 | 1977 | 4½ billion | .01 |
| 1960-D | 1½ billion | .01 | 1977-D | 4¼ billion | .01 |
| 1960-D | Small Date | .02 | 1977-S | proof only 3¼ million | 1.00 |
| 1961 | 753⅓ million | .01 | 1978 | 5½ billion | .01 |
| 1961-D | 1¾ billion | .01 | 1978-D | 4¼ billion | .01 |
| 1962 | 606 million | .01 | 1978-S | proof only 3 million | 1.00 |
| 1962-D | 1¾ billion | .01 | 1979 | 6 billion | .01 |
| 1963 | 754 million | .01 | 1979-D | 4¼ billion | .01 |
| 1963-D | 1¾ billion | .01 | 1979-S | proof only 3¾ million | 1.00 |
| 1964 | 2⅔ billion | .01 | 1980 | 7½ billion | .01 |
| 1964-D | 3¾ billion | .01 | 1980-D | 5 billion | .01 |
| 1965 | 1½ billion | .01 | 1980-S | proof only 3½ million | .50 |
| 1966 | 2¼ billion | .01 | 1981 | 7½ billion | .01 |
| 1967 | 3 billion | .01 | 1981-D | 5½ billion | .01 |
| 1968 | 1¾ billion | .01 | 1981-S | proof only 4 million | .50 |
| 1968-D | 2¾ billion | .01 | 1982 | copper, lg. date | .02 |
| 1968-S | 258¼ million | .01 | 1982 | copper, sm. date | .02 |
| 1969 | 1.2 billion | (unc.) .05 | 1982 | zinc, lg. date | .01 |
| 1969–D | 4 billion | .01 | 1982 | zinc, sm. date | .01 |
| 1969–S | 544⅓ million | .01 | | (9 billion, all types) | |
| 1970 | 1¾ billion | .01 | 1982-D | copper, lg. date | .01 |
| 1970-D | 2¾ billion | .01 | 1982-D | zinc, lg. date | .05 |
| 1970-S | 690½ million | .01 | 1982-D | zinc, sm. date | .01 |
| 1970-S | Small Date (unc) | 3.50 | | (6 billion, all types) | |
| 1971 | 2 billion | .01 | 1982-S | 3.8 million proofs | 1.00 |
| 1971-D | 3 billion | .01 | 1983 | 7½ billion | .01 |
| 1971-S | 525 million | .01 | 1983-D | 6½ billion | .01 |
| 1972 | 3 billion | .01 | 1983-S proof only 3¼ mil. | | 4.00 |
| 1972 | double die. (unc.) | 100.00 | 1984 | 8.1 billion | .01 |
| 1972-D | 2⅔ billion | .01 | 1984-D | 5.5 billion | .01 |
| 1972-S | 380 million | .01 | 1984-S | proof only | 3.75 |
| 1973 | 3¾ billion | .01 | 1985 | 5.5 billion | .01 |
| 1973-D | 3½ billion | .01 | 1985-D | 5.25 billion | .01 |
| 1973-S | 320 million | .01 | 1985-S | proof only | 3.50 |
| 1974 | 4¼ billion | .01 | 1986 | | .01 |
| 1974-D | 4¼ billion | .01 | 1986-D | | .01 |
| 1974-S | 412 million | .01 | 1986-S | proof only | 3.50 |
| 1975 | 5½ billion | .01 | 1987 | | .01 |
| 1975-D | 4½ billion | .01 | 1987-D | | .01 |
| 1975-S | proof only 3 million | 5.00 | 1987-S | proof only | 3.50 |

# 2 CENT PIECES

*Type: Bronze with shield on Obv. and the value on the Rev.*

| Date | Amount Minted | Value | Date | Amount Minted | Value |
|------|---------------|-------|------|---------------|-------|
| 1864 Large motto | 19¾ million | 1.75 | 1869 | 1½ million | 2.75 |
| 1864 Small motto | Part of above | 30.00 | 1870 | 861,250 | 3.00 |
| 1865 | 13⅔ million | 1.75 | 1871 | 721,250 | 4.00 |
| 1866 | 3¼ million | 2.00 | 1872 | 65,000 | 40.00 |
| 1867 | 3 million | 2.00 | 1873 | 600 proofs | 750.00 |
| 1868 | 3 million | 2.25 | | | |

60

# 3 CENT PIECES—SILVER

Plain star and plain III
1851-1853

Star with borders; sprig and arrows of the III
1854-1873

### Type: Large star, the Rev. has the Roman Numeral III for the value.

(The "O" mint mark is on the Rev., to the right of the III)

| Date | Amount Minted | Value | Date | Amount Minted | Value |
|------|---------------|-------|------|---------------|-------|
| 1851 | 5½ million | 4.00 | 1862 | 363,550 | 6.00 |
| 1851-O | 720,000 | 7.00 | 1863 | 21,500 proofs | 300.00 |
| 1852 | 18⅔ million | 4.00 | 1864 | 470 proofs | 300.00 |
| 1853 | 11½ million | 4.00 | 1865 | 8,500 proofs | 300.00 |
| 1854 | 671,000 | 5.00 | 1866 | 22,700 proofs | 300.00 |
| 1855 | 139,000 | 8.00 | 1867 | 4,625 proofs | 300.00 |
| 1856 | 1½ million | 4.50 | 1868 | 4,100 proofs | 300.00 |
| 1857 | 1 million | 4.50 | 1869 | 5,100 proofs | 300.00 |
| 1858 | 1⅔ million | 4.50 | 1870 | 4,000 proofs | 300.00 |
| 1859 | 365,000 | 6.00 | 1871 | 4,260 proofs | 300.00 |
| 1860 | 287,000 | 6.00 | 1872 | 1,950 proofs | 300.00 |
| 1861 | 498,000 | 6.00 | 1873 | 600 proofs | 600.00 |

# 3 CENT PIECES—NICKEL

**Type: Liberty head. The Rev. has the Roman numeral III
for the value.**

| Date | Amount Minted | Value | Date | Amount Minted | Value |
|------|---------------|-------|------|---------------|-------|
| 1865 | 11⅓ million | 2.00 | 1878 | 2,350 proofs | 600.00 |
| 1866 | 4¾ million | 2.00 | 1879 | 41,200 | 20.00 |
| 1867 | 4 million | 2.00 | 1880 | 25,000 | 30.00 |
| 1868 | 3¼ million | 2.00 | 1881 | 1⅛ million | 2.00 |
| 1869 | 1⅔ million | 2.00 | 1882 | 25,300 | 30.00 |
| 1870 | 1⅓ million | 2.00 | 1883 | 10,600 | 60.00 |
| 1871 | 604,000 | 2.50 | 1884 | 5,650 | 150.00 |
| 1872 | 862,000 | 2.50 | 1885 | 4,800 | 175.00 |
| 1873 | 1¼ million | 2.50 | 1886 | 4,300 proofs | 325.00 |
| 1874 | 790,000 | 3.00 | 1887 | 7,960 | 100.00 |
| 1875 | 228,000 | 4.00 | 1888 | 41,000 | 20.00 |
| 1876 | 162,000 | 4.50 | 1889 | 21,600 | 30.00 |
| 1877 | 510 proofs | 750.00 | | | |

# NICKELS

| With rays on Rev. | Without rays on Rev. |
|---|---|
| 1866-1867 | 1867-1883 |

### *Type: Shield. The U.S. shield is on the obv. and the value is on the Rev.*

| Date | Amount Minted | | Value | Date | Amount Minted | Value |
|---|---|---|---|---|---|---|
| 1866 | | 14¾ million | 5.50 | 1875 | 2 million | 5.00 |
| 1867 | With rays | 31 million | 5.75 | 1876 | 2½ million | 5.00 |
| 1867 | No rays | Part of above | 3.50 | 1877 | 510 proofs | 800.00 |
| 1868 | | 28¾ million | 3.50 | 1878 | 2,350 proofs | 400.00 |
| 1869 | | 16½ million | 3.50 | 1879 | 29,100 | 100.00 |
| 1870 | | 4¾ million | 4.00 | 1880 | 19,950 | 110.00 |
| 1871 | | 561,000 | 13.00 | 1881 | 72,400 | 125.00 |
| 1872 | | 6 million | 4.00 | 1882 | 11½ million | 3.50 |
| 1873 | | 4½ million | 4.00 | 1883 | 1½ million | 3.75 |
| 1874 | | 3½ million | 4.50 | | | |

| Without "Cents" on Rev. | With "Cents" on Rev. |
|---|---|
| 1883 | 1883 |

### *Type: Liberty head.*

(The mint marks of 1912 are on the Rev., to the left of "Cents" and under the dot)

| | | | | | |
|---|---|---|---|---|---|
| 1883 Without "Cents" | 5½ million | 1.00 | 1890 | 16¼ million | 1.75 |
| 1883 With "Cents" | 16 million | 3.00 | 1891 | 16¾ million | 1.50 |
| 1884 | 11¼ million | 3.50 | 1892 | 11½ million | 1.60 |
| 1885 | 1½ million | 90.00 | 1893 | 13⅓ million | 1.50 |
| 1886 | 3⅓ million | 25.00 | 1894 | 5½ million | 2.25 |
| 1887 | 15¼ million | 2.25 | 1895 | 10 million | 1.00 |
| 1888 | 10¾ million | 3.25 | 1896 | 8¾ million | 1.25 |
| 1889 | 15¾ million | 1.50 | 1897 | 20½ million | .45 |

# Liberty Head Nickels (continued)    63

| Date | Amount Minted | Value | Date | Amount Minted | Value |
|---|---|---|---|---|---|
| 1898 | 12½ million | .30 | 1909 | 11½ million | .20 |
| 1899 | 26 million | .30 | 1910 | 30¼ million | .20 |
| 1900 | 27¼ million | .20 | 1911 | 39½ million | .20 |
| 1901 | 26½ million | .20 | 1912 | 26¼ million | .20 |
| 1902 | 31½ million | .20 | 1912-D | 8½ million | .30 |
| 1903 | 28 million | .20 | 1912-S | 238,000 | 17.50 |
| 1904 | 21½ million | .20 | 1913 | 5 pieces struck. All are | |
| 1905 | 29¾ million | .20 | | accounted for in collec- | |
| 1906 | 38⅔ million | .20 | | tions and it is not pos- | |
| 1907 | 39¼ million | .20 | | sible to find one. | |
| 1908 | 22⅔ million | .20 | | | |

Type I. Buffalo on hilly mound
1913

Type II. Buffalo on more level mound
1913-1938

## *Type: Buffalo and Indian head.*

(The mint marks are on the Rev., under "Five Cents")

| Date | Amount Minted | Value | Date | Amount Minted | Value |
|---|---|---|---|---|---|
| 1913-I | 31 million | 1.50 | 1919 | 60¾ million | .25 |
| 1913-D-I | 5⅓ million | 3.00 | 1919-D | 8 million | 2.00 |
| 1913-S-I | 2 million | 4.00 | 1919-S | 7½ million | 1.25 |
| 1913-II | 29¾ million | 1.25 | 1920 | 63 million | .20 |
| 1913-D-II | 4¼ million | 15.00 | 1920-D | 9½ million | 1.50 |
| 1913-S-II | 1¼ million | 30.00 | 1920-S | 9⅔ million | .80 |
| 1914 | 20⅔ million | 2.00 | 1921 | 10⅔ million | .30 |
| 1914-D | 4 million | 15.00 | 1921-S | 1½ million | 6.00 |
| 1914-S | 3½ million | 2.50 | 1923 | 35¾ million | .20 |
| 1915 | 21 million | .90 | 1923-S | 6¼ million | .60 |
| 1915-D | 7½ million | 3.25 | 1924 | 21⅔ million | .15 |
| 1915-S | 7½ million | 5.25 | 1924-D | 5¼ million | 1.00 |
| 1916 | 63½ million | .25 | 1924-S | 1½ million | 2.25 |
| 1916, over 16 | | 300.00 | 1925 | 35½ million | .15 |
| 1916-D | 13⅓ million | 2.25 | 1925-D | 4½ million | 1.75 |
| 1916-S | 11¾ million | 1.50 | 1925-S | 6¼ million | .75 |
| 1917 | 51½ million | .20 | 1926 | 44⅔ million | .10 |
| 1917-D | 10 million | 2.25 | 1926-D | 5⅔ million | 1.00 |
| 1917-S | 4¼ million | 1.75 | 1926-S | 970,000 | 2.75 |
| 1918 | 32 million | .30 | 1927 | 38 million | .10 |
| 1918-D | 8⅓ million | 2.00 | 1927-D | 5¾ million | .40 |
| 1918-D, 8 over 7 | | 225.00 | | | |
| 1918-S | 4¾ million | 1.50 | | | |

| Date | Amount Minted | Value | Date | Amount Minted | Value |
|------|---------------|-------|------|---------------|-------|
| 1927-S | 3½ million | .25 | 1935 | 58¼ million | .10 |
| 1928 | 23½ million | .10 | 1935-D | 12 million | .10 |
| 1928-D | 6½ million | .25 | 1935-S | 10⅓ million | .10 |
| 1928-S | 7 million | .25 | 1936 | 119 million | .10 |
| 1929 | 36½ million | .10 | 1936-D | 24½ million | .10 |
| 1929-D | 8⅓ million | .25 | 1936-S | 15 million | .10 |
| 1929-S | 7¾ million | .12 | 1937 | 79½ million | .10 |
| 1930 | 22¾ million | .10 | 1937-D | 17¾ million | .10 |
| 1930-S | 5½ million | .15 | 1937-D | 3-legged buffalo | 40.00 |
| 1931-S | 1¼ million | 1.75 | 1937-S | 5⅔ million | .10 |
| 1934 | 20¼ million | .10 | 1938-D | 7 million | .10 |
| 1934-D | 7½ million | .10 | | | |

Normal type
1938-1942 & 1946 to date

Silver content type with large
Mint Mark on Rev.
1942-1945

### Type: Jefferson head.

(From 1938-1942 and 1946-1964, the mint marks are on the Rev. to the right of the building.
On the silver content nickels, 1942-1945, the mint marks are much larger and are over the
building. From 1968 to date, the mint marks are on the obverse under the date.)

| | | | | | |
|------|---------------|-------|------|---------------|-------|
| 1938 | 19½ million | .06 | 1940-D | 43½ million | .05 |
| 1938-D | 5⅓ million | .35 | 1940-S | 39⅔ million | .05 |
| 1938-S | 4 million | .75 | 1941 | 203¼ million | .05 |
| 1939 | 120⅔ million | .05 | 1941-D | 53½ million | .05 |
| 1939-D | 3½ million | 1.75 | 1941-S | 43½ million | .05 |
| 1939-S | 6⅔ million | .15 | 1942 | 49¾ million | .05 |
| 1940 | 176½ million | .05 | 1942-D | 14 million | .08 |

### Silver content Nickels with large mint mark on reverse.

| | | | | | |
|------|---------------|-------|------|---------------|-------|
| 1942-P | 56 million | .20 | 1944-D | 32⅓ million | .20 |
| 1942-S | 33 million | .20 | 1944-S | 21⅔ million | .20 |
| 1943-P | 27¼ million | .20 | 1945-P | 119½ million | .20 |
| 1943-D | 15¼ million | .20 | 1945-D | 37¼ million | .20 |
| 1943-S | 104 million | .20 | 1945-S | 59 million | .20 |
| 1944-P | 119¼ million | .20 | | | |

### Standard composition Nickels

(Prices are for uncirculated coins)

| | | | | | |
|------|---------------|-------|------|---------------|-------|
| 1946 | 161 million | .10 | 1947-D | 37¾ million | .25 |
| 1946-D | 45¼ million | .15 | 1947-S | 24¾ million | .20 |
| 1946-S | 13⅓ million | .25 | 1948 | 89⅓ million | .15 |
| 1947 | 95 million | .10 | 1948-D | 44¾ million | .30 |

| Date | Amount Minted | Value | Date | Amount Minted | Value |
|------|--------------|-------|------|--------------|-------|
| 1948-S | 11⅓ million | .25 | 1974-S | 2⅔ million proofs | .50 |
| 1949 | 60⅔ million | .30 | 1975 | 181¾ million | .05 |
| 1949-D | 35¼ million | .30 | 1975-D | 402 million | .05 |
| 1949-S | 9¾ million | .65 | 1975-S | 2¾ million proofs | .35 |
| 1950 | 9¾ million | .50 | 1976 | 367 million | .05 |
| 1950-D | 2⅔ million | 3.50 | 1976-D | 564 million | .05 |
| 1951 | 28⅔ million | .15 | 1976-S | 4¼ million proofs | .20 |
| 1951-D | 20½ million | .20 | 1977 | 585⅓ million | .05 |
| 1951-S | 7¾ million | .50 | 1977-D | 297⅓ million | .05 |
| 1952 | 64 million | .10 | 1977-S | 3¼ million proofs | .20 |
| 1952-D | 30¾ million | .50 | 1978 | 391⅓ million | .05 |
| 1952-S | 20½ million | .20 | 1978-D | 313 million | .05 |
| 1953 | 46¾ million | .07 | 1978-S | 3¼ million proofs | .20 |
| 1953-D | 59¾ million | .07 | 1979 | 463¼ million | .05 |
| 1953-S | 19¼ million | .08 | 1979-D | 325¾ million | .05 |
| 1954 | 48 million | .07 | 1979-S | 3⅔ million proofs | .20 |
| 1954-D | 117¼ million | .07 | 1980 | 600 million | .05 |
| 1954-S | 29⅓ million | .07 | 1980-S | 3½ million proofs | .20 |
| 1955 | 8¼ million | .08 | 1981 | 657½ million | .05 |
| 1955-D | 74½ million | .06 | 1981-D | 364¾ million | .05 |
| 1956 | 35⅓ million | .05 | 1981-S | 4 million proofs | .20 |
| 1956-D | 67¼ million | .05 | 1982 | 292⅓ million | .05 |
| 1957 | 38½ million | .05 | 1982-D | 373¾ million | .05 |
| 1957-D | 136¾ million | .05 | 1982-S | 3.8 million proofs | .40 |
| 1958 | 17 million | .05 | 1983 | 561½ million | .05 |
| 1958-D | 141¾ million | .05 | 1983-D | 536¾ million | .05 |
| 1959 | 27¼ million | .05 | 1983-S | 3¼ million proofs | .75 |
| 1959-D | 160¾ million | .05 | 1984 | 746 million | .05 |
| 1960 | 55½ million | .05 | 1984-D | 500 million | .05 |
| 1960-D | 192½ million | .05 | 1984-S | proof only | 1.00 |
| 1961 | 73⅔ million | .05 | 1985 | 647 million | .05 |
| 1961-D | 229⅓ million | .05 | 1985-D | 460 million | .05 |
| 1962 | 97⅓ million | .05 | 1985-S | proof only | .60 |
| 1962-D | 280¼ million | .05 | 1986 | | .05 |
| 1963 | 175¾ million | .05 | 1986-D | | .05 |
| 1963-D | 276¾ million | .05 | 1986-S | proof only | .60 |
| 1964 | 1 billion | .05 | 1987 | | .05 |
| 1964-D | 1¾ billion | .05 | 1987-D | | .05 |
| 1965 | 136 million | .05 | 1987-S | proof only | 1.00 |
| 1966 | 156¼ million | .05 | | | |
| 1967 | 107⅓ million | .05 | | | |
| 1968-D | 91¼ million | .05 | | | |
| 1968-S | 100⅓ million | .05 | | | |
| 1969-S | 120¼ million | .05 | | | |
| 1970-D | 515½ million | .05 | | | |
| 1970-S | 238¾ million | .05 | | | |
| 1971 | 106.8 million | .05 | | | |
| 1971-D | 316 million | .05 | | | |
| 1971-S | 3¼ million proofs | .35 | | | |
| 1972 | 202 million | .05 | | | |
| 1972-D | 351⅔ million | .05 | | | |
| 1972-S | 3¼ million proofs | .35 | | | |
| 1973 | 384⅓ million | .05 | | | |
| 1973-D | 261⅓ million | .05 | | | |
| 1973-S | 2¾ million proofs | .35 | | | |
| 1974 | 601¾ million | .05 | | | |
| 1974-D | 277⅓ million | .05 | | | |

# HALF DIMES

### Type: Liberty head with flowing hair.

| Date | Amount Minted | Value |
|------|---------------|-------|
| 1794 |               | **400.00** |
| 1795 |               | **350.00** |

(The combined coinage of 1794 and 1795 was 86,416 pieces. The exact amount of each year is not known)

### Type: Draped bust of Liberty; small eagle on Rev.

| Date | Amount Minted | Value |
|------|---------------|-------|
| 1796 | 10,200 | **400.00** |
| 1797 | 44,500 | **400.00** |

### Type: Draped bust of Liberty; large eagle on Rev.

| Date | Amount Minted | Value |
|------|---------------|-------|
| 1800 | 24,000 | **300.00** |
| 1801 | 33,900 | **300.00** |
| 1802 | 13,000 | **2,000.00** |
| 1803 | 37,800 | **300.00** |
| 1805 | 15,600 | **320.00** |

### Type: Bust of Liberty wearing cap.

| Date | Amount Minted | Value |
|------|---------------|-------|
| 1829 | 1¼ million | **6.00** |
| 1830 | 1¼ million | **6.00** |
| 1831 | 1¼ million | **6.00** |
| 1832 | 965,000 | **6.00** |
| 1833 | 1⅓ million | **6.00** |
| 1834 | 1½ million | **6.00** |
| 1835 | 2¾ million | **6.00** |
| 1836 | 2 million | **6.00** |
| 1837 | 2¼ million | **6.00** |

### Type: Liberty seated; no stars on Obv.

(The mint mark is under the value on the Rev.)

| Date | Amount Minted | Value |
|------|---------------|-------|
| 1837 | 2¼ million | **12.00** |
| 1838-O | 70,000 | **15.00** |

Without arrows at date
1838-1853 & 1856-1859

With arrows at date
1853-1855

## Type: Liberty seated; with stars on Obv.

(The mint mark is under the value on the Rev.)

| Date | Amount Minted | Value | Date | Amount Minted | Value |
|------|---------------|-------|------|---------------|-------|
| .1838 | 2¼ million | 2.50 | 1851-O | 860,000 | 4.50 |
| 1839 | 1 million | 2.50 | 1852 | 1 million | 2.50 |
| 1839-O | 1 million | 3.00 | 1852-O | 260,000 | 7.50 |
| 1840 | 1⅓ million | 2.50 | 1853 No Arr. | * | 10.00 |
| 1840-O | 935,000 | 2.75 | 1853-O No Arr. | * | 50.00 |
| 1841 | 1¼ million | 2.50 | 1853 Arr. | 13⅓ million | 2.00 |
| 1841-O | 815,000 | 4.00 | 1853-O Arr. | 2⅓ million | 2.00 |
| 1842 | 815,000 | 2.50 | 1854 | 5¾ million | 2.00 |
| 1842-O | 350,000 | 9.00 | 1854-O | 1½ million | 2.00 |
| 1843 | 1¼ million | 2.50 | 1855 | 1¾ million | 2.00 |
| 1844 | 430,000 | 3.00 | 1855-O | 600,000 | 3.50 |
| 1844-O | 220,000 | 20.00 | 1856 | 4¾ million | 2.00 |
| 1845 | 1½ million | 2.50 | 1856-O | 1 million | 2.50 |
| 1846 | 27,000 | 55.00 | 1857 | 7¼ million | 2.00 |
| 1847 | 1¼ million | 2.50 | 1857-O | 1⅓ million | 2.00 |
| 1848 | 668,000 | 3.00 | 1858 | 3½ million | 2.00 |
| 1848-O | 600,000 | 3.00 | 1858-O | 1⅔ million | 2.00 |
| 1849 | 1⅓ million | 2.50 | 1859 | 340,000 | 3.25 |
| 1849-O | 140,000 | 15.00 | 1859-O | 560,000 | 3.00 |
| 1850 | 955,000 | 2.50 | | | |
| 1850-O | 690,000 | 4.00 | | | |
| 1851 | 781,000 | 2.75 | | | |

*The figures for the No Arrow coinage are included in the figures for the Arrow coinage.

## Type: Liberty seated; with "United States of America" on Obv.

(The mint marks are on the Rev., under or within the wreath)

| Date | Amount Minted | Value | Date | Amount Minted | Value |
|------|---------------|-------|------|---------------|-------|
| 1860 | 799,000 | 2.00 | 1863-S | 100,000 | 6.50 |
| 1860-O | 1 million | 2.00 | 1864 | 48,470 | 85.00 |
| 1861 | 3¼ million | 2.00 | 1864-S | 90,000 | 10.00 |
| 1862 | 1½ million | 2.00 | 1865 | 13,500 | 80.00 |
| 1863 | 18,500 | 35.00 | 1865-S | 120,000 | 6.00 |

| Date | Amount Minted | Value | Date | Amount Minted | Value |
|------|--------------|-------|------|--------------|-------|
| 1866 | 10,700 | 50.00 | 1870 | 536,600 | 4.00 |
| 1866-S | 120,000 | 6.00 | 1871 | 1½ million | 2.00 |
| 1867 | 8,600 | 100.00 | 1871-S | 161,000 | 6.00 |
| 1867-S | 120,000 | 6.00 | 1872 | 3 million | 2.00 |
| 1868 | 85,900 | 12.00 | 1872-S | 837,000 | 3.75 |
| 1868-S | 280,000 | 4.25 | 1873 | 712,600 | 3.00 |
| 1869 | 208,600 | 4.00 | 1873-S | 324,000 | 3.50 |
| 1869-S | 230,000 | 4.00 | | | |

## DIMES

### Type: Draped bust of Liberty; small eagle on Rev.

| | | | | | |
|------|------|------|------|------|------|
| 1796 | 22,100 | 550.00 | 1797 | 25,300 | 500.00 |

### Type: Draped bust of Liberty; large eagle on Rev.

| Date | Amount | Value | Date | Amount | Value |
|------|--------|-------|------|--------|-------|
| 1798 | 27,500 | 250.00 | 1803 | 33,000 | 250.00 |
| 1800 | 21,800 | 250.00 | 1804 | 8,300 | 400.00 |
| 1801 | 34,600 | 250.00 | 1805 | 120,800 | 200.00 |
| 1802 | 11,000 | 250.00 | 1807 | 165,000 | 200.00 |

Large Size
1809-1828

Reduced Size
1828-1837

### Type: Bust of Liberty wearing cap.

| | | | | | |
|------|------|------|------|------|------|
| 1809 | 44,700 | 25.00 | 1811 | 65,200 | 17.50 |

| Date | Amount Minted | Value | Date | Amount Minted | Value |
|------|---------------|-------|------|---------------|-------|
| 1814 | 421,500 | 10.00 | 1829 | 770,000 | 5.00 |
| 1820 | 942,600 | 7.00 | 1830 | 510,000 | 5.00 |
| 1821 | 1¼ million | 7.00 | 1831 | 771,300 | 5.00 |
| 1822 | 100,000 | 30.00 | 1832 | 522,500 | 5.00 |
| 1823 | 440,000 | 9.50 | 1833 | 485,000 | 5.00 |
| 1824 | Unknown | 10.00 | 1834 | 635,000 | 5.00 |
| 1825 | 510,000 | 9.00 | 1835 | 1⅓ million | 5.00 |
| 1827 | 1¼ million | 7.00 | 1836 | 1¼ million | 5.00 |
| 1828 | 125,000 | 10.00 | 1837 | 1 million | 5.00 |

**Type: Liberty seated; no stars on Obv.**

(The mint mark is under the value on the Rev.)

| 1837 | Unknown | 12.00 | 1838-O | 402,400 | 15.00 |
|------|---------|-------|--------|---------|-------|

| Without arrows at date | With arrows at date |
|------------------------|---------------------|
| 1838-1853 & 1856-1860 | 1853-1855 |

**Type: Liberty seated; with stars on Obv.**

(The mint mark is under the value on the Rev.)

| 1838 | 2 million | 4.00 | 1846 | 31,300 | 30.00 |
|------|-----------|------|------|--------|-------|
| 1839 | 1 million | 3.25 | 1847 | 245,000 | 3.75 |
| 1839-O | 1¼ million | 3.75 | 1848 | 451,500 | 3.75 |
| 1840 | 1⅓ million | 3.00 | 1849 | 839,000 | 2.00 |
| 1840-O | 1¼ million | 3.75 | 1849-O | 300,000 | 3.75 |
| 1841 | 1⅔ million | 2.00 | 1850 | 2 million | 1.50 |
| 1841-O | 2 million | 2.00 | 1850-O | 510,000 | 1.50 |
| 1842 | 2 million | 2.00 | 1851 | 1 million | 1.50 |
| 1842-O | 2 million | 3.00 | 1851-O | 400,000 | 3.25 |
| 1843 | 1⅓ million | 2.00 | 1852 | 1½ million | 1.50 |
| 1843-O | 150,000 | 15.00 | 1852-O | 430,000 | 3.25 |
| 1844 | 72,500 | 15.00 | 1853 No Arr. | 12¼ million | 20.00 |
| 1845 | 1¾ million | 2.00 | 1853 Arr. | | 1.50 |
| 1845-O | 230,000 | 7.00 | 1853-O | 1 million | 2.00 |

| Date | Amount Minted | Value | Date | Amount Minted | Value |
|------|--------------|-------|------|--------------|-------|
| 1854 | 4½ million | 1.50 | 1858 | 1½ million | 1.50 |
| 1854-O | 1¾ million | 1.50 | 1858-O | 290,000 | 3.25 |
| 1855 | 2 million | 1.50 | 1858-S | 60,000 | 20.00 |
| 1856 | 5¾ million | 1.50 | 1859 | 430,000 | 1.50 |
| 1856-O | 1¼ million | 1.50 | 1859-O | 480,000 | 1.50 |
| 1856-S | 70,000 | 20.00 | 1859-S | 60,000 | 20.00 |
| 1857 | 5½ million | 1.50 | 1860-S | 140,000 | 6.00 |
| 1857-O | 1½ million | 1.50 | | | |

Without arrows at date
1860-1873 & 1875-1891

With arrows at date
1873-1874

## Type: Liberty seated; with "United States of America" on Obv.

(The mint marks are on the Rev., under or within the wreath)

| Date | Amount Minted | Value | Date | Amount Minted | Value |
|------|--------------|-------|------|--------------|-------|
| 1860 | 607,000 | 2.00 | 1872-CC | 24,000 | 75.00 |
| 1860-O | 40,000 | 185.00 | 1873 No Arr. | 1¾ million | 1.50 |
| 1861 | 2 million | 1.50 | 1873 Arr. | 2¼ million | 4.00 |
| 1861-S | 172,500 | 8.50 | 1873-S | 455,000 | 7.00 |
| 1862 | 847,500 | 2.00 | 1873-CC | 18,800 | 225.00 |
| 1862-S | 180,700 | 8.50 | 1874 | 3 million | 4.00 |
| 1863 | 14,500 | 50.00 | 1874-S | 240,000 | 8.00 |
| 1863-S | 157,500 | 8.50 | 1874-CC | 10,800 | 300.00 |
| 1864 | 39,000 | 50.00 | 1875 | 10⅓ million | 1.50 |
| 1864-S | 230,000 | 6.00 | 1875-S | 9 million | 1.50 |
| 1865 | 10,500 | 40.00 | 1875-CC | 4⅔ million | 1.50 |
| 1865-S | 175,000 | 6.00 | 1876 | 11½ million | 1.50 |
| 1866 | 8,700 | 65.00 | 1876-S | 10½ million | 1.50 |
| 1866-S | 135,000 | 6.00 | 1876-CC | 8¼ million | 1.50 |
| 1867 | 6,600 | 100.00 | 1877 | 7⅓ million | 1.50 |
| 1867-S | 140,000 | 6.00 | 1877-S | 2⅓ million | 1.50 |
| 1868 | 466,200 | 2.00 | 1877-CC | 7¾ million | 1.50 |
| 1868-S | 260,000 | 5.00 | 1878 | 1⅔ million | 1.50 |
| 1869 | 256,600 | 2.00 | 1878-CC | 200,000 | 12.00 |
| 1869-S | 450,000 | 2.50 | 1879 | 15,100 | 30.00 |
| 1870 | 471,500 | 2.00 | 1880 | 37,400 | 25.00 |
| 1870-S | 50,000 | 30.00 | 1881 | 25,000 | 26.00 |
| 1871 | 753,600 | 2.00 | 1882 | 4 million | 1.50 |
| 1871-S | 320,000 | 6.00 | 1883 | 7⅔ million | 1.50 |
| 1871-CC | 20,100 | 150.00 | 1884 | 3⅓ million | 1.50 |
| 1872 | 2⅓ million | 1.50 | 1884-S | 565,000 | 5.50 |
| 1872-S | 190,000 | 7.00 | 1885 | 2½ million | 1.50 |

| Date | Amount Minted | Value | Date | Amount Minted | Value |
|------|---------------|-------|------|---------------|-------|
| 1885-S | 43,700 | 55.00 | 1889 | 7⅓ million | 1.50 |
| 1886 | 6⅓ million | 1.50 | 1889-S | 972,700 | 3.50 |
| 1886-S | 206,500 | 3.50 | 1890 | 10 million | 1.50 |
| 1887 | 11¼ million | 1.50 | 1890-S | 1½ million | 1.50 |
| 1887-S | 4½ million | 1.50 | 1891 | 15⅓ million | 1.50 |
| 1888 | 5½ million | 1.50 | 1891-O | 4½ million | 1.50 |
| 1888-S | 1¾ million | 1.50 | 1891-S | 3¼ million | 1.50 |

## Type: Liberty head.

(The mint marks are on the Rev., under the wreath)

| Date | Amount Minted | Value | Date | Amount Minted | Value |
|------|---------------|-------|------|---------------|-------|
| 1892 | 12 million | 1.00 | 1901-S | 593,000 | 15.00 |
| 1892-O | 3¾ million | 2.50 | 1902 | 21⅓ million | .55 |
| 1892-S | 990,700 | 11.00 | 1902-O | 4½ million | .85 |
| 1893 | 3⅓ million | 2.50 | 1902-S | 2 million | 1.50 |
| 1893-O | 1¾ million | 6.00 | 1903 | 19½ million | .55 |
| 1893-S | 2½ million | 2.50 | 1903-O | 8¼ million | .85 |
| 1894 | 1⅓ million | 2.75 | 1903-S | 613,300 | 12.00 |
| 1894-O | 720,000 | 13.00 | 1904 | 14⅔ million | .55 |
| 1894-S | 24 | Rare | 1904-S | 800,000 | 8.50 |
| 1895 | 690,900 | 25.00 | 1905 | 14½ million | .55 |
| 1895-O | 440,000 | 60.00 | 1905-O | 3½ million | .85 |
| 1895-S | 1 million | 6.00 | 1905-S | 6¾ million | .85 |
| 1896 | 2 million | 2.00 | 1906 | 20 million | .55 |
| 1896-O | 610,000 | 17.50 | 1906-D | 4 million | .85 |
| 1896-S | 575,000 | 15.00 | 1906-O | 2⅔ million | 1.00 |
| 1897 | 10¾ million | .55 | 1906-S | 3¼ million | .75 |
| 1897-O | 666,000 | 15.00 | 1907 | 22¼ million | .55 |
| 1897-S | 1⅓ million | 3.00 | 1907-D | 4 million | .75 |
| 1898 | 16⅓ million | .55 | 1907-O | 5 million | .75 |
| 1898-O | 2¼ million | 1.50 | 1907-S | 3¼ million | 1.00 |
| 1898-S | 1¾ million | 1.50 | 1908 | 10⅔ million | .55 |
| 1899 | 19½ million | .55 | 1908-D | 7½ million | .55 |
| 1899-O | 2⅔ million | 1.50 | 1908-O | 1¾ million | 1.00 |
| 1899-S | 1¾ million | 1.50 | 1908-S | 3¼ million | .75 |
| 1900 | 17⅔ million | .55 | 1909 | 10¼ million | .55 |
| 1900-O | 2 million | 2.00 | 1909-D | 954,000 | 1.25 |
| 1900-S | 5¼ million | .85 | 1909-O | 2¼ million | .55 |
| 1901 | 18¾ million | .55 | 1909-S | 1 million | 1.25 |
| 1901-O | 5⅔ million | .85 | 1910 | 11½ million | .55 |

| Date | Amount Minted | Value | Date | Amount Minted | Value |
|------|--------------|-------|------|--------------|-------|
| 1910-D | 3½ million | .55 | 1913-S | 510,000 | 2.50 |
| 1910-D | 1¼ million | .55 | 1914 | 17⅓ million | .55 |
| 1911 | 19 million | .55 | 1914-D | 12 million | .55 |
| 1911-D | 11¼ million | .55 | 1914-S | 2 million | .85 |
| 1911-S | 3½ million | .55 | 1915 | 5⅔ million | .55 |
| 1912 | 19⅓ million | .55 | 1915-S | 960,000 | .75 |
| 1912-D | 11¾ million | .55 | 1916 | 18½ million | .55 |
| 1912-S | 3⅓ million | .55 | 1916-S | 5¾ million | .55 |
| 1913 | 19¾ million | .55 | | | |

### Type: Mercury head.

(The mint marks are on the bottom of the Rev. to the left of the branches)

| Date | Amount Minted | Value | Date | Amount Minted | Value |
|------|--------------|-------|------|--------------|-------|
| 1916 | 22¼ million | 1.00 | 1926-S | 1½ million | 2.75 |
| 1916-D | 264,000 | 150.00 | 1927 | 28 million | .50 |
| 1916-S | 10½ million | 1.25 | 1927-D | 4¾ million | 1.00 |
| 1917 | 55¼ million | .75 | 1927-S | 4¾ million | .75 |
| 1917-D | 9⅓ million | .85 | 1928 | 19½ million | .50 |
| 1917-S | 27⅓ million | .75 | 1928-D | 4¼ million | .75 |
| 1918 | 26⅔ million | .50 | 1928-S | 7⅓ million | .75 |
| 1918-D | 22⅔ million | .50 | 1929 | 26 million | .50 |
| 1918-S | 19⅓ million | .75 | 1929-D | 5 million | .75 |
| 1919 | 35¾ million | .75 | 1929-S | 4¾ million | .75 |
| 1919-D | 10 million | 1.25 | 1930 | 6¾ million | .75 |
| 1919-S | 8¾ million | 1.00 | 1930-S | 1¾ million | 1.25 |
| 1920 | 59 million | .50 | 1931 | 3¼ million | .75 |
| 1920-D | 19¼ million | .75 | 1931-D | 1¼ million | 2.25 |
| 1920-S | 13¾ million | .75 | 1931-S | 1¾ million | 1.00 |
| 1921 | 1¼ million | 10.00 | 1934 | 24 million | .45 |
| 1921-D | 1 million | 15.00 | 1934-D | 6¾ million | .45 |
| 1923 | 50¼ million | .50 | 1935 | 58¾ million | .45 |
| 1923-S | 6½ million | 1.00 | 1935-D | 10½ million | .45 |
| 1924 | 24 million | .50 | 1935-S | 15¾ million | .45 |
| 1924-D | 6¾ million | .75 | 1936 | 87½ million | .45 |
| 1924-S | 7 million | .75 | 1936-D | 16¼ million | .45 |
| 1925 | 25⅔ million | .50 | 1936-S | 9¼ million | .45 |
| 1925-D | 5 million | 1.50 | 1937 | 56¾ million | .45 |
| 1925-S | 5¾ million | .75 | 1937-D | 14¼ million | .45 |
| 1926 | 32¼ million | .50 | 1937-S | 9¾ million | .45 |
| 1926-D | 6¾ million | .75 | 1938 | 22¼ million | .45 |

**(The valuations in this book are based on the coins being in G-VG condition, unless otherwise noted.)**

| Date | Amount Minted | Value | Date | Amount Minted | Value |
|---|---|---|---|---|---|
| 1938-D | 5½ million | .45 | 1942/1 | | 80.00 |
| 1938-S | 8 million | .45 | 1942-D | 60¾ million | .45 |
| 1939 | 67¾ million | .45 | 1942-S | 49⅓ million | .45 |
| 1939-D | 24⅓ million | .45 | 1943 | 191¾ million | .45 |
| 1939-S | 10½ million | .45 | 1943-D | 72 million | .45 |
| 1940 | 65⅓ million | .45 | 1943-S | 60⅓ million | .45 |
| 1940-D | 21¼ million | .45 | 1944 | 231½ million | .45 |
| 1940-S | 21½ million | .45 | 1944-D | 62¼ million | .45 |
| 1941 | 175 million | .45 | 1944-S | 49½ million | .45 |
| 1941-D | 45⅔ million | .45 | 1945 | 159¼ million | .45 |
| 1941-S | 43 million | .45 | 1945-D | 40¼ million | .45 |
| 1942 | 205½ million | .45 | 1945-S | 42 million | .45 |

**Type: Roosevelt head.**

(From 1946-1964, the mint marks are on the Rev., at left bottom of torch. From 1968 to date, the mint marks are on the obverse above the date.)

| Date | Amount Minted | Value | Date | Amount Minted | Value |
|---|---|---|---|---|---|
| 1946 | 255¼ million | .45 | 1955-D | 14 million | .45 |
| 1946-D | 61 million | .50 | 1955-S | 18½ million | .45 |
| 1946-S | 28 million | .50 | 1956 | 108¾ million | .45 |
| 1947 | 121½ million | .45 | 1956-D | 108 million | .45 |
| 1947-D | 46¾ million | .50 | 1957 | 160¼ million | .45 |
| 1947-S | 34¾ million | .50 | 1957-D | 113⅓ million | .45 |
| 1948 | 75 million | .45 | 1958 | 32 million | .45 |
| 1948-D | 52¾ million | .50 | 1958-D | 136½ million | .45 |
| 1948-S | 35½ million | .50 | 1959 | 85¾ million | .45 |
| 1949 | 31 million | .50 | 1959-D | 165 million | .45 |
| 1949-D | 26 million | .50 | 1960 | 72 million | .45 |
| 1949-S | 13½ million | .75 | 1960-D | 200¼ million | .45 |
| 1950 | 50¼ million | .45 | 1961 | 93¾ million | .45 |
| 1950-D | 46¾ million | .45 | 1961-D | 209¼ million | .45 |
| 1950-S | 20½ million | .45 | 1962 | 72½ million | .45 |
| 1951 | 104 million | .45 | 1962-D | 353¼ million | .45 |
| 1951-D | 52¼ million | .45 | 1963 | 123⅔ million | .45 |
| 1951-S | 31⅔ million | .45 | 1963-D | 421½ million | .45 |
| 1952 | 92¼ million | .45 | 1964 | 929⅓ million | .45 |
| 1952-D | 122 million | .45 | 1964-D | 1⅓ billion | .45 |
| 1952-S | 44½ million | .45 | | | |
| 1953 | 53⅔ million | .45 | | | |
| 1953-D | 136½ million | .45 | **CLAD COINAGE** | | |
| 1953-S | 39¼ million | .45 | 1965 | 1⅔ billion | .10 |
| 1954 | 114¼ million | .45 | 1966 | 1½ billion | .10 |
| 1954-D | 106⅓ million | .45 | 1967 | 2¼ billion | .10 |
| 1954-S | 22¾ million | .45 | 1968 | 424½ million | .10 |
| 1955 | 12¾ million | .45 | 1968-D | 480¾ million | .10 |

| Date | Amount Minted | Value | Date | Amount Minted | Value |
|---|---|---|---|---|---|
| 1968-S | 3 million proofs | .20 | 1978-D | 282¾ million | .10 |
| 1969 | 145¾ million | .10 | 1978-S | 3¼ million proofs | .25 |
| 1969-D | 563⅓ million | .10 | 1979 | 315½ million | .10 |
| 1969-S | 3 million proofs | .20 | 1979-D | 391 million | .10 |
| 1970 | 345½ million | .10 | 1979-S | 3¾ million proofs | .25 |
| 1970-D | 755 million | .10 | 1980 | 73.5 million | .10 |
| 1970-S | 2½ million proofs | .30 | 1980-D | 719⅓ million | .10 |
| 1971 | 162⅔ million | .10 | 1980-S | 3½ million proofs | .20 |
| 1971-D | 378 million | .10 | 1981 | 676⅔ million | .10 |
| 1971-S | 3¼ million proofs | .30 | 1981-D | 712¼ million | .10 |
| 1972 | 431½ million | .10 | 1981-S | 4 million proofs | .25 |
| 1972-D | 330¼ million | .10 | 1982 | 519½ million | .10 |
| 1972-S | 3¼ million proofs | .30 | 1982-D | 542¾ million | .10 |
| 1973 | 315⅔ million | .10 | 1982-S | 3¾ million proofs | .25 |
| 1973-D | 455 million | .10 | 1983 | 647 million | .10 |
| 1973-S | 2¾ million | .40 | 1983-D | 730 million | .10 |
| 1974 | 470¼ million | .10 | 1983-S | 3¾ million proofs | .50 |
| 1974-D | 571 million | .10 | 1984 | 856½ million | .10 |
| 1974-S | 2⅔ million proofs | .25 | 1984-D | 700 million | .10 |
| 1975 | 585¾ million | .10 | 1984-S | proof | .40 |
| 1975-D | 313¾ million | .10 | 1985 | 705 million | .10 |
| 1975-S | 2¾ million proofs | .30 | 1985-D | 588 million | .10 |
| 1976 | 568¾ million | .10 | 1985-S | proof only | .40 |
| 1976-D | 695¼ million | .10 | 1986 | | .10 |
| 1976-S | 4¼ million proofs | .20 | 1986-D | | .10 |
| 1977 | 797 million | .10 | 1986-S | proof only | .30 |
| 1977-D | 376½ million | .10 | 1987 | | .10 |
| 1977-S | 3¼ million proofs | .20 | 1987-D | | .10 |
| 1978 | 664 million | .10 | 1987-S | proof only | .40 |

## 20 CENT PIECES

### Type: Liberty seated.

(The mint marks are on the Rev., under the eagle)

| | | | | | |
|---|---|---|---|---|---|
| 1875 | 39,700 | **25.00** | 1876-CC | 10,000* | —— |
| 1875-S | 1⅛ million | **20.00** | 1877 | 510 proofs | **1,900.00** |
| 1875-CC | 133,300 | **27.00** | 1878 | 600 proofs | **1,800.00** |
| 1876 | 15,900 | **35.00** | *About a dozen are actually known. | | |

## QUARTERS

*Type: Draped bust of Liberty; small eagle on Rev.*

| Date | Amount Minted | Value |
|------|---------------|-------|
| 1796 | 5,900 | **2,000.00** |

*Type: Draped bust of Liberty; large eagle on Rev.*

| Date | Amount Minted | Value | Date | Amount Minted | Value |
|------|---------------|-------|------|---------------|-------|
| 1804 | 6,700 | **200.00** | 1806 | 206,100 | **100.00** |
| 1805 | 121,400 | **100.00** | 1807 | 220,600 | **100.00** |

*Type: Bust of Liberty wearing cap; motto over the eagle.*

| Date | Amount Minted | Value | Date | Amount Minted | Value |
|------|---------------|-------|------|---------------|-------|
| 1815 | 69,200 | 20.00 | 1823 | 17,800 | 1,000.00 |
| 1818 | 361,200 | 20.00 | 1824 | Unknown | 20.00 |
| 1819 | 144,000 | 20.00 | 1825 | 168,000 | 20.00 |
| 1820 | 127,400 | 20.00 | 1827 | 4,000 | — |
| 1821 | 216,900 | 20.00 | 1828 | 102,000 | 20.00 |
| 1822 | 64,000 | 20.00 | | | |

*Type: Bust of Liberty wearing cap; without motto over the eagle.*

| | | | | | |
|------|---------|-------|------|------------------|-------|
| 1831 | 398,000 | 14.00 | 1835 | 2 million | 14.00 |
| 1832 | 320,000 | 14.00 | 1836 | 472,000 | 14.00 |
| 1833 | 156,000 | 14.00 | 1837 | 252,400 | 14.00 |
| 1834 | 286,000 | 14.00 | 1838 | Part of 832,000 | 14.00 |

Without arrows or rays
1838-1853 & 1856-1865

With arrows and rays 1853 only
With arrows only, 1854-1855

### Type: *Liberty seated; without motto over the eagle.*

(The mint marks are on the Rev., under the eagle)

| Date | Amount Minted | Value | Date | Amount Minted | Value |
|---|---|---|---|---|---|
| 1838 | Part of 832,000 | 5.50 | 1854-O | 1½ million | 3.50 |
| 1839 | 491,000 | 5.50 | 1855 | 2¾ million | 3.50 |
| 1840 | 188,127 | 10.00 | 1855-O | 176,000 | 25.00 |
| 1840-O | 425,200 | 6.50 | 1855-S | 396,400 | 25.00 |
| 1841 | 120,000 | 10.00 | 1856 | 7¼ million | 3.50 |
| 1841-O | 452,000 | 5.00 | 1856-O | 968,000 | 3.50 |
| 1842 | 88,000 | 30.00 | 1856-S | 286,000 | 15.00 |
| 1842-O | 769,000 | 4.00 | 1857 | 9⅔ million | 3.50 |
| 1843 | 645,600 | 4.00 | 1857-O | 1¼ million | 3.50 |
| 1843-O | 968,000 | 4.00 | 1857-S | 82,000 | 25.00 |
| 1844 | 421,200 | 4.00 | 1858 | 7⅓ million | 3.50 |
| 1844-O | 740,000 | 4.00 | 1858-O | 520,000 | 3.50 |
| 1845 | 922,000 | 4.00 | 1858-S | 121,000 | 15.00 |
| 1846 | 510,000 | 4.00 | 1859 | 1⅓ million | 3.50 |
| 1847 | 734,000 | 4.00 | 1859-O | 260,000 | 5.00 |
| 1847-O | 368,000 | 12.00 | 1859-S | 80,000 | 25.00 |
| 1848 | 146,000 | 12.00 | 1860 | 805,400 | 3.50 |
| 1849 | 340,000 | 10.00 | 1860-O | 388,000 | 3.50 |
| 1849-O | Unknown | 225.00 | 1860-S | 56,000 | 35.00 |
| 1850 | 190,800 | 4.00 | 1861 | 4¾ million | 3.50 |
| 1850-O | 412,000 | 15.00 | 1861-S | 96,000 | 12.00 |
| 1851 | 160,000 | 4.00 | 1862 | 932,600 | 3.50 |
| 1851-O | 88,000 | 90.00 | 1862-S | 67,000 | 15.00 |
| 1852 | 177,100 | 12.00 | 1863 | 192,100 | 10.00 |
| 1852-O | 96,000 | 90.00 | 1864 | 94,100 | 15.00 |
| 1853 Arr. & Rays | 15¼ million | 4.00 | 1864-S | 20,000 | 60.00 |
| 1853/3 No Arr. | Part of above | 75.00 | 1865 | 59,300 | 22.00 |
| 1853-O | 1⅓ million | 4.00 | 1865-S | 41,000 | 20.00 |
| 1854 | 12⅓ million | 3.50 | | | |

**(The valuations in this book are based on the coins
being in G-VG condition, unless otherwise noted.)**

Without arrows at date                          With arrows at date
1866-1873 & 1875-1891                             1873-1874

### Type: Liberty seated; with motto over the eagle.

(The mint marks are on the Rev., under the eagle)

| Date | Amount Minted | Value | Date | Amount Minted | Value |
|------|---------------|-------|------|---------------|-------|
| 1866 | 17,500 | 75.00 | 1876 | 17¾ million | 3.00 |
| 1866-S | 28,000 | 40.00 | 1876-S | 8½ million | 3.00 |
| 1867 | 20,600 | 40.00 | 1876-CC | 5 million | 3.00 |
| 1867-S | 48,000 | 20.00 | 1877 | 11 million | 3.00 |
| 1868 | 30,000 | 30.00 | 1877-S | 9 million | 3.00 |
| 1868-S | 96,000 | 15.00 | 1877-CC | 4¼ million | 3.00 |
| 1869 | 16,600 | 50.00 | 1878 | 2¼ million | 3.00 |
| 1869-S | 76,000 | 15.00 | 1878-S | 140,000 | 20.00 |
| 1870 | 87,400 | 12.00 | 1878-CC | 996,000 | 6.00 |
| 1870-CC | 8,300 | 325.00 | 1879 | 14,700 | 40.00 |
| 1871 | 171,200 | 3.50 | 1880 | 15,000 | 40.00 |
| 1871-S | 30,900 | 60.00 | 1881 | 13,000 | 40.00 |
| 1871-CC | 10,900 | 275.00 | 1882 | 16,300 | 40.00 |
| 1872 | 182,900 | 3.50 | 1883 | 15,400 | 40.00 |
| 1872-S | 83,000 | 50.00 | 1884 | 8,900 | 45.00 |
| 1872-CC | 9,100 | 150.00 | 1885 | 14,500 | 40.00 |
| 1873-No Arr. | 143,700 | 4.00 | 1886 | 5,900 | 75.00 |
| 1873-CC-No. Arr. | 4,000 | Rare | 1887 | 10,700 | 40.00 |
| 1873-Arr. | 1⅓ million | 3.50 | 1888 | 10,800 | 40.00 |
| 1873-S.Arr. | 156,000 | 8.00 | 1888-S | 1¼ million | 3.00 |
| 1873-CC-Arr. | 12,500 | 275.00 | 1889 | 12,700 | 40.00 |
| 1874 | 471,900 | 8.00 | 1890 | 80,600 | 20.00 |
| 1874-S | 392,000 | 8.00 | 1891 | 4 million | 3.00 |
| 1875 | 4¼ million | 3.00 | 1891-O | 68,000 | 75.00 |
| 1875-S | 680,000 | 4.00 | 1891-S | 2¼ million | 3.00 |
| 1875-CC | 140,000 | 20.00 | | | |

### Type: Liberty head.

(The mint marks are on the Rev., under the eagle)

| Date | Amount Minted | Value | Date | Amount Minted | Value |
|------|---------------|-------|------|---------------|-------|
| 1892 | 8¼ million | 1.25 | 1892-S | 964,100 | 6.00 |
| 1892-O | 2⅔ million | 2.25 | 1893 | 5½ million | 1.25 |

| Date | Amount Minted | Value | Date | Amount Minted | Value |
|---|---|---|---|---|---|
| 1893-O | 3½ million | 1.50 | 1905-O | 1¼ million | 2.00 |
| 1893-S | 1½ million | 2.00 | 1905-S | 1¾ million | 2.00 |
| 1894 | 3½ million | 1.50 | 1906 | 3⅔ million | 1.15 |
| 1894-O | 2¾ million | 1.75 | 1906-D | 3⅓ million | 1.25 |
| 1894-S | 2⅔ million | 1.75 | 1906-O | 2 million | 1.25 |
| 1895 | 4½ million | 1.25 | 1907 | 7¼ million | 1.15 |
| 1895-O | 2¾ million | 1.75 | 1907-D | 2½ million | 1.25 |
| 1895-S | 1¾ million | 1.90 | 1907-O | 4½ million | 1.25 |
| 1896 | 3¾ million | 1.50 | 1907-S | 1⅓ million | 1.90 |
| 1896-O | 1½ million | 2.00 | 1908 | 4¼ million | 1.15 |
| 1896-S | 188,000 | 90.00 | 1908-D | 5¾ million | 1.25 |
| 1897 | 8 million | 1.15 | 1908-O | 6¼ million | 1.25 |
| 1897-O | 1½ million | 3.00 | 1908-S | 784,000 | 3.00 |
| 1897-S | 542,200 | 4.00 | 1909 | 9¼ million | 1.15 |
| 1898 | 11 million | 1.15 | 1909-D | 5 million | 1.25 |
| 1898-O | 1¾ million | 2.00 | 1909-O | 712,000 | 4.00 |
| 1898-S | 1 million | 2.00 | 1909-S | 1⅓ million | 1.25 |
| 1899 | 12⅔ million | 1.15 | 1910 | 2¼ million | 1.15 |
| 1899-O | 2⅔ million | 1.90 | 1910-D | 1½ million | 1.15 |
| 1899-S | 708,000 | 3.00 | 1911 | 3¾ million | 1.15 |
| 1900 | 10 million | 1.15 | 1911-D | 933,600 | 1.25 |
| 1900-O | 3½ million | 2.25 | 1911-S | 988,000 | 1.25 |
| 1900-S | 1¾ million | 2.25 | 1912 | 4½ million | 1.15 |
| 1901 | 9 million | 1.15 | 1912-S | 708,000 | 1.15 |
| 1901-O | 1⅔ million | 5.50 | 1913 | 484,600 | 4.50 |
| 1901-S | 72,700 | 500.00 | 1913-D | 1½ million | 1.25 |
| 1902 | 12¼ million | 1.15 | 1913-S | 40,000 | 125.00 |
| 1902-O | 4¾ million | 1.90 | 1914 | 6¼ million | 1.25 |
| 1902-S | 1½ million | 3.50 | 1914-D | 3 million | 1.25 |
| 1903 | 9⅔ million | 1.15 | 1914-S | 264,000 | 6.50 |
| 1903-O | 3½ million | 1.90 | 1915 | 3½ million | 1.15 |
| 1903-S | 1 million | 3.25 | 1915-D | 3¾ million | 1.25 |
| 1904 | 9½ million | 1.15 | 1915-S | 704,000 | 1.90 |
| 1904-O | 2½ million | 1.90 | 1016 | 1¾ million | 1.15 |
| 1905 | 5 million | 1.15 | 1916-D | 6½ million | 1.25 |

Type I. No stars under eagle
1916–1917

Type II. Three stars under eagle
1917–1930

## *Type: Liberty standing*

(The mint marks are on the Obv., above and to left of the date)

| Date | Amount Minted | Value | Date | Amount Minted | Value |
|---|---|---|---|---|---|
| 1916 | 52,000 | 550.00 | 1917-II | 14 million | 6.00 |
| 1917-I | 8¾ million | 5.00 | 1917-D-II | 6¼ million | 9.00 |
| 1917-D-I | 1½ million | 7.00 | 1917-S-II | 5½ million | 7.50 |
| 1917-S-I | 2 million | 7.00 | 1918 | 14¼ million | 6.50 |

| Date | Amount Minted | Value | Date | Amount Minted | Value |
|---|---|---|---|---|---|
| 1918-D | 7⅓ million | 10.00 | 1925 | 12¼ million | 1.25 |
| 1918-S | 11 million | 7.00 | 1926 | 11¼ million | 1.25 |
| 1918-S over 17 | — | 600.00 | 1926-D | 1¾ million | 3.00 |
| 1919 | 11⅓ million | 13.00 | 1926-S | 2¾ million | 1.75 |
| 1919-D | 2 million | 20.00 | 1927 | 12 million | 1.25 |
| 1919-S | 1¾ million | 20.00 | 1927-D | 976,400 | 2.50 |
| 1920 | 28 million | 6.00 | 1927-S | 396,000 | 4.00 |
| 1920-D | 3½ million | 12.00 | 1928 | 6⅓ million | 1.25 |
| 1920-S | 6⅓ million | 7.00 | 1928-D | 1⅔ million | 1.50 |
| 1921 | 2 million | 30.00 | 1928-S | 2⅔ million | 1.25 |
| 1923 | 9¾ million | 7.00 | 1929 | 11 million | 1.25 |
| 1923-S | 1⅓ million | 50.00 | 1929-D | 1⅓ million | 1.25 |
| 1924 | 11 million | 7.00 | 1929-S | 1¾ million | 1.25 |
| 1924-D | 3 million | 10.00 | 1930 | 5⅔ million | 1.25 |
| 1924-S | 3 million | 7.00 | 1930-S | 1⅔ million | 1.25 |

| Reg. Obv. 1932–1974 | Reg. Rev. 1932–1974 | Bicentennial Obv.—1976 | Bicentennial Rev.—1976 |

## Type: Washington head

(From 1932–1964, the mint marks are on the Rev., under the eagle. From 1968 to date, the mint marks are on the obverse, to the right of Washington's neck)

| Date | Amount Minted | Value | Date | Amount Minted | Value |
|---|---|---|---|---|---|
| 1932 | 5½ million | 1.25 | 1940-S | 8¼ million | 1.15 |
| 1932-D | 436,800 | 20.00 | 1941 | 79 million | 1.15 |
| 1932-S | 408,000 | 17.50 | 1941-D | 16¾ million | 1.15 |
| 1934 | 32 million | 1.15 | 1941-S | 16 million | 1.15 |
| 1934-D | 3½ million | 1.15 | 1942 | 102 million | 1.15 |
| 1935 | 32½ million | 1.15 | 1942-D | 17½ million | 1.15 |
| 1935-D | 5¾ million | 1.15 | 1942-S | 19½ million | 1.15 |
| 1935-S | 5¾ million | 1.15 | 1943 | 99¾ million | 1.15 |
| 1936 | 41⅓ million | 1.15 | 1943-D | 16 million | 1.15 |
| 1936-D | 5½ million | 1.25 | 1943-S | 21¾ million | 1.15 |
| 1936-S | 3¾ million | 1.15 | 1944 | 105 million | 1.15 |
| 1937 | 19¾ million | 1.15 | 1944-D | 14⅔ million | 1.15 |
| 1937-D | 7¼ million | 1.15 | 1944-S | 12⅔ million | 1.15 |
| 1937-S | 1¾ million | 1.75 | 1945 | 74½ million | 1.15 |
| 1938 | 9½ million | 1.15 | 1945-D | 12⅓ million | 1.15 |
| 1938-S | 2¾ million | 1.15 | 1945-S | 17 million | 1.15 |
| 1939 | 33½ million | 1.15 | 1946 | 53½ million | 1.15 |
| 1939-D | 7 million | 1.15 | 1946-D | 9 million | 1.15 |
| 1939-S | 2⅔ million | 1.15 | 1946-S | 4¼ million | 1.15 |
| 1940 | 35¾ million | 1.15 | 1947 | 22⅔ million | 1.15 |
| 1940-D | 2¾ million | 1.15 | 1947-D | 15⅓ million | 1.15 |

| Date | Amount Minted | Value | Date | Amount Minted | Value |
|------|---------------|-------|------|---------------|-------|
| 1947-S | 5½ million | 1.15 | 1970-S | 2½ million proofs | .35 |
| 1948 | 35¼ million | 1.15 | 1971 | 109¼ million | .25 |
| 1948-D | 16¾ million | 1.15 | 1971-D | 258⅔ million | .25 |
| 1948-S | 16 million | 1.15 | 1971-S | 3¼ million proofs | .35 |
| 1949 | 9⅓ million | 1.15 | 1972 | 215 million | .25 |
| 1949-D | 10 million | 1.15 | 1972-D | 311 million | .25 |
| 1950 | 25 million | 1.15 | 1972-S | 3¼ million proofs | .35 |
| 1950-D | 21 million | 1.15 | 1973 | 347 million | .25 |
| 1950-S | 10⅓ million | 1.15 | 1973-D | 233 million | .25 |
| 1951 | 43½ million | 1.15 | 1973-S | 2¾ million proofs | .30 |
| 1951-D | 35½ million | 1.15 | 1974 | 801½ million | .25 |
| 1951-S | 9 million | 1.15 | 1974-D | 353¼ million | .25 |
| 1952 | 39 million | 1.15 | 1974-S | 2⅔ million proofs | .30 |
| 1952-D | 49¾ million | 1.15 | 1975 | none minted | — |
| 1952-S | 13¾ million | 1.15 | 1976 | 809¾ million | .25 |
| 1953 | 18¾ million | 1.15 | 1976-D | 860 million | .25 |
| 1953-D | 56 million | 1.15 | 1976-S | cupro-nickel,proof,7 | .30 |
| 1953-S | 14 million | 1.15 | 1976-S | silver | .75 |
| 1954 | 54⅔ million | 1.15 | 1976-S | silver, proof | 1.25 |
| 1954-D | 46⅙ million | 1.15 | 1077 | 460½ million | .25 |
| 1954-S | 11¾ million | 1.15 | 1977-D | 256½ million | .25 |
| 1955 | 18⅔ million | 1.15 | 1977-S | 3¼ million proofs | .30 |
| 1955-D | 3¼ million | 1.15 | 1978 | 521½ million | .25 |
| 1956 | 44⅓ million | 1.15 | 1978-D | 287¼ million | .25 |
| 1956-D | 32⅓ million | 1.15 | 1978-S | 3¼ million proofs | .30 |
| 1957 | 46½ million | 1.15 | 1979 | 515¾ million | .25 |
| 1957-D | 78 million | 1.15 | 1979-D | 489¾ million | .25 |
| 1958 | 6⅓ million | 1.15 | 1979-S | 3¾ million proofs | .30 |
| 1958-D | 78¼ million | 1.15 | 1980 | 635¾ million | .25 |
| 1959 | 24⅓ million | 1.15 | 1980-D | 518⅓ million | .25 |
| 1959-D | 62 million | 1.15 | 1980-S,proof | 3½ million proofs | .30 |
| 1960 | 30¾ million | 1.15 | 1981 | 601¾ million | .25 |
| 1960-D | 63 million | 1.15 | 1981-D | 575¾ million | .25 |
| 1961 | 37 million | 1.15 | 1981-S | 4 million proofs | .30 |
| 1961-D | 80¼ million | 1.15 | 1982 | 501 million | .25 |
| 1962 | 36¼ million | 1.15 | 1982-D | 480 million | .25 |
| 1962-D | 127½ million | 1.15 | 1982-S | 3.8 million proofs | .30 |
| 1963 | 74⅓ million | 1.15 | 1983 | 673½ million | .25 |
| 1963-D | 135¼ million | 1.15 | 1983-D | 618 million | .25 |
| 1964 | 560⅓ million | 1.15 | 1983-S | 3.8 million proofs | .40 |
| 1964 | 704 million | 1.15 | 1984 | 673½ million | .25 |
| | CLAD COINAGE | | 1984-D | 546½ million | .25 |
| 1965 | 1¾ billion | .25 | 1984-S | proof only | .35 |
| 1966 | 821 million | .25 | 1985 | 776 million | .25 |
| 1967 | 1½ billion | .25 | 1985-D | 520 million | .25 |
| 1968 | 220¾ million | .25 | 1985-S | proof only | .35 |
| 1968-D | 101½ million | .25 | 1986 | | .25 |
| 1968-S | 3 million proofs | .30 | 1986-D | | .25 |
| 1969 | 176¼ million | .25 | 1986-S | proof only | .40 |
| 1969-D | 114⅓ million | .25 | 1987 | | .25 |
| 1969-S | 3 million proofs | .35 | 1987-D | | .25 |
| 1970 | 136½ million | .25 | 1987-S | proof only | .50 |
| 1970-D | 417⅓ million | .25 | | | |

## HALF DOLLARS

***Type: Liberty head with flowing hair.***

| Date | Amount Minted | Value | Date | Amount Minted | Value |
|------|---------------|-------|------|---------------|-------|
| 1794 | 5,300 | **275.00** | 1795 | 317,800 | **240.00** |

***Type: Draped bust of Liberty; small eagle on Rev.***

| Date | Amount Minted | Value | Date | Amount Minted | Value |
|------|---------------|-------|------|---------------|-------|
| 1796 | Unknown | **6,000.00** | 1797 | | **6,000.00** |

***Type: Draped bust of Liberty; large eagle on Rev.***

| Date | Amount Minted | Value | Date | Amount Minted | Value |
|------|---------------|-------|------|---------------|-------|
| 1801 | 30,300 | **85.00** | 1805 | 211,700 | **40.00** |
| 1802 | 29,900 | **50.00** | 1806 | 839,600 | **35.00** |
| 1803 | 31,700 | **45.00** | 1807 | 301,100 | **35.00** |

***(The valuations in this book are based on the coins
being in G-VG condition, unless otherwise noted.)***

*Type: Bust of Liberty wearing cap; motto over eagle lettered edge; large size.*

| Date | Amount Minted | Value | Date | Amount Minted | Value |
|------|--------------|-------|------|--------------|-------|
| 1807 | 750,500 | 20.00 | 1823 | 1⅔ million | 12.00 |
| 1808 | 1⅓ million | 17.50 | 1824 | 3½ million | 12.00 |
| 1809 | 1½ million | 17.50 | 1825 | 3 million | 12.00 |
| 1810 | 1¼ million | 17.50 | 1826 | 4 million | 12.00 |
| 1811 | 1¼ million | 17.50 | 1827 | 5½ million | 12.00 |
| 1812 | 1⅔ million | 17.50 | 1828 | 3 million | 12.00 |
| 1813 | 1¼ million | 17.50 | 1829 | 3¾ million | 12.00 |
| 1814 | 1 million | 17.50 | 1830 | 4¾ million | 12.00 |
| 1815 | 47,100 | 135.00 | 1831 | 5¾ million | 12.00 |
| 1817 | 1¼ million | 16.00 | 1832 | 4¾ million | 12.00 |
| 1818 | 2 million | 16.00 | 1833 | 5¼ million | 12.00 |
| 1819 | 2¼ million | 16.00 | 1834 | 6⅓ million | 12.00 |
| 1820 | 751,100 | 20.00 | 1835 | 5½ million | 12.00 |
| 1821 | 1⅓ million | 12.00 | 1836 | Part of 6½ million | 12.00 |
| 1822 | 1½ million | 12.00 | | | |

*Type: Bust of Liberty wearing cap; no motto over eagle; reeded edge; reduced size; value expressed as "50" cents."*

| | | | | | |
|------|------|------|------|------|------|
| 1836 | Part of 6½ million | 175.00 | 1837 | 3⅔ million | 16.00 |

*Type: Same as above; but value is expressed as "Half Dol."*

(The mint marks are on the Obv., over the date)

| Date | Amount Minted | Value | Date | Amount Minted | Value |
|------|---------------|-------|------|---------------|-------|
| 1838 | 3½ million | **18.00** | 1839 | Part of 3⅓ million | **18.00** |
| 1838-O | About 20 | **Rare** | 1839-O | 163,000 | **40.00** |

Without arrows or rays, 1839-1853 & 1856-1866
With arrows and rays, 1853 only
With arrows only, 1854-1855

*Type: Liberty seated; without motto over the eagle.*

(The mint marks are on the Rev., under the eagle)

| Date | Amount Minted | Value | Date | Amount Minted | Value |
|------|---------------|-------|------|---------------|-------|
| 1839 | Part of 3⅓ million | **14.00** | 1847-O | 2½ million | 6.00 |
| 1840 | 1½ million | **10.00** | 1848 | 580,000 | 6.00 |
| 1840-O | 855,100 | **13.00** | 1848-O | 3¼ million | 6.00 |
| 1841 | 310,000 | **15.00** | 1849 | 1¼ million | 6.00 |
| 1841-O | 401,000 | 6.00 | 1849-O | 2⅓ million | 6.00 |
| 1842 | 2 million | 6.00 | 1850 | 227,000 | 22.00 |
| 1842-O | 957,000 | 6.00 | 1850-O | 2½ million | 7.00 |
| 1843 | 3¾ million | 6.00 | 1851 | 200,700 | 22.00 |
| 1843-O | 2¼ million | 6.00 | 1851-O | 402,000 | 7.00 |
| 1844 | 1¾ million | 6.00 | 1852 | 77,100 | 45.00 |
| 1844-O | 2 million | 6.00 | 1852-O | 144,000 | 25.00 |
| 1845 | 589,000 | 6.00 | 1853-Arr. & Rays | 3½ million | 8.00 |
| 1845-O | 2 million | 6.00 | 1853-O-No Arr & Rays | 1⅓ million | **Rare** |
| 1846 | 2¼ million | 6.00 | 1853-O-Arr. & Rays | Part of above | 8.00 |
| 1846-O | 2⅓ million | 6.00 | 1854 | 3 million | 7.00 |
| 1847 | 1¼ million | 6.00 | 1854-O | 5¼ million | 7.00 |

| Date | Amount Minted | Value | Date | Amount Minted | Value |
|------|--------------|-------|------|--------------|-------|
| 1855 | 759,500 | 7.00 | 1860 | 303,700 | 10.00 |
| 1855-O | 3⅔ million | 7.00 | 1860-O | 1¼ million | 6.00 |
| 1855-S | 129,900 | 125.00 | 1860-S | 472,000 | 6.00 |
| 1856 | 938,000 | 6.00 | 1861 | 2¾ million | 6.00 |
| 1856-O | 2⅔ million | 6.00 | 1861-O | 2½ million | 6.00 |
| 1856-S | 211,000 | 12.00 | 1861-S | 939,500 | 6.00 |
| 1857 | 2 million | 6.00 | 1862 | 252,300 | 10.00 |
| 1857-O | 818,000 | 6.00 | 1862-S | 1⅓ million | 6.00 |
| 1857-S | 158,000 | 15.00 | 1863 | 503,700 | 10.00 |
| 1858 | 4¼ million | 6.00 | 1863-S | 916,000 | 6.00 |
| 1858-O | 7¼ million | 6.00 | 1864 | 379,600 | 10.00 |
| 1858-S | 476,000 | 9.00 | 1864-S | 658,000 | 6.00 |
| 1859 | 748,000 | 6.00 | 1865 | 511,900 | 10.00 |
| 1859-O | 2¾ million | 6.00 | 1865-S | 675,000 | 6.00 |
| 1859-S | 566,000 | 9.00 | 1866-S | Part of 1 million | 25.00 |

Without arrows at date, 1866-1873 & 1875-1891
With arrows at date, 1873-1874

## Type: Liberty seated; with motto over the eagle.

(The mint marks are on the Rev., under the eagle)

| Date | Amount Minted | Value | Date | Amount Minted | Value |
|------|--------------|-------|------|--------------|-------|
| 1866 | 745,600 | 5.00 | 1872-S | 580,000 | 5.00 |
| 1866-S | Part of 1 million | 5.00 | 1872-CC | 272,000 | 20.00 |
| 1867 | 424,300 | 10.00 | 1873-No Arr. | 820,800 | 5.00 |
| 1867-S | 1¼ million | 5.00 | 1873-CC-No Arr. | 122,500 | 30.00 |
| 1868 | 378,200 | 12.00 | 1873-Arr. | 1¾ million | 10.00 |
| 1868-S | 1¼ million | 5.00 | 1873-S-Arr. | 228,000 | 12.00 |
| 1869 | 795,900 | 5.00 | 1873-CC-Arr. | 214,600 | 15.00 |
| 1869-S | 656,000 | 5.00 | 1874 | 2⅓ million | 10.00 |
| 1870 | 600,900 | 5.00 | 1874-S | 394,000 | 12.00 |
| 1870-S | 1 million | 5.00 | 1874-CC | 59,000 | 45.00 |
| 1870-CC | 54,600 | 125.00 | 1875 | 6 million | 5.00 |
| 1871 | 1¼ million | 5.00 | 1875-S | 3¼ million | 5.00 |
| 1871-S | 2¼ million | 5.00 | 1875-CC | 1 million | 7.00 |
| 1871-CC | 139,900 | 35.00 | 1876 | 8½ million | 5.00 |
| 1872 | 881,500 | 5.00 | 1876-S | 4½ million | 5.00 |

| Date | Amount Minted | Value | Date | Amount Minted | Value |
|------|--------------|-------|------|--------------|-------|
| 1876-CC | 2 million | 5.00 | 1882 | 5,500 | 75.00 |
| 1877 | 8⅓ million | 5.00 | 1883 | 9,000 | 70.00 |
| 1877-S | 5⅓ million | 5.00 | 1884 | 5,300 | 75.00 |
| 1877-CC | 1½ million | 5.00 | 1885 | 6,100 | 75.00 |
| 1878 | 1⅓ million | 5.00 | 1886 | 5,900 | 75.00 |
| 1878-S | 12,000 | 900.00 | 1887 | 5,700 | 75.00 |
| 1878-CC | 62,000 | 90.00 | 1888 | 12,800 | 65.00 |
| 1879 | 5,900 | 75.00 | 1889 | 12,700 | 65.00 |
| 1880 | 9,800 | 70.00 | 1890 | 12,600 | 65.00 |
| 1881 | 11,000 | 70.00 | 1891 | 200,600 | 10.00 |

## Type: Liberty Head.

(The mint marks are on the Rev., under the eagle)

| Date | Amount Minted | Value | Date | Amount Minted | Value |
|------|--------------|-------|------|--------------|-------|
| 1892 | 1 million | 6.00 | 1900 | 4¾ million | 2.50 |
| 1892-O | 390,000 | 35.00 | 1900-O | 2¾ million | 3.75 |
| 1892-S | 1 million | 50.00 | 1900-S | 2½ million | 3.75 |
| 1893 | 1¾ million | 4.00 | 1901 | 4¼ million | 2.50 |
| 1893-O | 1⅓ million | 7.00 | 1901-O | 1 million | 3.75 |
| 1893-S | 740,000 | 21.00 | 1901-S | 847,000 | 5.00 |
| 1894 | 1¼ million | 3.75 | 1902 | 5 million | 2.50 |
| 1894-O | 2¼ million | 3.75 | 1902-O | 2½ million | 3.75 |
| 1894-S | 4 million | 3.75 | 1902-S | 1½ million | 3.75 |
| 1895 | 1¾ million | 3.75 | 1903 | 2¼ million | 2.50 |
| 1895-O | 1¾ million | 3.75 | 1903-O | 2 million | 2.75 |
| 1895-S | 1 million | 6.00 | 1903-S | 2 million | 2.75 |
| 1896 | 950,800 | 3.75 | 1904 | 3 million | 2.50 |
| 1896-O | 924,000 | 6.00 | 1904-O | 1 million | 4.00 |
| 1896-S | 1¼ million | 20.00 | 1904-S | 553,000 | 5.00 |
| 1897 | 2½ million | 2.50 | 1905 | 663,000 | 4.50 |
| 1897-O | 632,000 | 20.00 | 1905-O | 505,000 | 5.00 |
| 1897-S | 933,900 | 40.00 | 1905-S | 2½ million | 3.00 |
| 1898 | 3 million | 2.50 | 1906 | 2½ million | 2.50 |
| 1898-O | 874,000 | 6.00 | 1906-D | 4 million | 2.50 |
| 1898-S | 2⅓ million | 3.75 | 1906-O | 2½ million | 2.50 |
| 1899 | 5½ million | 2.50 | 1906-S | 1¾ million | 2.50 |
| 1899-O | 1¾ million | 3.75 | 1907 | 2½ million | 2.50 |
| 1899-S | 1½ million | 3.75 | 1907-D | 3¾ million | 2.50 |

# Half Dollars (continued)

| Date | Amount Minted | Value | Date | Amount Minted | Value |
|------|---------------|-------|------|---------------|-------|
| 1907-O | 4 million | 2.50 | 1911-S | 1¼ million | 2.50 |
| 1907-S | 1¼ million | 2.50 | 1912 | 1½ million | 2.50 |
| 1908 | 1⅓ million | 2.50 | 1912-D | 2⅓ million | 2.50 |
| 1908-D | 3¼ million | 2.50 | 1912-S | 1⅓ million | 2.50 |
| 1908-O | 5⅓ million | 2.50 | 1913 | 189,000 | 8.00 |
| 1908-S | 1⅔ million | 2.50 | 1913-D | 534,000 | 2.50 |
| 1909 | 2⅓ million | 2.50 | 1913-S | 604,000 | 2.50 |
| 1909-O | 925,000 | 2.50 | 1914 | 125,000 | 10.00 |
| 1909-S | 1¾ million | 2.50 | 1914-S | 1 million | 2.50 |
| 1910 | 419,000 | 4.00 | 1915 | 138,000 | 10.00 |
| 1910-S | 2 million | 2.50 | 1915-D | 1¼ million | 2.50 |
| 1911 | 1½ million | 2.50 | 1915-S | 1⅔ million | 2.50 |
| 1911-D | 695,000 | 2.50 | | | |

### Type: Liberty Walking.

(Mint marks: on the coins of 1916 and the early coinage of 1917, the mint marks are on the Obv., under the motto. On the later coinage of 1917 and thereafter, the mint marks are on the Rev., to the left of "Half Dollar.")

| Date | Amount Minted | Value | Date | Amount Minted | Value |
|------|---------------|-------|------|---------------|-------|
| 1916 | 608,000 | 7.00 | 1923-S | 2¼ million | 4.00 |
| 1916-D | 1 million | 6.00 | 1927-S | 2⅓ million | 2.50 |
| 1916-S | 508,000 | 15.00 | 1928-S | 2 million | 3.00 |
| 1917 | 12¼ million | 3.75 | 1929-D | 1 million | 3.00 |
| 1917-D (Obv.) | 765,000 | 5.00 | 1929-S | 2 million | 2.50 |
| 1917-D (Rev.) | 2 million | 3.75 | 1933-S | 1¾ million | 2.50 |
| 1917-S (Obv.) | 1 million | 5.00 | 1934 | 7 million | 2.25 |
| 1917-S (Rev.) | 5½ million | 3.75 | 1934-D | 2⅓ million | 2.25 |
| 1918 | 6⅔ million | 3.75 | 1934-S | 3⅔ million | 2.25 |
| 1918-D | 3¾ million | 4.00 | 1935 | 9¼ million | 2.25 |
| 1918-S | 10¼ million | 3.75 | 1935-D | 3 million | 2.25 |
| 1919 | 962,000 | 5.00 | 1935-S | 3¾ million | 2.25 |
| 1919-D | 1¼ million | 4.00 | 1936 | 12⅓ million | 2.25 |
| 1919-S | 1½ million | 3.75 | 1936-D | 4¼ million | 2.25 |
| 1920 | 6⅓ million | 3.75 | 1936-S | 4 million | 2.25 |
| 1920-D | 1½ million | 4.00 | 1937 | 9½ million | 2.25 |
| 1920-S | 4⅔ million | 3.75 | 1937-D | 1¾ million | 2.25 |
| 1921 | 246,000 | 22.50 | 1937-S | 2 million | 2.25 |
| 1921-D | 208,000 | 34.00 | 1938 | 4 million | 2.25 |
| 1921-S | 548,000 | 7.00 | 1938-D | 491,600 | 9.00 |

| Date | Amount Minted | Value | Date | Amount Minted | Value |
|------|--------------|-------|------|--------------|-------|
| 1939 | 6¾ million | 2.25 | 1943-S | 13½ million | 2.25 |
| 1939-D | 4¼ million | 2.25 | 1944 | 28¼ million | 2.25 |
| 1939-S | 2½ million | 2.25 | 1944-D | 9¾ million | 2.25 |
| 1940 | 9¼ million | 2.25 | 1944-S | 9 million | 2.25 |
| 1940-S | 4½ million | 2.25 | 1945 | 31½ million | 2.25 |
| 1941 | 24¼ million | 2.25 | 1945-D | 10 million | 2.25 |
| 1941-D | 11¼ million | 2.25 | 1945-S | 10¼ million | 2.25 |
| 1941-S | 8 million | 2.25 | 1946 | 12 million | 2.25 |
| 1942 | 47¾ million | 2.25 | 1946-D | 2¼ million | 2.25 |
| 1942-D | 11 million | 2.25 | 1946-S | 3¾ million | 2.25 |
| 1942-S | 12¾ million | 2.25 | 1947 | 4 million | 2.25 |
| 1943 | 53¼ million | 2.25 | 1947-D | 4 million | 2.25 |
| 1943-D | 11⅓ million | 2.25 | | | |

### Type: Franklin Head.

(The mint marks are on the Rev., above the Liberty Bell)

| Date | Amount Minted | Value | Date | Amount Minted | Value |
|------|--------------|-------|------|--------------|-------|
| 1948 | 3 million | 2.50 | 1954-S | 5 million | 2.25 |
| 1948-D | 4 million | 2.50 | 1955 | 3 million | 2.25 |
| 1949 | 5¾ million | 2.50 | 1956 | 4¼ million | 2.25 |
| 1949-D | 4 million | 2.50 | 1957 | 5 million | 2.25 |
| 1949-S | 3¾ million | 3.00 | 1957-D | 20 million | 2.25 |
| 1950 | 7¾ million | 2.25 | 1958 | 4 million | 2.25 |
| 1950-D | 8 million | 2.25 | 1958-D | 24 million | 2.25 |
| 1951 | 16¾ million | 2.25 | 1959 | 6¼ million | 2.25 |
| 1951-D | 9½ million | 2.25 | 1959-D | 13 million | 2.25 |
| 1951-S | 13⅔ million | 2.25 | 1960 | 7¾ million | 2.25 |
| 1952 | 21¼ million | 2.25 | 1960-D | 18¼ million | 2.25 |
| 1952-D | 25⅓ million | 2.25 | 1961 | 8¼ million | 2.25 |
| 1952-S | 5½ million | 2.25 | 1961-D | 20¼ million | 2.25 |
| 1953 | 2¾ million | 2.25 | 1962 | 9¾ million | 2.25 |
| 1953-D | 21 million | 2.25 | 1962-D | 35½ million | 2.25 |
| 1953-S | 4¼ million | 2.25 | 1963 | 22 million | 2.25 |
| 1954 | 13½ million | 2.25 | 1963-D | 67 million | 2.25 |
| 1954-D | 24½ million | 2.25 | | | |

| Reg. Obv. | Reg. Rev. | Bicentennial | Bicentennial |
|-----------|-----------|--------------|--------------|
| 1964-1974 | 1964-1974 | Obv.—1976 | Rev.—1976 |

## Type: Kennedy Head

(In 1964 the mint mark is on the Rev., under the eagle's right talon. From 1968 to date, the mint marks are on the obverse, just below the base of Kennedy's neck)

| Date | Amount Minted | Value | Date | Amount Minted | Value |
|------|---------------|-------|------|---------------|-------|
| | SILVER | | 1977 | 43½ million | .50 |
| 1964 | 277¼ million | 2.25 | 1977-D | 31½ million | .50 |
| 1964-D | 156¼ million | 2.25 | 1977-S | 3¼ million proofs | .85 |
| | SILVER CLAD | | 1978 | 14⅓ million | .50 |
| 1965 | 65¾ million | .70 | 1978-D | 13¾ million | .50 |
| 1966 | 109 million | .70 | 1978-S | 3¼ million proofs | 1.00 |
| 1967 | 295 million | .70 | 1979 | 68⅓ million | .50 |
| 1968-D | 247 million | .70 | 1979-D | 15¾ million | .50 |
| 1968-S | 3 million proofs | 2.00 | 1979-S | 3¾ million proofs | .85 |
| 1969-D | 129¾ million | .70 | 1980 | 44 million | .50 |
| 1969-S | 3 million proofs | 2.00 | 1980-D | 33½ million | .50 |
| 1970-D | 2¼ million | 10.00 | 1980-S proof | 3½ million proofs | .85 |
| 1970-S | 2½ million proofs | 6.00 | 1981 | 29½ million | .50 |
| | COPPER-NICKEL CLAD | | 1981-D | 27¾ million | .50 |
| 1971 | 155¼ million | .50 | 1981-S | 4 million proofs | .85 |
| 1971-D | 302 million | .50 | 1982 | 10.8 million | .50 |
| 1971-S | 3¼ million proofs | .90 | 1982-D | 13 million | .50 |
| 1972 | 153 million | .50 | 1982-S | 3.8 million proofs | 2.50 |
| 1972-D | 141¾ million | .50 | 1983 | 34 million | .50 |
| 1972-S | 3¼ million proofs | 1.00 | 1983-D | 32½ million | .50 |
| 1973 | 65 million | .50 | 1983-S | 3.8 million proofs | 3.50 |
| 1973-D | 83 million | .50 | 1984 | 26 million | .50 |
| 1973-S | 2¾ million proofs | 1.00 | 1984-D | 26¼ million | .50 |
| 1974 | 201½ million | .50 | 1984-S | proof | 2.50 |
| 1974-D | 79 million | .50 | 1985 | 18.7 million | .50 |
| 1974-S | 2⅔ million proofs | 1.00 | 1985-D | 19.8 million | .50 |
| 1975 | none minted | | 1985-S | proof only | 3.00 |
| 1976 | 234⅓ million | .50 | 1986 | | .50 |
| 1976-D | 287½ million | .50 | 1986-D | | .50 |
| 1976-S cupro-nickel, proof | | | 1986-S | proof only | 2.00 |
| | 7 million | .75 | 1987 | | .50 |
| 1976-S | silver | 1.25 | 1987-D | | .50 |
| 1976-S | silver, proof | 1.75 | 1987-S | proof only | 3.00 |

## SILVER DOLLARS

*Type: Head of Liberty with flowing hair.*

| Date | Amount Minted | Value | Date | Amount Minted | Value |
|------|--------------|-------|------|--------------|-------|
| 1794 | 1,758 | **3,250.00** | 1795 | Part of 184,000 | **500.00** |

*Type: Draped bust of Liberty; with small eagle on Rev.*

| Date | Amount Minted | Value | Date | Amount Minted | Value |
|------|--------------|-------|------|--------------|-------|
| 1795 | Part of 184,000 | **350.00** | 1797 | 7,800 | **350.00** |
| 1796 | 72,900 | **350.00** | 1798 | Part of 327,500 | **400.00** |

*Type: Draped bust of Liberty; with large eagle on Rev.*

| Date | Amount Minted | Value | Date | Amount Minted | Value |
|------|---------------|-------|------|---------------|-------|
| 1798 | Part of 327,500 | **200.00** | 1803 | 66,100 | **200.00** |
| 1799 | 423,500 | **200.00** | 1804 | —— | —— |
| 1800 | 220,900 | **200.00** | (less than 15 specimens are known of the |
| 1801 | 54,500 | **200.00** | 1804 Dollar.) |
| 1802 | 41,600 | **200.00** | | | |

*Type: Liberty seated; with flying eagle on Rev.—the*
*Gobrecht design.*

| 1836 | About 1,000 | **1,000.00** | 1839 | About 300 | **1,300.00** |
|------|-------------|-------------|------|-----------|-------------|
| 1838 | About 100 | **2,000.00** | | | |

### *Type: Liberty seated; without motto over the eagle.*

(The mint marks are on the Rev., under the eagle)

| Date | Amount Minted | Value | Date | Amount Minted | Value |
|------|--------------:|------:|------|--------------:|------:|
| 1840 | 61,000 | 42.00 | 1854 | 33,100 | 75.00 |
| 1841 | 173,000 | 40.00 | 1855 | 26,000 | 120.00 |
| 1842 | 184,600 | 40.00 | 1856 | 63,500 | 70.00 |
| 1843 | 165,100 | 40.00 | 1857 | 94,000 | 70.00 |
| 1844 | 20,000 | 75.00 | 1858 | Proof, About 100 | 3,000.00 |
| 1845 | 24,500 | 75.00 | 1859 | 256,500 | 40.00 |
| 1846 | 110,600 | 40.00 | 1859-O | 360,000 | 40.00 |
| 1846-O | 59,000 | 70.00 | 1859-S | 20,000 | 50.00 |
| 1847 | 140,700 | 40.00 | 1860 | 218,900 | 40.00 |
| 1848 | 15,000 | 50.00 | 1860-O | 515,000 | 40.00 |
| 1849 | 62,600 | 40.00 | 1861 | 78,500 | 70.00 |
| 1850 | 7,500 | 90.00 | 1862 | 12,100 | 125.00 |
| 1850-O | 40,000 | 40.00 | 1863 | 27,700 | 75.00 |
| 1851 | 1,300 | 600.00 | 1864 | 31,200 | 75.00 |
| 1852 | 1,100 | Rare | 1865 | 47,000 | 75.00 |
| 1853 | 46,100 | 45.00 | | | |

### *Type: Liberty seated: with motto over the eagle.*

(The mint marks are on the Rev., under the eagle)

| Date | Amount Minted | Value | Date | Amount Minted | Value |
|------|--------------|-------|------|--------------|-------|
| 1866 | 49,600 | **50.00** | 1871 | 1 million | 40.00 |
| 1867 | 60,300 | **50.00** | 1871-CC | 1,400 | **350.00** |
| 1868 | 182,700 | **45.00** | 1872 | 1 million | 40.00 |
| 1869 | 424,300 | **40.00** | 1872-S | 9,000 | 50.00 |
| 1870 | 433,000 | **40.00** | 1872-CC | 3,100 | 175.00 |
| 1870-S | Unknown | **Rare** | 1873 | 293,600 | 40.00 |
| 1870-CC | 12,500 | **90.00** | 1873-CC | 2,300 | **450.00** |

## Type: *Liberty Head.*

(The mint marks are on the Rev., under the eagle)

| Date | Amount Minted | Very Fine | Unc | Date | Amount Minted | Very Fine | Unc |
|------|--------------|-----------|-----|------|--------------|-----------|-----|
| 1878 | 10½ million | 9.00 | 30.00 | 1885-O | 9¼ million | 8.00 | 22.00 |
| 1878-S | 9¾ million | 9.00 | 30.00 | 1885-S | 1½ million | 9.00 | 50.00 |
| 1878-CC | 2¼ million | 11.00 | 65.00 | 1885-CC | 228,000 | 90.00 | 150.00 |
| 1879 | 14¾ million | 8.00 | 25.00 | 1886 | 20 million | 8.00 | 22.00 |
| 1879-O | 3 million | 8.00 | 25.00 | 1886-O | 10¾ million | 8.00 | 200.00 |
| 1879-S | 9 million | 9.00 | 28.00 | 1886-S | 750,000 | 9.00 | 75.00 |
| 1879-CC | 756,000 | 18.00 | 750.00 | 1887 | 20¼ million | 8.00 | 22.00 |
| 1880 | 12⅔ million | 8.00 | 25.00 | 1887-O | 11½ million | 8.00 | 25.00 |
| 1880-O | 5⅓ million | 8.00 | 25.00 | 1887-S | 1¾ million | 9.00 | 25.00 |
| 1880-S | 9 million | 9.00 | 27.00 | 1888 | 19¼ million | 8.00 | 22.00 |
| 1880-CC | 591,000 | 20.00 | 110.00 | 1888-O | 12¼ million | 8.00 | 25.00 |
| 1881 | 9¼ million | 8.00 | 24.00 | 1888-S | 657,000 | 11.50 | 90.00 |
| 1881-O | 5¾ million | 8.00 | 22.00 | 1889 | 21¾ million | 8.00 | 22.00 |
| 1881-S | 12¾ million | 9.00 | 26.00 | 1889-O | 11¾ million | 8.00 | 45.00 |
| 1881-CC | 296,000 | 35.00 | 120.00 | 1889-S | 700,000 | 11.00 | 65.00 |
| 1882 | 11 million | 8.00 | 22.00 | 1889-CC | 350,000 | 100.00 | 3,250.00 |
| 1882-O | 6 million | 8.00 | 22.00 | 1890 | 16¾ million | 8.00 | 25.00 |
| 1882-S | 9¼ million | 9.00 | 31.00 | 1890-O | 10¾ million | 8.00 | 28.00 |
| 1882-CC | 1¼ million | 15.00 | 60.00 | 1890-S | 8¼ million | 8.00 | 40.00 |
| 1883 | 12¼ million | 8.00 | 22.00 | 1890-CC | 2⅓ million | 12.00 | 125.00 |
| 1883-O | 8¾ million | 8.00 | 22.00 | 1891 | 8¾ million | 8.00 | 25.00 |
| 1883-S | 6¼ million | 9.00 | 200.00 | 1891-O | 8 million | 8.00 | 30.00 |
| 1883-CC | 1¼ million | 15.00 | 60.00 | 1891-S | 5¼ million | 8.00 | 25.00 |
| 1884 | 14 million | 8.00 | 24.00 | 1891-CC | 1⅔ million | 15.00 | 100.00 |
| 1884-O | 9¾ million | 8.00 | 22.00 | 1892 | 1 million | 8.00 | 65.00 |
| 1884-S | 3¼ million | 10.00 | 700.00 | 1892-O | 2¾ million | 8.00 | 65.00 |
| 1884-CC | 1¼ million | 15.00 | 60.00 | 1892-S | 1¼ million | 9.00 | 2,500.00 |
| 1885 | 17¾ million | 8.00 | 22.00 | 1892-CC | 1⅓ million | 15.00 | 175.00 |

| Date | Amount Minted | Very Fine | Unc | Date | Amount Minted | Very Fine | Unc |
|---|---|---|---|---|---|---|---|
| 1893 | 379,000 | 20.00 | 150.00 | 1899-O | 12¼ million | 8.00 | 22.00 |
| 1893-O | 300,000 | 35.00 | 500.00 | 1899-S | 2½ million | 11.00 | 70.00 |
| 1893-S | 100,000 | 500.00 | 12,000.00 | 1900 | 8¾ million | 8.00 | 22.00 |
| 1893-CC | 677,000 | 40.00 | 375.00 | 1900-O | 12½ million | 8.00 | 22.00 |
| 1894 | 111,000 | 125.00 | 550.00 | 1900-S | 3½ million | 11.00 | 70.00 |
| 1894-O | 1¾ million | 10.00 | 300.00 | 1901 | 7 million | 13.00 | 550.00 |
| 1894-S | 1¼ million | 17.00 | 175.00 | 1901-O | 13⅓ million | 8.00 | 22.00 |
| 1895 | 880 proofs | | 10,000.00 | 1901-S | 2¼ million | 12.00 | 65.00 |
| 1895-O | 450,000 | 30.00 | 1,200.00 | 1902 | 8 million | 11.00 | 25.00 |
| 1895-S | 400,000 | 70.00 | 500.00 | 1902-O | 8⅔ million | 8.00 | 22.00 |
| 1896 | 10 million | 8.00 | 20.00 | 1902-S | 1½ million | 25.00 | 120.00 |
| 1896-O | 5 million | 11.00 | 450.00 | 1903 | 4⅔ million | 8.00 | 25.00 |
| 1896-S | 5 million | 18.00 | 200.00 | 1903-O | 4½ million | 90.00 | 150.00 |
| 1897 | 2¾ million | 8.00 | 20.00 | 1903-S | 1¼ million | 25.00 | 800.00 |
| 1897-O | 4 million | 8.00 | 240.00 | 1904 | 2¾ million | 8.00 | 45.00 |
| 1897-S | 5¾ million | 11.00 | 25.00 | 1904-O | 3¾ million | 8.00 | 22.00 |
| 1898 | 5¾ million | 8.00 | 22.00 | 1904-S | 2½ million | 20.00 | 500.00 |
| 1898-O | 4½ million | 8.00 | 22.00 | 1921 | 44⅔ million | 8.00 | 18.00 |
| 1898-S | 4 million | 8.00 | 75.00 | 1921-D | 20⅓ million | 8.00 | 20.00 |
| 1899 | 331,000 | 15.00 | 50.00 | 1921-S | 21⅔ million | 8.00 | 22.00 |

**Type: The Peace Dollar**

(The mint marks are on the bottom of the Rev., to left of the eagle's wing)

| Date | Amount Minted | Very Fine | Unc | Date | Amount Minted | Very Fine | Unc |
|---|---|---|---|---|---|---|---|
| 1921 | 1 million | 14.00 | 125.00 | 1926-D | 2⅓ million | 9.00 | 35.00 |
| 1922 | 51¾ million | 8.00 | 18.00 | 1926-S | 7 million | 8.00 | 22.00 |
| 1922-D | 15 million | 8.00 | 22.00 | 1927 | 848,000 | 9.00 | 50.00 |
| 1922-S | 17½ million | 8.00 | 22.00 | 1927-D | 1¼ million | 9.00 | 100.00 |
| 1923 | 30¾ million | 8.00 | 18.00 | 1927-S | 866,000 | 9.00 | 65.00 |
| 1923-D | 6¾ million | 8.00 | 22.00 | 1928 | 361,000 | 55.00 | 135.00 |
| 1923-S | 19 million | 8.00 | 22.00 | 1928-S | 1⅔ million | 9.00 | 60.00 |
| 1924 | 11¾ million | 8.00 | 20.00 | 1934 | 954,000 | 9.00 | 45.00 |
| 1924-S | 1¾ million | 9.00 | 75.00 | 1934-D | 1½ million | 9.00 | 55.00 |
| 1925 | 10¼ million | 8.00 | 21.00 | 1934-S | 1 million | 20.00 | 750.00 |
| 1925-S | 1⅔ million | 8.00 | 60.00 | 1935 | 1½ million | 8.00 | 30.00 |
| 1926 | 2 million | | 22.00 | 1935-S | 2 million | 8.00 | 80.00 |

Reg. Obv.
1971-1974

Reg. Rev.
1971-1974

Bicentennial
Obv.—1976

Bicentennial
Rev.—1976

## Type: The Eisenhower Dollar

(The mint marks are on the obverse, below Eisenhower's neck)
(The valuations are for uncirculated coins)

| Date | Amount Minted | Value | Date | Amount Minted | Value |
|---|---|---|---|---|---|
| 1971 cupro-nickel, | 47¾ million | 1.25 | 1974-Sc.n., proof, | 2⅔ million | 2.50 |
| 1971-Dcupro-nickel, | 68½ million | 1.25 | 1974-Ssilver, | 2 million | 6.00 |
| 1971-Ssilver, | 6¾ million | 2.50 | 1974-Ssilver, proof, | 1⅓ million | 7.50 |
| 1971-Ssilver, proof, | 4¼ million | 3.00 | 1975 | none minted | |
| 1972 cupro-nickel, | 75¾ million | 1.25 | 1976 | | 1.00 |
| 1972-Dcupro-nickel, | 92½ million | 1.25 | 1976-D | | 1.00 |
| 1972-Ssilver, | 2¼ million | 5.00 | 1976-S cupro-nickel, proof | | 2.00 |
| 1972-Ssilver, proof, | 2 million | 6.00 | 1976-S silver | | 3.50 |
| 1973 cupro-nickel, | 2 million | 2.50 | 1976-Ssilver, proof | | 6.00 |
| 1973-D cupro-nickel, | 2 million | 2.50 | 1977 cupro-nickel, | 12½ million | 1.00 |
| 1973-S cupro-nickel, proof, | | | 1977-Dcupro-nickel, | 33 million | 1.00 |
| | 2¾ million | 2.50 | 1977-Sc.n., proof, | 3¼ million | 2.00 |
| 1973-Ssilver, | 1¾ million | 8.00 | 1978 cupro-nickel, | 25¾ million | 1.00 |
| 1973-Ssilver, proof, | 1 million | 30.00 | 1978-D cupro-nickel, | 23 million | 1.00 |
| 1974 cupro-nickel, | 27⅓ million | 1.00 | 1978-S c.n. | 3 million | 2.25 |
| 1974-Dcupro-nickel, | 45½ million | 1.00 | | | |

## Type: The Anthony Dollar

(The mint marks are on the Obv., to the left of Anthony's neck.
The valuations are for Uncirculated coins)

Type I—Mint mark is not distinct. Type II—Mint mark is clear.

| Date | Amount Minted | Value | Date | Amount Minted | Value |
|------|---------------|-------|------|---------------|-------|
| 1979-P | 360¼ million | 1.00 | 1980-S | 20½ million | 1.10 |
| 1979-D | 288 million | 1.00 | 1980-S | 3½ million proofs | 4.00 |
| 1979-S | 109½ million | 1.10 | 1981-P | 3 million | 2.00 |
| 1979-S Ty. I | 3½ million proofs | 4.00 | 1981-D | 3¼ million | 2.00 |
| 1979-S Ty. II | proof | 45.00 | 1981-S | 3½ million | 2.00 |
| 1980-P | 27½ million | 1.00 | 1981-S Ty. I | 4 million proofs | 4.00 |
| 1980-D | 41½ million | 1.00 | 1981-S Ty. II | proof | 40.00 |

## Type: The Trade Dollar

(The mint marks are on the Rev., under the eagle)

| Date | Amount Minted | Value | Date | Amount Minted | Value |
|------|---------------|-------|------|---------------|-------|
| 1873 | 397,500 | 25.00 | 1877-S | 9½ million | 25.00 |
| 1873-S | 703,000 | 25.00 | 1877-CC | 534,000 | 35.00 |
| 1873-CC | 124,500 | 35.00 | 1878 | 900 Proofs | 2,000.00 |
| 1874 | 987,800 | 25.00 | 1878-S | 4¼ million | 25.00 |
| 1874-S | 2½ million | 25.00 | 1878-CC | 97,000 | 70.00 |
| 1874-CC | 1⅓ million | 25.00 | 1879 | 1,500 Proofs | 2,000.00 |
| 1875 | 218,900 | 40.00 | 1880 | 2,000 Proofs | 2,000.00 |
| 1875-S | 4½ million | 25.00 | 1881 | 1,000 Proofs | 2,000.00 |
| 1875-CC | 1½ million | 25.00 | 1882 | 1,100 Proofs | 2,000.00 |
| 1876 | 456,100 | 25.00 | 1883 | 1,000 Proofs | 2,000.00 |
| 1876-S | 5¼ million | 25.00 | 1884 | 10 Proofs | ——— |
| 1876-CC | 509,000 | 35.00 | 1885 | 5 Proofs | ——— |
| 1877 | 3 million | 25.00 | | | |

# U.S. Silver Commemorative Coins

(All are Half Dollars of standard size and weight except the Isabella Quarter
of 1893, the Lafayette Dollar of 1900, the Olympic coins of 1984, the
Immigrant Half Dollar of 1986, and the Ellis Island Dollar.)

IMPORTANT NOTE: **The valuations below are for coins in bright, new, uncirculated
condition.** Pieces in used or circulated condition are worth less. The amount of coins minted
or in existence is shown to the left of the valuation. Because of speculation, the valuations are
subject to fluctuation. Coins in exceptionally choice condition are worth considerably more
than the prices listed.

## COLUMBIAN, 1892-1893

For the World's Columbian Exposition of
Chicago, where it was issued on the 400th
year of the discovery of America. Head of
Columbus. Rev. His flagship, the Santa
Maria, over global hemispheres.

| | | |
|---|---|---|
| 1892 | 950,000 (used **4.50**) | **35.00** |
| 1893 | 1½ million (used **4.50**) | **35.00** |

## ISABELLA QUARTER, 1893

For the same event as the Columbian Half
Dollar. Crowned head of Queen Isabella of
Spain. Rev. Female spinner kneeling.

| | | |
|---|---|---|
| 1893 | 24,191 | **300.00** |

## LAFAYETTE DOLLAR, 1900

On the gift by the youth of
America to France of an eques-
trian statue of Lafayette. Conjoined heads of Washington
and Lafayette. Rev. The statue
as erected in Paris.

| | | |
|---|---|---|
| 1900 | 36,026 | **500.00** |

## PANAMA-PACIFIC, 1915

For the Panama-Pacific Exposition in San
Francisco on the opening of the Panama
Canal. Columbia and child standing at the
Golden Gate. Rev. Eagle and shield.

| | | |
|---|---|---|
| 1915-S | 27,134 | **350.00** |

### ILLINOIS, 1918

On the 100th year of Illinois statehood.
Head of Lincoln. Rev. Eagle standing to left.

| 1918 | 100,058 | **60.00** |

### MAINE, 1920

On the 100th year of Maine statehood. The
coat-of-arms of Maine. Rev. Wreath formed
of pines and cones.

| 1920 | 50,028 | **70.00** |

### PILGRIM, 1920-1921

On the 300th year of the Landing of the
Pilgrims at Plymouth Rock. Governor Brad-
ford in Pilgrim dress. Rev. The ship May-
flower.

| 1920 | 152,000 | **30.00** |
| 1921 | 20,053 | **85.00** |

### MISSOURI, 1921

On the 100th year of Missouri statehood.
Bust of a Missouri pioneer. Rev. Pioneer
and Indian standing. The "2 × 4" is located
in front of the bust.

| 1921 | 15,400 | **300.00** |
| 1921 2 × 4 | 5,000 | **325.00** |

### ALABAMA, 1921

n the 100th year of Alabama statehood.
onjoined heads of Gov. Bibb (1821) and
ov. Kilby (1921). Rev. Eagle. The "2 × 2"
located in the back of the busts.

| | | |
|---|---|---|
| 921 | 49,000 | **150.00** |
| 921 2 × 2 | 5,000 | **210.00** |

### GRANT, 1922

n the 100th year of his birth. Uniformed
ust of the General. Rev. A log cabin in the
oods. The * is located on the obverse, over
e word, "Grant." Beware of added star.

| | | |
|---|---|---|
| 922 | 67,200 | **70.00** |
| 922* | 4,250 | **450.00** |

### MONROE DOCTRINE, 1923

n the 100th year of Monroe's famous
octrine. Conjoined heads of Monroe and
hn Q. Adams. Rev. Allegories depicting
orth and South America.

| | | |
|---|---|---|
| 923-S | 274,077 | **40.00** |

### HUGUENOT-WALLOON, 1924

n the 300th year of the settlement of New
etherlands by the Dutch. Conjoined heads
Admiral Coligny and William the Silent.
ev. The ship New Netherlands.

| | | |
|---|---|---|
| 24 | 142,080 | **60.00** |

### LEXINGTON-CONCORD, 1925

On the 150th year of these famous battles of 1775. Armed Minute Man standing. Rev. View of Old Belfry.

| | | |
|---|---|---|
| 1925 | 162,099 | **27.50** |

### STONE MOUNTAIN, 1925

On the erection of a Memorial on Stone Mountain to the valor of the Soldier of the South. Gen. "Stonewall" Jackson and Gen. Robert E. Lee on horseback. Rev. Eagle on mountain peak.

| | | |
|---|---|---|
| 1925 | 1⅓ million (used **9.00**) | **27.00** |

### CALIFORNIA JUBILEE, 1925

On the 75th year of California Statehood. A "forty-niner" panning gold. Rev. Grizzly bear.

| | | |
|---|---|---|
| 1925-S | 86,500 | **85.00** |

### FORT VANCOUVER, 1925

On the 100th year of the erection of Fort Vancouver. Head of Dr. John McLoughlin, who built the Fort. Rev. Armed pioneer standing before mountain.

| | | |
|---|---|---|
| 1925 | 14,994 | **250.00** |

## U.S. INDEPENDENCE, 1926

On the 150th year of the Declaration of Independence. Conjoined heads of Washington and Coolidge. Rev. The Liberty Bell.

| | | |
|---|---|---|
| 1926 | 141,120 | **30.00** |

## OREGON TRAIL, 1926-1939

In commemoration of this popular but perilous highway to the west. Indian Chief standing before a map of the U.S. Rev. The famous covered wagon of the Trail.

| | | |
|---|---|---|
| 1926 | 48,030 | **75.00** |
| 1926-S | 86,354 | **75.00** |
| 1928 | 6,028 | **180.00** |
| 1933-D | 5,008 | **175.00** |
| 1934-D | 7,006 | **135.00** |
| 1936 | 10,006 | **100.00** |
| 1936-S | 5,006 | **150.00** |
| 1937-D | 12,008 | **90.00** |
| 1938-P-D-S | 6,005 sets, set of 3 | **400.00** |
| 1939-P-D-S | 3,004 sets, set of 3 | **625.00** |

## VERMONT, 1927

On the 150th year both of the Battle of Bennington and of Vermont's independence. Head of Ira Allen. Rev. Vermont mountain lion.

| | | |
|---|---|---|
| 1927 | 28,142 | **160.00** |

## HAWAII, 1928

On the 150th year of Captain Cook's discovery of the Hawaiian Islands. Bust of the Captain. Rev. Hawaiian Chief in native dress.

| | | |
|---|---|---|
| 1928 | 10,008 | **550.00** |

## MARYLAND, 1934

On the 300th year of the founding of the Colony. Head of Lord Baltimore, the founder. Rev. The coat-of-arms of Maryland.

| | | |
|---|---|---|
| 1934 | 25,015 | **95.00** |

## BOONE, 1934–1938

On the 200th year of the birth of Daniel Boone. Head of Boone. Rev. Standing figures of Boone and Indian Chief, Black Fish.

| | | | |
|---|---|---|---|
| 1934 | 10,007 | | **70.00** |
| 1935 | 10,010 | Set of | |
| 1935-D-S | 5,005 per mint | 3 | **700.00** |

The following have the date "1934" on the reverse about "Pioneer Year."

| | | | |
|---|---|---|---|
| 1935 | 10,008 | Set of | |
| 1935-D-S | 2,003 per Mint | 3 | **275.00** |
| 1936 | 12,012 | Set of | |
| 1036-D-S | 5,006 per Mint | 3 | **275.00** |
| 1937 | 9,810 | Set of | |
| 1937-D-S | 2,506 per Mint | 3 | **500.00** |
| 1938-P-D-S | 2,100 | Set of 3 | **750.00** |
| Type coin (any date) | | | **70.00** |

## TEXAS, 1934-1938

On the 100th year of the Independence of Texas. Eagle on a "lone star." Rev. Winged Victory between heads of Sam Houston and Stephen Austin.

| | | |
|---|---|---|
| 1934 | 61,350 | **70.00** |
| 1935 | 9,934 | **80.00** |
| 1935-D | 10,007 | **80.00** |
| 1935-S | 10,008 | **80.00** |
| 1936 | 8,911 | **80.00** |
| 1936-D | 9,039 | **80.00** |
| 1936-S | 9,064 | **80.00** |
| 1937-P-D-S | | |
| | 6,571 sets, set of 3 | **250.00** |
| 1938-P-D-S | | |
| | 3,775 sets, set of 3 | **500.00** |

## ARKANSAS, 1935-1939

On the 100th year of Arkansas Statehood.
Liberty head and Indian head conjoined.
Rev. Eagle.

| | | |
|---|---|---|
| 1935 | 13,012 | **50.00** |
| 1935-D-S | 5,505 pair, set of 2 | **120.00** |
| 1936-P-D-S | 9,660 sets, set of 3 | **180.00** |
| 1937-P-D-S | 5,505 sets, set of 3 | **190.00** |
| 1938-P-D-S | 3,155 sets, set of 3 | **350.00** |
| 1939-P-D-S | 2,104 sets, set of 3 | **700.00** |

## CONNECTICUT, 1935

On the 300th year of the founding of the
Colony. The famous Charter Oak Tree. Rev.
Eagle.

| | | |
|---|---|---|
| 1935 | 25,018 | **150.00** |

## HUDSON, 1935

On the 150th year of the founding of the city
of Hudson, N.Y. Hudson's ship, the Half
Moon. Rev. Neptune on whale, a mermaid
in the background.

| | | |
|---|---|---|
| 1935 | 10,008 | **350.00** |

## SAN DIEGO, 1935-1936

For the California-Pacific International Exposition in San Diego. Seated female and
bear. View of Exposition buildings.

| | | |
|---|---|---|
| 1935-S | 70,132 | **50.00** |
| 1936-D | 30,092 | **65.00** |

### OLD SPANISH TRAIL, 1935

On the 400th year of the de Vaca Expedition across the land area of the Gulf of Mexico. Skull of a cow. Rev. Yucca tree and map of the Trail.

| | | |
|---|---|---|
| 1935 | 10,008 | **500.00** |

### ALBANY, 1936

On the 250th year of Albany's City Charter. Beaver gnawing on maple twigs. Rev. Standing figures of Gov. Dongan, Peter Schuyler and Robert Livingston.

| | | |
|---|---|---|
| 1936 | 16,887 | **155.00** |

### BRIDGEPORT, 1936

On the 100th year of Bridgeport, Conn. as a city. Head of P. T. Barnum. Rev. Modern style eagle.

| | | |
|---|---|---|
| 1936 | 25,015 | **100.00** |

### CINCINNATI, 1936

On the 50th year of Cincinnati as a music center. Head of Stephen Foster. Rev. Girl playing harp.

| | | |
|---|---|---|
| 1936 | 5,005 | **175.00** |
| 1936-D | 5,005 | **175.00** |
| 1936-S | 5,006 | **175.00** |

### COLUMBIA, S.C., 1936

On the 150th year of the founding of the city. Standing figure of Justice between the Capitol buildings of 1786 and 1936. Rev. Palmetto tree.

| | | |
|---|---|---|
| 1936 | 9.007 | **175.00** |
| 1936-D | 8,009 | **175.00** |
| 1936-S | 8,007 | **175.00** |

### DELAWARE, 1936

On the 300th year of the Swedish landing in Wilmington. The Swedish ship Kalmar Nyckel. Rev. Old Swede's Church in Wilmington.

| | | |
|---|---|---|
| 1936 | 25,015 | **150.00** |

### ELGIN, ILLINOIS, 1936

On the 100th year of the founding of the city. Bearded head of a pioneer. Rev. Four pioneers standing.

| | | |
|---|---|---|
| 1936 | 25,015 | **175.00** |

### GETTYSBURG, 1936

For the 75th Anniversary of the Battle of Gettysburg, 1863-1938. Conjoined heads of a Union and Confederate soldier. Rev. Union and Confederate shields.

| | | |
|---|---|---|
| 1936 | 26,928 | **175.00** |

### GREAT LAKES, 1936

For the Great Lakes Exposition on the 100th year of Cleveland, Ohio. Head of Moses Cleaveland. Rev. Map of the Great Lakes.

| | | |
|---|---|---|
| 1936 | 50,030 | **60.00** |

### LONG ISLAND, 1936

On the 300th year of the landing at Jamaica Bay, Long Island by Dutch Settlers. Conjoined heads of a Dutchman and Indian. Rev. Sailing ship.

| | | |
|---|---|---|
| 1936 | 81,773 | **55.00** |

### LYNCHBURG, 1936

On the 150th year of the city charter given to Lynchburg, Virginia. Head of Senator Carter Glass. Rev. Liberty standing at old courthouse.

| | | |
|---|---|---|
| 1936 | 20,013 | **125.00** |

### NORFOLK, 1936

On the 200th year of Norfolk, Virginia, becoming a royal borough. Sailing ship as on the city shield. Rev. A large mace.

| | | |
|---|---|---|
| 1936 | 15,000 | **400.00** |

## RHODE ISLAND, 1936

On the 300th year of the founding of Providence by Roger Williams. Roger Williams in canoe being welcomed by Indian. Rev. Large anchor.

| | | |
|---|---|---|
| 1936 | 20,013 | **65.00** |
| 1936-D | 15,010 | **65.00** |
| 1936-S | 15,011 | **65.00** |

## ROBINSON, 1936

On the 100th year of Arkansas statehood. Head of Senator Joseph T. Robinson. Rev. Eagle. (Identical to the reverse of the Arkansas issues of 1935-1939; the only instance of the same event being commemorated by two different types of Half Dollars.)

| | | |
|---|---|---|
| 1936 | 25,265 | **70.00** |

## SAN FRANCISCO, 1936

On the opening of the San Francisco-Oakland Bay Bridge. California grizzly bear. Rev. View of the bridge.

| | | |
|---|---|---|
| 1936-S | 71,369 | **125.00** |

## WISCONSIN, 1936

On the 100th year of the formation of Wisconsin Territory. Forearm holding pickaxe over ore. Rev. Badger on log.

| | | |
|---|---|---|
| 1936 | 25,015 | **160.00** |

### YORK COUNTY, ME., 1936

On the 300th year of the founding of York County, Maine. Brown's Garrison at Saco. Rev. The seal of the County.

1936            25,015        **140.00**

### ANTIETAM, 1937

On the 75th year of the Battle of Antietam. Conjoined heads of the Union's Gen. Mc-Clellan and the Confederacy's Gen. Lee. Rev. Burnside Bridge for which the battle was fought.

1937            18,028        **250.00**

### ROANOKE, 1937

On the 350th year of the colonization of Roanoke Island by Sir Walter Raleigh; also on the birth of Virginia Dare in 1587, the first white child born in America. Bust of Sir Walter Raleigh. Rev. Mother holding Virginia Dare.

1937            29,030        **110.00**

### NEW ROCHELLE, 1938

On the 250th year of the founding of New Rochelle, New York, by the Huguenots. Lord Pell holding fatted calf. Rev. Fleur-de-lis.

1938            15,266        **275.00**

## IOWA, 1946

On the 100th year of Iowa Statehood. Eagle on scroll. Rev. The old Capitol Statehouse at Iowa City.

| | | |
|---|---|---|
| 1946 | 100,057 | **60.00** |

## B.T.W., 1946-1951

In honor of this great black leader and educator. Head of Booker T. Washington. Rev. View of the log cabin of his birth and of the Hall of Fame where he is inscribed.

| | | |
|---|---|---|
| 1946 | 1 million | **6.00** |
| 1946-D | 200,113 | **8.00** |
| 1946-S | 500,279 | **7.00** |
| 1947-P-D-S | 100,017 sets, set of 3 | **35.00** |
| 1948-P-D-S | 8,005 sets, set of 3 | **75.00** |
| 1949-P-D-S | 6,004 sets, set of 3 | **85.00** |
| 1950-P-D-S | 6,004 sets, set of 3 | **85.00** |
| 1950-S | 403,996 | **8.00** |
| 1951 | 503,078 | **8.00** |
| 1951-P-D-S | 7,004 sets, set of 3 | **50.00** |

## G.W.C.-B.T.W., 1951-1954

In honor of the famous black leaders, George Washington Carver and Booker T. Washington. Their conjoined heads. Rev. Map of the United States.

| | | |
|---|---|---|
| 1951 | 100,014 | **7.00** |
| 1951-P-D-S | 10,004 sets, set of 3 | **60.00** |
| 1952 | 2 million | **7.00** |
| 1952-P-D-S | 8,000 sets, set of 3 | **70.00** |
| 1953-P-D-S | 8,000 sets, set of 3 | **95.00** |
| 1953-S | 100,000 | **9.00** |
| 1954-P-D-S | 12,000 sets, set of 3 | **60.00** |
| 1954-S | 110,000 | **9.00** |

## GEORGE WASHINGTON, 1982

On the 250th Anniversary of the birth of the first President. Washington on horseback. Rev. View of Mount Vernon.

| | | |
|---|---|---|
| 1982-D | Uncirculated | **6.00** |
| 1982-S | Proof | **6.00** |

## LOS ANGELES OLYMPIC GAMES, 1983–1984

Issued to help raise funds for the staging of the 1984 Summer Olympic Games in Los Angeles. Both issues bear an eagle on the obverse, with the reverse of the 1983 coin depicting a discus thrower and the 1984 coin the gateway to the Los Angeles Coliseum.

| | | | |
|---|---|---|---|
| 1 Dollar | 1983-P Unc. | 920,485 | **16.00** |
| 1 Dollar | 1983-D Unc. | 597,157 | **30.00** |
| 1 Dollar | 1983-S Unc. | 662,837 | **24.00** |
| 1 Dollar | 1983-S Proof | 4,575,603 | **16.00** |
| 1 Dollar | 1984-P Unc. | 470,131 | **15.00** |
| 1 Dollar | 1984-D Unc. | 316,778 | **75.00** |
| 1 Dollar | 1984-S Unc. | 339,970 | **40.00** |
| 1 Dollar | 1984-S Proof | 2,623,609 | **16.00** |

## IMMIGRANT, 1986

On the centennial of the Statue of Liberty. Commemorates the immigrants who passed through Ellis Island before entering New York. Rising sun behind statue. Rev. Immigrant Family on Ellis Island.

| | | |
|---|---|---|
| 1986-D | Uncirculated | **4.00** |
| 1986-S | Proof | **5.00** |

## ELLIS ISLAND, 1986

On the centennial of the Statue of Liberty. Commemorates Ellis Island, the "Gateway to America." Statue in front of the Ellis Island immigration facility. Rev. Liberty's hand holding torch.

| | | |
|---|---|---|
| 1986-P | Uncirculated | **15.00** |
| 1986-S | Proof | **16.00** |

*Coins shown at approximately 4/5 actual size.*

## CONSTITUTION BICENTENNIAL, 1988

On the 200th anniversary of the Constitution of the United States. Quill pen superimposed over a copy of the Constitution. Rev. A group of American men and women from the past two centuries.

| | | |
|---|---|---|
| 1987-P | Uncirculated | **20.00** |
| 1987-S | Proof | **25.00** |

*Coins shown at approximately 85% of actual size.*

### 1988 OLYMPICS

To raise money for the 1988 American Olympic Teams. Two torches. Rev. Rings.

| | | |
|---|---|---|
| 1988-D | Uncirculated | **17.50** |
| 1988-S | Proof | **20.00** |

# U.S. Gold Commemorative Coins

IMPORTANT NOTE: The valuations below are for coins in bright, new, uncirculated condition. Pieces in used or circulated condition are worth less. The amount of coins minted or in existence is shown to the left of the valuation.

## LOUISIANA PURCHASE ISSUE, 1903

Two types of Gold Dollars were struck to commemorate the Centennial of the Louisiana Purchase. The same reverse appears on both.

| | | | |
|---|---|---|---|
| 1 Dollar 1903 | Head of Jefferson | 17,375 | **500.00** |
| 1 Dollar 1903 | Head of McKinley | 17,375 | **500.00** |

## LEWIS AND CLARK ISSUE, 1904–1905

Two dates of a Gold Dollar were struck to commemorate the Centennial of the Lewis and Clark Expedition. The head of Lewis appears on one side and that of Clark on the other.

| | | |
|---|---|---|
| 1 Dollar 1904 | 9,997 | **700.00** |
| 1 Dollar 1905 | 10,000 | **700.00** |

## PANAMA PACIFIC ISSUE, 1915

Four types of gold coins were struck for the Panama-Pacific Exposition commemorating the opening of the Panama Canal.

| 1 Dollar 1915-S | Head of worker | 25,000 | **400.00** |
|---|---|---|---|

| 2½ Dollars 1915-S | Columbia on hippocampus | 6,749 | **1,000.00** |
|---|---|---|---|

| 50 Dollars 1915-S, round | Head of Minerva | 483 | **17,000.00** |
| 50 Dollars 1915-S, octagonal | Head of Minerva | 645 | **15,000.00** |

## McKINLEY MEMORIAL ISSUE, 1916–1917

Two dates of a Gold Dollar were struck to commemorate the erection of the McKinley Memorial at Niles, Ohio. The obverse shows his head, and the reverse the memorial building.

| 1 Dollar 1916 | | 9,977 | **500.00** |
| 1 Dollar 1917 | | 10,000 | **525.00** |

### GRANT CENTENNIAL ISSUE, 1922

Two varieties of a Gold Dollar were struck to commemorate the 100th year of Grant's birth. His head appears on the obverse and a log cabin on the reverse. The star is located on the obverse, over the word, "Grant."

| | | |
|---|---|---|
| 1 Dollar 1922 | 5,000 | **900.00** |
| 1 Dollar 1922 with star | 5,000 | **900.00** |

### U.S. INDEPENDENCE ISSUE, 1926

A 2½ Dollar gold piece was struck to commemorate the Sesquicentennial (150th year) of the Declaration of Independence. The obverse shows Liberty standing; the reverse a view of Independence Hall in Philadelphia.

| | | |
|---|---|---|
| 2½ Dollars 1926 | 46,019 | **400.00** |

### LOS ANGELES OLYMPIC GAMES, 1984

To raise funds for the staging of the Games. Struck at the West Point, NY Mint facility.

| | | | |
|---|---|---|---|
| 10 Dollars | 1984-W Unc. | 100,000 | **240.00** |
| 10 Dollars | 1984-W Proof | 661,000 | **200.00** |
| 10 Dollars | 1984-P Proof only | 40,000 | **650.00** |
| 10 Dollars | 1984-D Proof only | 44,000 | **425.00** |
| 10 Dollars | 1984-S Proof only | 55,000 | **325.00** |

## STATUE OF LIBERTY, 1986

On the centennial of the Statue of Liberty. Head of statue. Rev. American eagle in flight.

| 5 Dollars | 1986-W | Uncirculated | 500,000 | **220.00** |
| 5 Dollars | 1986-W | Proof | 500,000 | **150.00** |

## CONSTITUTION BICENTENNIAL, 1988

*Coins shown at approximately 150% of actual size.*

On the 200th anniversary of the U.S. Constitution. Eagle holding quill pen. Rev. Quill pen under "We the People."

| 5 Dollars | 1987-W | Uncirculated | **115.00** |
| 5 Dollars | 1987-W | Proof | **125.00** |

## 1988 OLYMPICS

To raise money for the 1988 American Olympic Teams. Head of Liberty. Rev. Flame.

| 5 Dollars | 1988-W | Uncirculated | **150.00** |
| 5 Dollars | 1988-W | Proof | **175.00** |

***(The valuations in this book are based on the coins being in G-VG condition, unless otherwise noted.)***

# United States Gold Coins

(The valuations are for coins in choice VF-EF condition. Americans traveling abroad are cautioned to beware of counterfeit U.S. gold pieces in all denominations, which are being produced in many parts of Europe and Asia.)

## 1 DOLLAR GOLD PIECES

### Type: Liberty head with coronet. Small size.

(The mint marks are on the Rev., under the wreath)

| Date | Amount minted | Value | Date | Amount minted | Value |
|---|---|---|---|---|---|
| 1849 | 688,600 | 110.00 | 1852 | 2 million | 110.00 |
| 1849-O | 215,000 | 110.00 | 1852-O | 140,000 | 110.00 |
| 1849-C | 11,600 | 150.00 | 1852-C | 9,400 | 125.00 |
| 1849-D | 21,600 | 150.00 | 1852-D | 6,400 | 130.00 |
| 1850 | 482,000 | 110.00 | 1853 | 4 million | 110.00 |
| 1850-O | 14,000 | 110.00 | 1853-O | 290,000 | 110.00 |
| 1850-C | 7,000 | 200.00 | 1853-C | 11,500 | 115.00 |
| 1850-D | 8,400 | 175.00 | 1853-D | 6,600 | 125.00 |
| 1851 | 3⅓ million | 110.00 | 1854 | Part of 1⅔ million | 110.00 |
| 1851-O | 290,000 | 110.00 | 1854-D | 2,900 | 250.00 |
| 1851-C | 41,300 | 115.00 | 1854-S | 14,600 | 110.00 |
| 1851-D | 9,900 | 125.00 | | | |

### Type: Small Liberty head with feather head-dress. Large size.

(The mint marks are on the Rev., under the wreath)

| Date | Amount Minted | Value | Date | Amount Minted | Value |
|---|---|---|---|---|---|
| 1854 | Part of 1⅔ million | 200.00 | 1855-C | 9,800 | 375.00 |
| 1855 | 758,300 | 200.00 | 1855-D | 1,800 | 1,500.00 |
| 1855-O | 55,000 | 225.00 | 1856-S | 24,600 | 225.00 |

*Type: Large Liberty head with feather head-dress.*
*Large size.*

(The mint marks are on the Rev., under the wreath)

| Date | Amount Minted | Value | Date | Amount Minted | Value |
|---|---|---|---|---|---|
| 1856 | 1¾ million | 100.00 | 1868 | 10,500 | 125.00 |
| 1856-D | 1,500 | 1,500.00 | 1869 | 5,900 | 125.00 |
| 1857 | 774,800 | 100.00 | 1870 | 6,300 | 125.00 |
| 1857-C | 13,300 | 125.00 | 1870-S | 3,000 | 300.00 |
| 1857-D | 3,500 | 250.00 | 1871 | 3,900 | 125.00 |
| 1857-S | 10,000 | 150.00 | 1872 | 3,500 | 125.00 |
| 1858 | 118,000 | 100.00 | 1873 | 125,100 | 100.00 |
| 1858-D | 3,500 | 300.00 | 1874 | 198,800 | 100.00 |
| 1858-S | 10,000 | 125.00 | 1875 | 400 | 1,500.00 |
| 1859 | 168,200 | 100.00 | 1876 | 3,200 | 125.00 |
| 1859-C | 5,200 | 200.00 | 1877 | 3,900 | 125.00 |
| 1859-D | 5,000 | 400.00 | 1878 | 3,000 | 125.00 |
| 1859-S | 15,000 | 125.00 | 1879 | 3,000 | 125.00 |
| 1860 | 36,700 | 100.00 | 1880 | 1,600 | 125.00 |
| 1860-D | 1,600 | 1,400.00 | 1881 | 7,700 | 100.00 |
| 1860-S | 13,000 | 125.00 | 1882 | 5,000 | 100.00 |
| 1861 | 527,500 | 100.00 | 1883 | 10,800 | 100.00 |
| 1861-D | Unknown | 2,000.00 | 1884 | 6,200 | 100.00 |
| 1862 | 1⅓ million | 100.00 | 1885 | 12,200 | 100.00 |
| 1863 | 6,200 | 150.00 | 1886 | 6,000 | 100.00 |
| 1864 | 5,900 | 150.00 | 1887 | 8,500 | 100.00 |
| 1865 | 3,700 | 150.00 | 1888 | 16,100 | 100.00 |
| 1866 | 7,200 | 125.00 | 1889 | 30,700 | 100.00 |
| 1867 | 5,200 | 125.00 | | | |

## 2½ DOLLAR GOLD PIECES (QUARTER EAGLES)

*Type: Liberty head; without stars on Obv.*

| Date | Amount Minted | Value |
|---|---|---|
| 1796 | Part of 1,400 | 6,000.00 |

**2½ Dollar Gold Pieces (continued)** **117**

### Type: Liberty head; with stars on Obv.

| Date | Amount Minted | Value | Date | Amount Minted | Value |
|------|------|------|------|------|------|
| 1796 | Part of 1,400 | 4,000.00 | 1804 | 3,300 | 1,500.00 |
| 1797 | 1,700 | 3,000.00 | 1805 | 1,800 | 1,800.00 |
| 1798 | 600 | 2,000.00 | 1806 | 1,600 | 1,800.00 |
| 1802 over 1 | 2,600 | 1,500.00 | 1807 | 6,800 | 1,500.00 |

### Type: Draped bust of Liberty with round cap.

| Date | Amount Minted | Value |
|------|------|------|
| 1808 | 2,700 | 5,000.00 |

### Type: Undraped head of Liberty with round cap; with motto over eagle.

| Date | Amount Minted | Value | Date | Amount Minted | Value |
|------|------|------|------|------|------|
| 1821 | 6,400 | 1,500.00 | 1831 | 4,500 | 1,000.00 |
| 1824 over 21 | 2,600 | 1,500.00 | 1832 | 4,400 | 1,000.00 |
| 1825 | 4,400 | 1,500.00 | 1833 | 4,200 | 1,000.00 |
| 1826 over 25 | 800 | 2,000.00 | 1834 | 4,000 | 3,000.00 |
| 1827 | 2,800 | 1,500.00 | | | |
| 1829 | 3,400 | 1,000.00 | | | |
| 1830 | 4,500 | 1,000.00 | | | |

## Type: Liberty head with ribbon; without motto over eagle.

(The mint marks are on the Obv., over the date)

| Date | Amount Minted | Value | Date | Amount Minted | Value |
|------|---------------|-------|------|---------------|-------|
| 1834 | 112,200 | 150.00 | 1838-C | 7,900 | 275.00 |
| 1835 | 131,400 | 150.00 | 1839 | 27,000 | 150.00 |
| 1836 | 548,000 | 150.00 | 1839-O | 17,800 | 250.00 |
| 1837 | 45,100 | 150.00 | 1839-C | 18,200 | 275.00 |
| 1838 | 47,000 | 150.00 | 1839-D | 13,700 | 300.00 |

## Type: Liberty head with coronet.

(The mint marks are on the Rev., under the eagle. The "CAL" on the 1848 is over the eagle and represents gold mined in California)

| Date | Amount Minted | Value | Date | Amount Minted | Value |
|------|---------------|-------|------|---------------|-------|
| 1840 | 18,900 | 150.00 | 1846-C | 4,800 | 250.00 |
| 1840-O | 26,200 | 150.00 | 1846-D | 19,300 | 160.00 |
| 1840-C | 12,800 | 275.00 | 1847 | 29,800 | 150.00 |
| 1840-D | 3,500 | 500.00 | 1847-O | 124,000 | 150.00 |
| 1841 | A few proofs | — | 1847-C | 23,200 | 160.00 |
| 1841-C | 10,300 | 300.00 | 1847-D | 15,800 | 160.00 |
| 1841-D | 4,200 | 400.00 | 1848 | 7,500 | 300.00 |
| 1842 | 2,800 | 300.00 | 1848-CAL | 1,400 | 2,500.00 |
| 1842-O | 19,800 | 150.00 | 1848-C | 16,800 | 200.00 |
| 1842-C | 6,700 | 300.00 | 1848-D | 13,800 | 250.00 |
| 1842-D | 4,600 | 400.00 | 1849 | 23,300 | 120.00 |
| 1843 | 100,500 | 150.00 | 1849-C | 10,200 | 200.00 |
| 1843-O | 368,000 | 150.00 | 1849-D | 10,900 | 200.00 |
| 1843-C | 26,100 | 300.00 | 1850 | 252,900 | 120.00 |
| 1843-D | 36,200 | 300.00 | 1850-O | 84,000 | 120.00 |
| 1844 | 6,800 | 150.00 | 1850-C | 9,100 | 200.00 |
| 1844-C | 11,600 | 160.00 | 1850-D | 12,100 | 200.00 |
| 1844-D | 17,300 | 160.00 | 1851 | 1⅓ million | 120.00 |
| 1845 | 91,100 | 150.00 | 1851-O | 148,000 | 120.00 |
| 1845-O | 4,000 | 250.00 | 1851-C | 14,900 | 200.00 |
| 1845-D | 19,500 | 160.00 | 1851-D | 11,300 | 200.00 |
| 1846 | 21,600 | 150.00 | 1852 | 1¼ million | 120.00 |
| 1846-O | 66,000 | 150.00 | 1852-O | 142,000 | 120.00 |

| Date | Amount Minted | Value | Date | Amount Minted | Value |
|------|---------------|-------|------|---------------|-------|
| 1852-C | 9,800 | 200.00 | 1867 | 3,200 | 175.00 |
| 1852-D | 4,000 | 275.00 | 1867-S | 28,000 | 120.00 |
| 1853 | 1⅓ million | 120.00 | 1868 | 3,600 | 165.00 |
| 1853-D | 3,200 | 275.00 | 1868-S | 34,000 | 120.00 |
| 1854 | 596,300 | 120.00 | 1869 | 4,300 | 150.00 |
| 1854-O | 153,000 | 120.00 | 1869-S | 29,500 | 120.00 |
| 1854-C | 7,300 | 200.00 | 1870 | 4,600 | 150.00 |
| 1854-D | 1,800 | 1,000.00 | 1870-S | 16,000 | 120.00 |
| 1854-S | 246 | 10,000.00 | 1871 | 5,300 | 150.00 |
| 1855 | 235,500 | 120.00 | 1871-S | 22,000 | 120.00 |
| 1855-C | 3,700 | 375.00 | 1872 | 3,000 | 165.00 |
| 1855-D | 1,100 | 900.00 | 1872-S | 18,000 | 120.00 |
| 1856 | 384,200 | 120.00 | 1873 | 178,000 | 120.00 |
| 1856-O | 21,100 | 140.00 | 1873-S | 27,000 | 120.00 |
| 1856-C | 7,900 | 200.00 | 1874 | 3,900 | 160.00 |
| 1856-D | 874 | 1,500.00 | 1875 | 420 | 1,000.00 |
| 1856-S | 71,100 | 140.00 | 1875-S | 11,600 | 120.00 |
| 1857 | 214,100 | 120.00 | 1876 | 4,200 | 150.00 |
| 1857-O | 34,000 | 120.00 | 1876-S | 5,000 | 140.00 |
| 1857-D | 2,400 | 250.00 | 1877 | 1,700 | 200.00 |
| 1857-S | 68,000 | 120.00 | 1877-S | 35,400 | 120.00 |
| 1858 | 47,400 | 120.00 | 1878 | 286,300 | 120.00 |
| 1858-C | 9,100 | 175.00 | 1878-S | 178,000 | 120.00 |
| 1859 | 39,400 | 120.00 | 1879 | 89,000 | 120.00 |
| 1859-D | 2,200 | 250.00 | 1879-S | 43,500 | 120.00 |
| 1859-S | 15,200 | 120.00 | 1880 | 3,000 | 120.00 |
| 1860 | 22,700 | 120.00 | 1881 | 680 | 300.00 |
| 1860-C | 7,500 | 175.00 | 1882 | 4,000 | 140.00 |
| 1860-S | 35,600 | 120.00 | 1883 | 2,000 | 165.00 |
| 1861 | 1¼ million | 120.00 | 1884 | 2,000 | 165.00 |
| 1861-S | 24,000 | 140.00 | 1885 | 887 | 300.00 |
| 1862 | 112,400 | 120.00 | 1886 | 4,100 | 150.00 |
| 1862-S | 8,000 | 140.00 | 1887 | 6,300 | 120.00 |
| 1863 | 30 proofs | —— | 1888 | 16,100 | 120.00 |
| 1863-S | 10,800 | 120.00 | 1889 | 17,600 | 120.00 |
| 1864 | 2,900 | 375.00 | 1890 | 8,800 | 120.00 |
| 1865 | 1,500 | 375.00 | 1891 | 11,000 | 120.00 |
| 1865-S | 23,400 | 120.00 | 1892 | 2,500 | 120.00 |
| 1866 | 3,100 | 175.00 | 1893 | 30,100 | 120.00 |
| 1866-S | 39,000 | 120.00 | 1894 | 4,100 | 140.00 |

| Date | Amount Minted | Value | Date | Amount Minted | Value |
|------|--------------:|------:|------|--------------:|------:|
| 1895 | 6,100  | 140.00 | 1902 | 133,700 | 120.00 |
| 1896 | 19,200 | 120.00 | 1903 | 201,300 | 120.00 |
| 1897 | 29,900 | 120.00 | 1904 | 161,000 | 120.00 |
| 1898 | 24,200 | 120.00 | 1905 | 217,900 | 120.00 |
| 1899 | 27,300 | 120.00 | 1906 | 176,500 | 120.00 |
| 1900 | 67,200 | 120.00 | 1907 | 336,400 | 120.00 |
| 1901 | 91,300 | 120.00 |      |         |        |

### Type: Indian Head

(The mint marks are on the Rev., to the left of the value)

| Date | Amount Minted | Value | Date | Amount Minted | Value |
|------|--------------:|------:|------|--------------:|------:|
| 1908   | 565,000 | 120.00 | 1914-D | 448,000 | 120.00 |
| 1909   | 441,900 | 120.00 | 1915   | 606,100 | 120.00 |
| 1910   | 492,700 | 120.00 | 1925-D | 578,000 | 120.00 |
| 1911   | 704,200 | 120.00 | 1926   | 446,000 | 120.00 |
| 1911-D | 55,700  | 650.00 | 1927   | 388,000 | 120.00 |
| 1912   | 616,200 | 120.00 | 1928   | 416,000 | 120.00 |
| 1913   | 722,200 | 120.00 | 1929   | 532,200 | 120.00 |
| 1914   | 240,100 | 120.00 |        |         |        |

# 3 DOLLAR GOLD PIECES

### Type: Liberty head with feather head-dress

(The mint marks are on the Rev., under the wreath)

| Date | Amount Minted | Value | Date | Amount Minted | Value |
|------|--------------:|------:|------|--------------:|------:|
| 1854   | 138,600 | 400.00   | 1856-S | 34,500 | 400.00 |
| 1854-O | 24,000  | 400.00   | 1857   | 20,900 | 400.00 |
| 1854-D | 1,100   | 1,500.00 | 1857-S | 14,000 | 400.00 |
| 1855   | 50,600  | 400.00   | 1858   | 2,100  | 425.00 |
| 1855-S | 6,600   | 400.00   | 1859   | 15,600 | 400.00 |
| 1856   | 26,000  | 400.00   | 1860   | 7,200  | 400.00 |

| Date | Amount Minted | Value | Date | Amount Minted | Value |
|------|--------------|-------|------|--------------|-------|
| 1860-S | 7,000 | **400.00** | 1875 | About 50 proofs | — |
| 1861 | 6,100 | **400.00** | 1876 | About 50 proofs | — |
| 1862 | 5,800 | **400.00** | 1877 | 1,500 | **500.00** |
| 1863 | 5,000 | **400.00** | 1878 | 82,300 | **600.00** |
| 1864 | 2,700 | **525.00** | 1879 | 3,000 | **500.00** |
| 1865 | 1,200 | **600.00** | 1880 | 1,000 | **425.00** |
| 1866 | 4,000 | **400.00** | 1881 | 550 | **425.00** |
| 1867 | 2,600 | **400.00** | 1882 | 1,500 | **425.00** |
| 1868 | 4,900 | **400.00** | 1883 | 900 | **425.00** |
| 1869 | 2,500 | **400.00** | 1884 | 1,100 | **425.00** |
| 1870 | 3,500 | **400.00** | 1885 | 900 | **425.00** |
| 1870-S | 2 | — | 1886 | 1,100 | **425.00** |
| 1871 | 1,300 | **500.00** | 1887 | 6,200 | **400.00** |
| 1872 | 2,000 | **400.00** | 1888 | 5,300 | **400.00** |
| 1873 | About 100 proofs | — | 1889 | 2,400 | **400.00** |
| 1874 | 41,800 | **400.00** | | | |

# 4 DOLLAR GOLD PIECES (STELLAS)

### Type: Liberty head with flowing hair.

| 1879 | 415 proofs | **14,000.00** | 1880 | 15 proofs | — |
|------|-----------|---------------|------|-----------|---|

### Type: Liberty head with coiled hair.

| 1879 | 10 proofs | — | 1880 | 10 proofs | — |
|------|-----------|---|------|-----------|---|

# 5 DOLLAR GOLD PIECES (HALF EAGLES)

**Type: Liberty head; with small eagle on Rev.**

| Date | Amount Minted | Value | Date | Amount Minted | Value |
|---|---|---|---|---|---|
| 1795 | Part of 8,700 | 3,000.00 | 1797 | Part of 6,400 | 3,500.00 |
| 1796 | 3,400 | 3,000.00 | 1798 | Part of 24,900 | —— |

**Type: Liberty head to right; with large eagle on Rev.**

| 1795 | Part of 8,700 | 2,500.00 | 1803 | 33,500 | 600.00 |
|---|---|---|---|---|---|
| 1797 | Part of 6,400 | 2,000.00 | 1804 | 30,500 | 600.00 |
| 1798 | Part of 24,900 | 600.00 | 1805 | 33,200 | 600.00 |
| 1799 | 7,500 | 600.00 | 1806 | 64,100 | 600.00 |
| 1800 | 11,600 | 600.00 | 1807 | Part of 84,100 | 600.00 |
| 1802 | 53,200 | 600.00 | | | |

**Type: Draped bust of Liberty to left with round cap.**

| 1807 | Part of 84,100 | 650.00 | 1810 | 100,300 | 600.00 |
|---|---|---|---|---|---|
| 1808 | 55,600 | 600.00 | 1811 | 99,600 | 600.00 |
| 1809 | 33,900 | 600.00 | 1812 | 58,100 | 600.00 |

*Type: Liberty head with round cap; with motto over eagle.*

| Date | Amount Minted | Value | Date | Amount Minted | Value |
|------|---------------|-------|------|---------------|-------|
| 1813 | 95,400 | 600.00 | 1825 | 29,100 | 1,500.00 |
| 1814 | 15,500 | 800.00 | 1826 | 18,100 | 1,600.00 |
| 1815 | 635 | —— | 1827 | 24,900 | —— |
| 1818 | 48,600 | 800.00 | 1828 | 28,000 | —— |
| 1819 | 51,700 | —— | 1829 | 57,400 | —— |
| 1820 | 263,800 | 800.00 | 1830 | 126,400 | 1,000.00 |
| 1821 | 34,600 | 1,500.00 | 1831 | 140,600 | 1,000.00 |
| 1822 | 17,800 | —— | 1832 | 157,500 | 1,500.00 |
| 1823 | 14,500 | 1,000.00 | 1833 | 193,600 | 1,000.00 |
| 1824 | 17,300 | 3,500.00 | 1834 | Part of 732,200 | 1,000.00 |

*Type: Liberty head with ribbon; without motto over eagle.*

(The mint marks are on the Obv., over the date)

| Date | Amount Minted | Value | Date | Amount Minted | Value |
|------|---------------|-------|------|---------------|-------|
| 1834 | Part of 732,200 | 175.00 | 1838 | 286,600 | 175.00 |
| 1835 | 371,500 | 175.00 | 1838-C | 12,900 | 500.00 |
| 1836 | 553,100 | 175.00 | 1838-D | 20,600 | 500.00 |
| 1837 | 207,100 | 175.00 | | | |

*Type: Liberty head with coronet; without motto over eagle.*

(The mint marks are on the Rev., under the eagle)

**5 Dollar Gold Pieces (continued)**

| Date | Amount Minted | Value | Date | Amount Minted | Value |
|------|--------------:|------:|------|--------------:|------:|
| 1839 | 118,100 | **130.00** | 1852-D | 91,500 | **175.00** |
| 1839-C | 23,500 | **175.00** | 1853 | 305,800 | **120.00** |
| 1839-D | 18,900 | **175.00** | 1853-C | 65,600 | **175.00** |
| 1840 | 137,400 | **130.00** | 1853-D | 89,700 | **175.00** |
| 1840-O | 30,400 | **130.00** | 1854 | 160,700 | **120.00** |
| 1840-C | 19,000 | **150.00** | 1854-O | 46,000 | **130.00** |
| 1840-D | 22,900 | **150.00** | 1854-C | 39,300 | **150.00** |
| 1841 | 15,800 | **130.00** | 1854-D | 56,400 | **150.00** |
| 1841-O | 8,300 | —— | 1854-S | 268 | — |
| 1841-C | 21,500 | **150.00** | 1855 | 117,100 | **120.00** |
| 1841-D | 30,500 | **150.00** | 1855-O | 11,100 | **175.00** |
| 1842 | 27,600 | **130.00** | 1855-C | 39,800 | **160.00** |
| 1842-O | 16,400 | **150.00** | 1855-D | 22,400 | **160.00** |
| 1842-C | 27,500 | **150.00** | 1855-S | 61,000 | **130.00** |
| 1842-D | 59,600 | **150.00** | 1856 | 198,000 | **120.00** |
| 1843 | 611,200 | **120.00** | 1856-O | 10,000 | **200.00** |
| 1843-O | 101,100 | **130.00** | 1856-C | 28,500 | **160.00** |
| 1843-C | 44,400 | **150.00** | 1856-D | 19,800 | **160.00** |
| 1843-D | 98,500 | **150.00** | 1856-S | 105,100 | **120.00** |
| 1844 | 340,300 | **120.00** | 1857 | 98,200 | **120.00** |
| 1844-O | 364,600 | **130.00** | 1857-O | 13,000 | **130.00** |
| 1844-C | 23,600 | **150.00** | 1857-C | 31,400 | **160.00** |
| 1844-D | 89,000 | **150.00** | 1857-D | 17,000 | **160.00** |
| 1845 | 417,100 | **120.00** | 1857-S | 87,000 | **130.00** |
| 1845-O | 41,000 | **130.00** | 1858 | 15,100 | **150.00** |
| 1845-D | 90,600 | **150.00** | 1858-C | 38,900 | **150.00** |
| 1846 | 395,900 | **120.00** | 1858-D | 15,400 | **175.00** |
| 1846-O | 58,000 | **130.00** | 1858-S | 18,600 | **130.00** |
| 1846-C | 13,000 | **175.00** | 1859 | 16,800 | **130.00** |
| 1846-D | 80,300 | **150.00** | 1859-C | 31,800 | **175.00** |
| 1847 | 916,000 | **120.00** | 1859-D | 10,400 | **190.00** |
| 1847-O | 12,000 | **150.00** | 1859-S | 13,200 | **130.00** |
| 1847-C | 84,200 | **175.00** | 1860 | 19,800 | **130.00** |
| 1847-D | 64,400 | **175.00** | 1860-C | 14,800 | **175.00** |
| 1848 | 260,800 | **120.00** | 1860-D | 14,600 | **175.00** |
| 1848-C | 64,500 | **175.00** | 1860-S | 21,200 | **130.00** |
| 1848-D | 47,500 | **175.00** | 1861 | 639,900 | **120.00** |
| 1849 | 133,100 | **120.00** | 1861-C | 6,900 | **400.00** |
| 1849-C | 64,800 | **175.00** | 1861-D | 1,600 | **1,500.00** |
| 1849-D | 39,000 | **175.00** | 1861-S | 18,000 | **130.00** |
| 1850 | 64,500 | **120.00** | 1862 | 4,500 | **175.00** |
| 1850-C | 63,600 | **175.00** | 1862-S | 9,500 | **130.00** |
| 1850-D | 43,900 | **175.00** | 1863 | 2,500 | **250.00** |
| 1851 | 377,500 | **120.00** | 1863-S | 17,000 | **130.00** |
| 1851-O | 41,000 | **130.00** | 1864 | 4,200 | **200.00** |
| 1851-C | 49,200 | **175.00** | 1864-S | 3,900 | **500.00** |
| 1851-D | 62,700 | **175.00** | 1865 | 1,300 | **400.00** |
| 1852 | 573,900 | **120.00** | 1865-S | 27,600 | **130.00** |
| 1852-C | 72,600 | **175.00** | 1866-S | Part of 43,900 | **150.00** |

### Type: Liberty head with coronet; with motto over eagle.

(The mint marks are on the Rev., under the eagle)

| Date | Amount Minted | Value | Date | Amount Minted | Value |
|---|---|---|---|---|---|
| 1866 | 6,700 | 175.00 | 1879-CC | 17,300 | 150.00 |
| 1866-S | Part of 43,900 | 150.00 | 1880 | 3¼ million | 110.00 |
| 1867 | 6,900 | 150.00 | 1880-S | 1⅓ million | 110.00 |
| 1867-S | 29,000 | 120.00 | 1880-CC | 51,000 | 150.00 |
| 1868 | 5,700 | 175.00 | 1881 | 5⅔ million | 110.00 |
| 1868-S | 52,000 | 110.00 | 1881-S | 969,000 | 110.00 |
| 1869 | 1,800 | 225.00 | 1881-CC | 13,900 | 150.00 |
| 1860 S | 31,000 | 110.00 | 1882 | 2½ million | 110.00 |
| 1870 | 4,000 | 150.00 | 1882-S | 970,000 | 110.00 |
| 1870-S | 17,000 | 140.00 | 1882-CC | 82,800 | 150.00 |
| 1870-CC | 7,700 | 800.00 | 1883 | 233,400 | 110.00 |
| 1871 | 3,200 | 175.00 | 1883-S | 83,200 | 110.00 |
| 1871-S | 25,000 | 110.00 | 1883-CC | 13,000 | 150.00 |
| 1871-CC | 20,800 | 190.00 | 1884 | 191,000 | 110.00 |
| 1872 | 1,700 | 250.00 | 1884-S | 177,000 | 110.00 |
| 1872-S | 36,400 | 110.00 | 1884-CC | 16,400 | 150.00 |
| 1872-CC | 17,000 | 190.00 | 1885 | 601,500 | 110.00 |
| 1873 | 112,500 | 110.00 | 1885-S | 1¼ million | 110.00 |
| 1873-S | 31,000 | 110.00 | 1886 | 388,400 | 110.00 |
| 1873-CC | 7,400 | 250.00 | 1886-S | 3¼ million | 110.00 |
| 1874 | 3,500 | 190.00 | 1887 | 87 proofs | —— |
| 1874-S | 16,000 | 110.00 | 1887-S | 2 million | 110.00 |
| 1874-CC | 21,200 | 160.00 | 1888 | 18,300 | 150.00 |
| 1875 | 220 | —— | 1888-S | 293,900 | 110.00 |
| 1875-S | 9,000 | 150.00 | 1889 | 7,600 | 175.00 |
| 1875-CC | 11,800 | 190.00 | 1890 | 4,300 | 190.00 |
| 1876 | 1,500 | 225.00 | 1890-CC | 53,800 | 150.00 |
| 1876-S | 4,000 | 150.00 | 1891 | 61,400 | 110.00 |
| 1876-CC | 6,900 | 225.00 | 1891-CC | 208,000 | 150.00 |
| 1877 | 1,200 | 250.00 | 1892 | 753,600 | 110.00 |
| 1877-S | 26,700 | 110.00 | 1892-O | 10,000 | 250.00 |
| 1877-CC | 8,700 | 200.00 | 1892-S | 298,400 | 110.00 |
| 1878 | 131,700 | 110.00 | 1892-CC | 83,000 | 150.00 |
| 1878-S | 144,700 | 110.00 | 1893 | 1½ million | 110.00 |
| 1878-CC | 9,100 | 600.00 | 1893-O | 110,000 | 110.00 |
| 1879 | 301,900 | 110.00 | 1893-S | 224,000 | 110.00 |
| 1879-S | 426,200 | 110.00 | 1893-CC | 60,000 | 150.00 |

| Date | Amount Minted | Value | Date | Amount Minted | Value |
|---|---|---|---|---|---|
| 1894 | 958,000 | **110.00** | 1901-S | 3⅔ million | **110.00** |
| 1894-O | 16,600 | **150.00** | 1902 | 172,600 | **110.00** |
| 1894-S | 55,900 | **110.00** | 1902-S | 939,000 | **110.00** |
| 1895 | 1⅓ million | **110.00** | 1903 | 227,000 | **110.00** |
| 1895-S | 112,000 | **110.00** | 1903-S | 1¾ million | **110.00** |
| 1896 | 59,100 | **110.00** | 1904 | 392,100 | **110.00** |
| 1896-S | 155,400 | **110.00** | 1904-S | 97,000 | **110.00** |
| 1897 | 867,900 | **110.00** | 1905 | 302,300 | **110.00** |
| 1897-S | 354,000 | **110.00** | 1905-S | 880,700 | **110.00** |
| 1898 | 633,500 | **110.00** | 1906 | 348,800 | **110.00** |
| 1898-S | 1⅓ million | **110.00** | 1906-S | 598,000 | **110.00** |
| 1899 | 1¾ million | **110.00** | 1906-D | 320,000 | **110.00** |
| 1899-S | 1½ million | **110.00** | 1907 | 626,200 | **110.00** |
| 1900 | 1⅓ million | **110.00** | 1907-D | 888,000 | **110.00** |
| 1900-S | 329,000 | **110.00** | 1908 | 421,900 | **110.00** |
| 1901 | 616,000 | **110.00** | | | |

### Type: Indian head.

(The mint marks are on the Rev., to the left of the value)

| Date | Amount Minted | Value | Date | Amount Minted | Value |
|---|---|---|---|---|---|
| 1908 | 578,000 | **140.00** | 1911-S | 1½ million | **140.00** |
| 1908-D | 148,000 | **140.00** | 1912 | 790,100 | **140.00** |
| 1908-S | 82,000 | **235.00** | 1912-S | 392,000 | **140.00** |
| 1909 | 627,100 | **140.00** | 1913 | 916,100 | **140.00** |
| 1909-O | 34,200 | **650.00** | 1913-S | 408,000 | **140.00** |
| 1909-D | 3½ million | **140.00** | 1914 | 247,100 | **140.00** |
| 1909-S | 297,200 | **140.00** | 1914-D | 247,000 | **140.00** |
| 1910 | 604,200 | **140.00** | 1914-S | 263,000 | **140.00** |
| 1910-D | 193,600 | **140.00** | 1915 | 588,100 | **140.00** |
| 1910-S | 770,200 | **140.00** | 1915-S | 164,000 | **140.00** |
| 1911 | 915,100 | **140.00** | 1916-S | 240,000 | **140.00** |
| 1911-D | 72,500 | **250.00** | 1929 | 662,000 | **2,000.00** |

The valuations listed in this book closely approximate how much established coin dealers will pay for any material needed in their stock.

# 10 DOLLAR GOLD PIECES (EAGLES)

### Type: Liberty head; with small eagle on Rev.

| Date | Amount Minted | Value | Date | Amount Minted | Value |
|------|--------------|-------|------|--------------|-------|
| 1795 | 2,800 | **3,000.00** | 1797 | Part of 9,200 | **3,000.00** |
| 1796 | 6,100 | **3,000.00** | | | |

### Type: Liberty head; with large eagle on Rev.

| Date | Amount Minted | Value | Date | Amount Minted | Value |
|------|--------------|-------|------|--------------|-------|
| 1797 | Part of 9,200 | **1,300.00** | 1801 | 29,300 | **1,000.00** |
| 1798 | 8,000 | **2,000.00** | 1803 | 9,000 | **1,100.00** |
| 1799 | 17,500 | **1,000.00** | 1804 | 9,800 | **1,300.00** |
| 1800 | 26,000 | **1,100.00** | | | |

### Type: Liberty head; without motto on Rev.

(The mint marks are on the Rev., under the eagle)

| Date | Amount Minted | Value | Date | Amount Minted | Value |
|------|--------------|-------|------|--------------|-------|
| 1838 | 7,200 | **400.00** | 1840 | 47,300 | **225.00** |
| 1839 | 38,200 | **300.00** | 1841 | 63,100 | **225.00** |

| Date | Amount Minted | Value | Date | Amount Minted | Value |
|------|--------------:|------:|------|--------------:|------:|
| 1841-O | 2,500 | 250.00 | 1855-O | 18,000 | 225.00 |
| 1842 | 81,500 | 225.00 | 1855-S | 9,000 | 250.00 |
| 1842-O | 27,400 | 225.00 | 1856 | 60,500 | 225.00 |
| 1843 | 75,500 | 225.00 | 1856-O | 14,500 | 225.00 |
| 1843-O | 175,200 | 225.00 | 1856-S | 68,000 | 225.00 |
| 1844 | 6,400 | 250.00 | 1857 | 16,600 | 225.00 |
| 1844-O | 118,700 | 225.00 | 1857-O | 5,500 | 250.00 |
| 1845 | 26,200 | 225.00 | 1857-S | 26,000 | 225.00 |
| 1845-O | 47,500 | 225.00 | 1858 | 2,500 | 2,000.00 |
| 1846 | 20,100 | 225.00 | 1858-O | 20,000 | 225.00 |
| 1846-O | 81,800 | 225.00 | 1858-S | 11,800 | 225.00 |
| 1847 | 862,300 | 225.00 | 1859 | 16,100 | 225.00 |
| 1847-O | 571,500 | 225.00 | 1859-O | 2,300 | 500.00 |
| 1848 | 145,500 | 225.00 | 1859-S | 7,000 | 300.00 |
| 1848-O | 35,800 | 225.00 | 1860 | 11,800 | 225.00 |
| 1849 | 653,600 | 225.00 | 1860-O | 11,100 | 225.00 |
| 1849-O | 23,900 | 225.00 | 1860-S | 5,000 | 400.00 |
| 1850 | 291,500 | 225.00 | 1861 | 113,200 | 225.00 |
| 1850-O | 57,500 | 225.00 | 1861-S | 15,500 | 225.00 |
| 1851 | 176,300 | 225.00 | 1862 | 11,000 | 225.00 |
| 1851-O | 263,000 | 225.00 | 1862-S | 12,500 | 225.00 |
| 1852 | 263,100 | 225.00 | 1863 | 1,200 | 1,000.00 |
| 1852-O | 18,000 | 225.00 | 1863-S | 10,000 | 225.00 |
| 1853 | 201,300 | 225.00 | 1864 | 3,600 | 400.00 |
| 1853-O | 51,000 | 225.00 | 1864-S | 2,500 | 700.00 |
| 1854 | 54,200 | 225.00 | 1865 | 4,000 | 300.00 |
| 1854-O | 52,500 | 225.00 | 1865-S | 16,700 | 300.00 |
| 1854-S | 123,800 | 225.00 | 1866-S | Part of 20,000 | 400.00 |
| 1855 | 121,700 | 225.00 | | | |

## Type: Liberty head; with motto on Rev.

(The mint marks are on the Rev., under the eagle)

| Date | Amount Minted | Value | Date | Amount Minted | Value |
|------|--------------:|------:|------|--------------:|------:|
| 1866 | 3,800 | 225.00 | 1869 | 1,900 | 350.00 |
| 1866-S | Part of 20,000 | 225.00 | 1869-S | 6,400 | 200.00 |
| 1867 | 3,100 | 225.00 | 1870 | 2,500 | 225.00 |
| 1867-S | 9,000 | 225.00 | 1870-S | 8,000 | 200.00 |
| 1868 | 10,700 | 200.00 | 1870-CC | 5,900 | 450.00 |
| 1868-S | 13,500 | 200.00 | 1871 | 1,800 | 225.00 |

| Date | Amount Minted | Value | Date | Amount Minted | Value |
|------|--------------:|------:|------|--------------:|------:|
| 1871-S | 16,500 | 225.00 | 1886-S | 826,000 | 175.00 |
| 1871-CC | 7,200 | 350.00 | 1887 | 53,700 | 200.00 |
| 1872 | 1,600 | 400.00 | 1887-S | 817,000 | 175.00 |
| 1872-S | 17,300 | 225.00 | 1888 | 133,000 | 175.00 |
| 1872-CC | 5,500 | 350.00 | 1888-O | 21,300 | 200.00 |
| 1873 | 825 | 1000.00 | 1888-S | 648,700 | 175.00 |
| 1873-S | 12,000 | 225.00 | 1889 | 4,500 | 300.00 |
| 1873-CC | 4,500 | 500.00 | 1889-S | 425,400 | 175.00 |
| 1874 | 53,200 | 200.00 | 1890 | 58,000 | 200.00 |
| 1874-S | 10,000 | 200.00 | 1890-CC | 17,500 | 200.00 |
| 1874-CC | 16,800 | 200.00 | 1891 | 91,900 | 175.00 |
| 1875 | 120 | —— | 1891-CC | 103,700 | 175.00 |
| 1875-CC | 7,700 | 300.00 | 1892 | 797,600 | 175.00 |
| 1876 | 732 | 1,000.00 | 1892-O | 28,700 | 175.00 |
| 1876-S | 5,000 | 300.00 | 1892-S | 115,500 | 175.00 |
| 1876-CC | 4,700 | 400.00 | 1892-CC | 40,000 | 225.00 |
| 1877 | 817 | 1,000.00 | 1893 | 1¾ million | 175.00 |
| 1877-S | 17,000 | 250.00 | 1893-O | 17,000 | 200.00 |
| 1877-CC | 3,300 | 500.00 | 1893-S | 141,300 | 175.00 |
| 1878 | 73,800 | 200.00 | 1893-CC | 14,000 | 200.00 |
| 1878-S | 26,100 | 200.00 | 1894 | 2½ million | 175.00 |
| 1878-CC | 3,200 | 500.00 | 1894-O | 107,500 | 175.00 |
| 1879 | 384,800 | 175.00 | 1894-S | 25,000 | 200.00 |
| 1879-O | 1,500 | 600.00 | 1895 | 567,800 | 175.00 |
| 1879-S | 224,000 | 175.00 | 1895-O | 98,000 | 175.00 |
| 1879-CC | 1,800 | 1,000.00 | 1895-S | 49,000 | 200.00 |
| 1880 | 1⅔ million | 175.00 | 1896 | 76,300 | 200.00 |
| 1880-O | 9,200 | 250.00 | 1896-S | 123,700 | 200.00 |
| 1880-S | 506,200 | 175.00 | 1897 | 1 million | 175.00 |
| 1880-CC | 11,200 | 225.00 | 1897-O | 42,500 | 200.00 |
| 1881 | 3¾ million | 175.00 | 1897-S | 234,700 | 175.00 |
| 1881-O | 8,300 | 225.00 | 1898 | 812,200 | 175.00 |
| 1881-S | 970,000 | 175.00 | 1898-S | 473,600 | 175.00 |
| 1881-CC | 24,000 | 200.00 | 1899 | 1¼ million | 175.00 |
| 1882 | 2⅓ million | 175.00 | 1899-O | 37,000 | 200.00 |
| 1882-O | 10,800 | 200.00 | 1899-S | 841,000 | 175.00 |
| 1882-S | 132,000 | 200.00 | 1900 | 294,000 | 175.00 |
| 1882-CC | 6,800 | 225.00 | 1900-S | 81,000 | 200.00 |
| 1883 | 208,700 | 175.00 | 1901 | 1¾ million | 175.00 |
| 1883-O | 800 | 1,000.00 | 1901-O | 72,000 | 200.00 |
| 1883-S | 38,000 | 200.00 | 1901-S | 2¾ million | 175.00 |
| 1883-CC | 12,000 | 225.00 | 1902 | 82,500 | 200.00 |
| 1884 | 76,900 | 200.00 | 1902-S | 469,500 | 175.00 |
| 1884-S | 124,200 | 175.00 | 1903 | 125,900 | 175.00 |
| 1884-CC | 9,900 | 225.00 | 1903-O | 112,800 | 175.00 |
| 1885 | 253,500 | 175.00 | 1903-S | 538,000 | 175.00 |
| 1885-S | 228,000 | 175.00 | 1904 | 162,000 | 175.00 |
| 1886 | 236,200 | 175.00 | 1904-O | 108,900 | 175.00 |

| Date | Amount Minted | Value | Date | Amount Minted | Value |
|------|--------------:|------:|------|--------------:|------:|
| 1905 | 201,000 | 175.00 | 1906-D | 981,000 | 175.00 |
| 1905-S | 369,200 | 175.00 | 1907 | 1¼ million | 175.00 |
| 1906 | 165,500 | 175.00 | 1907-S | 210,500 | 175.00 |
| 1906-O | 86,900 | 200.00 | 1907-D | 1 million | 175.00 |
| 1906-S | 457,000 | 175.00 | | | |

### Type: Indian head; without motto on Rev.

(The Mint marks are on the Rev., to the left of the value. The "1907 Periods"
indicates a period at each end of "United States of America" on the Rev.)

| Date | Amount Minted | Value | Date | Amount Minted | Value |
|------|--------------:|------:|------|--------------:|------:|
| 1907 | 239,400 | 350.00 | 1908 | 33,500 | 375.00 |
| 1907 Periods | 542 | 2,000.00 | 1908-D | 210,000 | 350.00 |

*Type: Indian head; with motto on Rev.*

| Date | Amount Minted | Value | Date | Amount Minted | Value |
|------|--------------|-------|------|--------------|-------|
| 1908 | 341,500 | 350.00 | 1913 | 442,100 | 350.00 |
| 1908-D | 836,500 | 350.00 | 1913-S | 66,000 | 350.00 |
| 1908-S | 59,900 | 500.00 | 1914 | 151,000 | 350.00 |
| 1909 | 184,900 | 350.00 | 1914-D | 343,500 | 350.00 |
| 1909-D | 121,500 | 350.00 | 1914-S | 208,000 | 350.00 |
| 1909-S | 292,300 | 350.00 | 1915 | 351,100 | 350.00 |
| 1910 | 318,700 | 350.00 | 1915-S | 59,000 | 400.00 |
| 1910-D | 2⅓ million | 350.00 | 1916-S | 138,500 | 400.00 |
| 1910-S | 811,000 | 350.00 | 1920-S | 126,500 | 4,500.00 |
| 1911 | 505,600 | 350.00 | 1926 | 1 million | 350.00 |
| 1911-D | 30,100 | 400.00 | 1930-S | 96,000 | 2,500.00 |
| 1911-S | 51,000 | 400.00 | 1932 | 4½ million | 350.00 |
| 1912 | 405,000 | 350.00 | 1933 | 312,500 | —— |
| 1912-S | 300,000 | 350.00 | | | |

## 20 DOLLAR GOLD PIECES (DOUBLE EAGLES)

### Type: Liberty head; without motto on Rev.

(The mint marks are on the Rev., under the eagle)

| Date | Amount Minted | Value | Date | Amount Minted | Value |
|---|---|---|---|---|---|
| 1850 | 1¼ million | 525.00 | 1858-O | 35,200 | 450.00 |
| 1850-O | 141,000 | 450.00 | 1858-S | 846,700 | 400.00 |
| 1851 | 2 million | 400.00 | 1859 | 43,600 | 425.00 |
| 1851-O | 315,000 | 425.00 | 1859-O | 9,100 | 1,000.00 |
| 1852 | 2 million | 400.00 | 1859-S | 636,400 | 400.00 |
| 1852-O | 190,000 | 425.00 | 1860 | 577,700 | 400.00 |
| 1853 | 1¼ million | 400.00 | 1860-O | 6,600 | 1,200.00 |
| 1853-O | 71,000 | 550.00 | 1860-S | 544,900 | 400.00 |
| 1854 | 757,900 | 400.00 | 1861 | 3 million | 400.00 |
| 1854-O | 3,200 | — | 1861-O | 5,000 | 800.00 |
| 1854-S | 141,500 | 400.00 | 1861-S | 768,000 | 400.00 |
| 1855 | 364,700 | 400.00 | 1862 | 92,100 | 400.00 |
| 1855-O | 8,000 | 900.00 | 1862-S | 854,200 | 400.00 |
| 1855-S | 879,700 | 400.00 | 1863 | 142,800 | 400.00 |
| 1856 | 329,900 | 400.00 | 1863-S | 966,600 | 400.00 |
| 1856-O | 2,200 | — | 1864 | 204,300 | 400.00 |
| 1856-S | 1¼ million | 400.00 | 1864-S | 793,700 | 400.00 |
| 1857 | 439,400 | 400.00 | 1865 | 351,200 | 400.00 |
| 1857-O | 30,000 | 400.00 | 1865-S | 1 million | 400.00 |
| 1857-S | 970,500 | 400.00 | 1866-S | Part of 842,200 | 525.00 |
| 1858 | 211,700 | 400.00 | | | |

### Type: Liberty head; with motto on Rev. and "Twenty D."

(The mint marks are on the Rev., under the eagle)

| Date | Amount Minted | Value | Date | Amount Minted | Value |
|------|---------------|-------|------|---------------|-------|
| 1866 | 698,800 | 375.00 | 1872-S | 780,000 | 375.00 |
| 1866-S | Part of 842,200 | 375.00 | 1872-CC | 29,600 | 550.00 |
| 1867 | 251,065 | 375.00 | 1873 | 1¾ million | 375.00 |
| 1867-S | 920,700 | 375.00 | 1873-S | 1 million | 375.00 |
| 1868 | 98,600 | 375.00 | 1873-CC | 22,400 | 550.00 |
| 1868-S | 837,500 | 375.00 | 1874 | 366,800 | 375.00 |
| 1869 | 171,200 | 375.00 | 1874-S | 1¼ million | 375.00 |
| 1869-S | 686,700 | 375.00 | 1874-CC | 115,100 | 400.00 |
| 1870 | 155,200 | 375.00 | 1875 | 295,700 | 375.00 |
| 1870-S | 982,000 | 375.00 | 1875-S | 1¼ million | 375.00 |
| 1870-CC | 3,800 | — | 1875-CC | 111,100 | 400.00 |
| 1871 | 80,100 | 375.00 | 1876 | 583,900 | 375.00 |
| 1871-S | 928,000 | 375.00 | 1876-S | 1½ million | 375.00 |
| 1871-CC | 14,700 | 800.00 | 1876-CC | 138,400 | 525.00 |
| 1872 | 251,900 | 375.00 | | | |

## Type: Liberty head; with motto on Rev. and "Twenty Dollars."

(The mint marks are on the Rev., under the eagle)

| Date | Amount Minted | Value | Date | Amount Minted | Value |
|------|---------------|-------|------|---------------|-------|
| 1877 | 397,700 | 375.00 | 1885-S | 683,500 | 375.00 |
| 1877-S | 1¾ million | 375.00 | 1885-CC | 9,500 | 550.00 |
| 1877-CC | 42,600 | 525.00 | 1886 | 1,100 | 2,000.00 |
| 1878 | 543,600 | 375.00 | 1887 | 121 proofs | —— |
| 1878-S | 1¾ million | 375.00 | 1887-S | 283,000 | 3,350.00 |
| 1878-CC | 13,200 | 535.00 | 1888 | 226,300 | 375.00 |
| 1879 | 207,600 | 375.00 | 1888-S | 859,600 | 375.00 |
| 1879-O | 2,300 | 1,500.00 | 1889 | 44,100 | 375.00 |
| 1879-S | 1¼ million | 375.00 | 1889-S | 774,700 | 375.00 |
| 1879-CC | 10,700 | 550.00 | 1889-CC | 30,900 | 375.00 |
| 1880 | 51,500 | 475.00 | 1890 | 76,000 | 375.00 |
| 1880-S | 836,000 | 375.00 | 1890-S | 802,700 | 375.00 |
| 1881 | 2,300 | 1,650.00 | 1890-CC | 91,200 | 375.00 |
| 1881-S | 727,000 | 375.00 | 1891 | 1,400 | 1,000.00 |
| 1882 | 630 | 3,000.00 | 1891-S | 1¼ million | 375.00 |
| 1882-S | 1¼ million | 375.00 | 1891-CC | 5,000 | 1,000.00 |
| 1882-CC | 39,100 | 500.00 | 1892 | 4,500 | 700.00 |
| 1883 | About 100 proofs | —— | 1892-S | 930,100 | 375.00 |
| 1883-S | 1¼ million | 375.00 | 1892-CC | 27,300 | 375.00 |
| 1883-CC | 60,000 | 500.00 | | | |
| 1884 | 71 proofs | —— | | | |
| 1884-S | 916,000 | 375.00 | | | |
| 1884-CC | 81,100 | 500.00 | | | |
| 1885 | 828 | 2,000.00 | | | |

| Date | Amount Minted | Value | Date | Amount Minted | Value |
|------|---------------|-------|------|---------------|-------|
| 1893 | 344,300 | 375.00 | 1901 | 111,500 | 375.00 |
| 1893-S | 996,200 | 375.00 | 1901-S | 1½ million | 375.00 |
| 1893-CC | 18,400 | 375.00 | 1902 | 31,300 | 375.00 |
| 1894 | 1⅓ million | 375.00 | 1902-S | 1¾ million | 375.00 |
| 1894-S | 1 million | 375.00 | 1903 | 287,400 | 375.00 |
| 1895 | 1 million | 375.00 | 1903-S | 954,000 | 375.00 |
| 1895-S | 1¼ million | 375.00 | 1904 | 6¼ million | 375.00 |
| 1896 | 792,700 | 375.00 | 1904-S | 5¼ million | 375.00 |
| 1896-S | 1½ million | 375.00 | 1905 | 59,000 | 375.00 |
| 1897 | 1⅓ million | 375.00 | 1905-S | 1¾ million | 375.00 |
| 1897-S | 1½ million | 375.00 | 1906 | 69,700 | 375.00 |
| 1898 | 170,500 | 375.00 | 1906-S | 2 million | 375.00 |
| 1898-S | 2½ million | 375.00 | 1906-D | 620,200 | 375.00 |
| 1899 | 1⅔ million | 375.00 | 1907 | 1½ million | 375.00 |
| 1899-S | 2 million | 375.00 | 1907-S | 2¼ million | 375.00 |
| 1900 | 1¾ million | 375.00 | 1907-D | 842,200 | 375.00 |
| 1900-S | 2½ million | 375.00 | | | |

**Type: Liberty standing (St. Gaudens design).
Date in Roman Numerals, MCMVII.**

| | | |
|------|--------|----------|
| 1907 | 11,200 | 2,000.00 |

### Type: Liberty standing; date in normal numerals; without motto on Rev.

(The mint mark is on the Obv., over the date)

| Date | Amount Minted | Value | Date | Amount Minted | Value |
|------|--------------:|------:|------|--------------:|------:|
| 1907 | 361,700 | **485.00** | 1908-D | 663,700 | **450.00** |
| 1908 | 4¼ million | **450.00** | | | |

### Type: Liberty standing; with motto on Rev.

(The mint marks are on the Obv., over the date)

| Date | Amount Minted | Value | Date | Amount Minted | Value |
|------|--------------:|------:|------|--------------:|------:|
| 1908 | 156,400 | **425.00** | 1914 | 95,300 | **425.00** |
| 1908-D | 349,500 | **425.00** | 1914-D | 453,000 | **425.00** |
| 1908-S | 22,000 | **650.00** | 1914-S | 1½ million | **425.00** |
| 1909 | Part of 161,300 | **425.00** | 1915 | 152,000 | **450.00** |
| 1909 over 8 | Part of 161,300 | **450.00** | 1915-S | 567,500 | **450.00** |
| 1909-D | 52,500 | **550.00** | 1916-S | 796,000 | **450.00** |
| 1909-S | 2¾ million | **425.00** | 1920 | 228,200 | **450.00** |
| 1910 | 482,200 | **425.00** | 1920-S | 558,000 | **4,500.00** |
| 1910-D | 429,000 | **425.00** | 1921 | 528,500 | **6,500.00** |
| 1910-S | 2¼ million | **425.00** | 1922 | 1⅓ million | **425.00** |
| 1911 | 197,300 | **425.00** | 1922-S | 2⅔ million | **550.00** |
| 1911-D | 846,500 | **425.00** | 1923 | 566,000 | **425.00** |
| 1911-S | 775,700 | **425.00** | 1923-D | 1⅔ million | **425.00** |
| 1912 | 149,800 | **425.00** | 1924 | 4⅓ million | **425.00** |
| 1913 | 168,800 | **425.00** | 1924-D | 3 million | **725.00** |
| 1913-D | 393,500 | **425.00** | 1924-S | 3 million | **675.00** |
| 1913-S | 34,000 | **425.00** | 1925 | 2¾ million | **425.00** |

| Date | Amount Minted | Value | Date | Amount Minted | Value |
|------|--------------|-------|------|--------------|-------|
| 1925-D | 3 million | 650.00 | 1928 | 8¾ million | 450.00 |
| 1925-S | 3¾ million | 600.00 | 1929 | 1¾ million | 2,000.00 |
| 1926 | 816,700 | 425.00 | 1930-S | 74,000 | 3,000.00 |
| 1926-D | 481,000 | 650.00 | 1931 | 3 million | 4,000.00 |
| 1926-S | 2 million | 525.00 | 1931-D | 106,500 | 4,500.00 |
| 1927 | 3 million | 425.00 | 1932 | 1 million | 4,000.00 |
| 1927-D | 180,000 | —— | 1933 | 445,500 | not issued |
| 1927-S | 3 million | 2,000.00 | | | |

# Pioneer Gold Coins

## Coinage of the Territorial and Private Mints

(The valuations are for coins in VG to F condition)
(Beware of Copies)

### BALDWIN & CO.

#### San Francisco, California

*Horseman with lariat. Rev. Eagle.*

10 Dollars 1850 . . . . . . . . . . . . . . . . . . . . . . . . . . . . . . . . . . . . . . . . . . . . . . . . . . . **6,500.00**

*"Baldwin & Co" on head band of Liberty. Rev. Eagle.*

5 Dollars 1850 . . . . . . . . . . . . . . . . . . . . . . . . . . . . . . . . . . . . . . . . . . . . . . . **1,500.00**
10 Dollars 1851 . . . . . . . . . . . . . . . . . . . . . . . . . . . . . . . . . . . . . . . . . . . . . . . **4,000.00**
20 Dollars 1851 . . . . . . . . . . . . . . . . . . . . . . . . . . . . . . . . . . . . . . . . . . . . . . . ——

## AUGUST BECHTLER

### *Rutherford, North Carolina*

Value and legend. Rev. Weight and legend. The coins are
undated but were struck from 1842 to 1852.

1 Dollar ND. One variety ............................................................ 350.00
5 Dollars ND. Three varieties ...................................................... 950.00

## CHRISTOPHER BECHTLER

### *Rutherford, North Carolina*

*Value and legend. Rev. Weight and legend. The coins are
undated, but were struck from 1831 to 1842.*

| | | |
|---|---|---|
| 1 | Dollar ND. Four varieties ................................................. | 400.00 |
| 2½ | Dollars ND. Seven varieties ............................................. | 750.00 |
| 5 | Dollars ND. Six varieties ................................................. | 950.00 |
| 5 | Dollars August 1, 1834. Two varieties ................................. | 950.00 |

The valuations listed in this book closely approximate how
much established coin dealers will pay for any material needed in
their stock.

## EPHRAIM BRASHER

### *New York*

*Radiant sun over mountains. Rev. Eagle with "EB" punched on
either the wing or breast. The famous Brasher Doubloon.*

Doubloon 1787    Extremely Rare .................................................. ——
½ Doubloon 1787 Extremely Rare .................................................. ——

## CINCINNATI MINING & TRADING CO.

### *San Francisco, California*

*Indian Head. Rev. Eagle*

 5 Dollars 1849 .................................................................. ——
10 Dollars 1849 .................................................................. ——

## CLARK, GRUBER & CO.

### *Denver, Colorado*

*View of Pikes Peak. Rev. Eagle*

10 Dollars 1860  ............................................................. 1,000.00
20 Dollars 1860  ............................................................. 5,000.00

*"Clark & Co." on head band of Liberty. Rev. Eagle.*

| | | | |
|---|---|---|---|
| 2½ | Dollars 1860 | ............................................................ | 350.00 |
| 5 | Dollars 1860 | ............................................................ | 500.00 |

*"Pikes Peak" on head band of Liberty. Rev. Eagle.*

| | | | |
|---|---|---|---|
| 2½ | Dollars 1861 | ............................................................ | 400.00 |
| 5 | Dollars 1861 | ............................................................ | 500.00 |
| 10 | Dollars 1861 | ............................................................ | 500.00 |
| 20 | Dollars 1861 | ............................................................ | 1,250.00 |

## J. J. CONWAY & CO.

### *Georgia Gulch, Colorado*

*Name of company. Rev. Value and "Pikes Peak."*
*Undated but struck in 1861.*

| | | | |
|---|---|---|---|
| 2½ | Dollars ND | ............................................................ | — |
| 5 | Dollars ND | ............................................................ | — |
| 10 | Dollars ND | ............................................................ | — |

## DUBOSQ & CO.

### *San Francisco, California*

*"Dubosq & Co." on head band of Liberty. Rev. Eagle.*

5 Dollars 1850 ............................................................. ——
10 Dollars 1850 ............................................................ ——

## DUNBAR & CO.

### *San Francisco, California*

*"Dunbar & Co." on head band of Liberty. Rev. Eagle.*

5 Dollars 1851 ............................................................. ——

## AUGUSTUS HUMBERT

### *U.S. Assayer of gold, San Francisco, California*

*Eagle. Rev. Four line legend in tablet.*

10 Dollars 1852 ........................................................ **750.00**
20 Dollars 1852 ...................................................... **1,250.00**

*Eagle. Rev. Small 50, star or circle in center of otherwise blank*
*Rev. Octagonal shaped with lettered edge.*
50 Dollars 1851. Five varieties . . . . . . . . . . . . . . . . . . . . . . . . . . . . . . . . . . . . . . . . . . . . **3,500.00**

*Eagle. Rev. Machine made criss-cross of circular lines. Octagonal*
*shaped with reeded edge.*
50 Dollars 1851, 52. Three varieties . . . . . . . . . . . . . . . . . . . . . . . . . . . . . . . . . . . . . . . **3,500.00**

# KELLOGG & CO.

## *San Francisco, California*

*"Kellogg & Co." on head band of Liberty. Rev. Standard Eagle.*
20 Dollars 1854, 55 . . . . . . . . . . . . . . . . . . . . . . . . . . . . . . . . . . . . . . . . . . . . . . . . . . . . **700.00**

*Obv. Similar to above. Rev. Eagle holding shield.*
50 Dollars 1855 . . . . . . . . . . . . . . . . . . . . . . . . . . . . . . . . . . . . . . . . . . . . . . . . . . . . ——

# MASSACHUSETTS & CALIFORNIA CO.

## *San Francisco, California*

*Arms supported by bear and stag. Value in wreath.*
5 Dollars 1849. Four varieties . . . . . . . . . . . . . . . . . . . . . . . . . . . . . . . . . . . . . . . . ——

## MINERS BANK

### *San Francisco, California*

Name and value. Rev. Eagle.

10 Dollars 1849 . . . . . . . . . . . . . . . . . . . . . . . . . . . . . . . . . . . . . . . . . . . . . . . . . . . . 2,000.00

## MOFFAT & CO.

### *San Francisco, California*

*"Moffat & Co." on head band of Liberty. Rev. Eagle.*

5 Dollars 1849, 50 . . . . . . . . . . . . . . . . . . . . . . . . . . . . . . . . . . . . . . . . . . . . . . . . . . . 300.00
10 Dollars 1849, 52 . . . . . . . . . . . . . . . . . . . . . . . . . . . . . . . . . . . . . . . . . . . . . . . . . . 650.00
20 Dollars 1853 . . . . . . . . . . . . . . . . . . . . . . . . . . . . . . . . . . . . . . . . . . . . . . . . . . . . . 800.00

## THE MORMONS

### *Salt Lake City, Utah*

*Eye and Bishop's Mitre. Rev. Clasped hands.*

2½ Dollars 1849 . . . . . . . . . . . . . . . . . . . . . . . . . . . . . . . . . . . . . . . . . . . . . . . . . . . 1,200.00
5    Dollars 1849, 50 . . . . . . . . . . . . . . . . . . . . . . . . . . . . . . . . . . . . . . . . . . . . . . . 1,000.00
10   Dollars 1849 . . . . . . . . . . . . . . . . . . . . . . . . . . . . . . . . . . . . . . . . . . . . . . . . . . . ——
20   Dollars 1849 . . . . . . . . . . . . . . . . . . . . . . . . . . . . . . . . . . . . . . . . . . . . . . . . . . . ——

*Lion. Rev. Beehive on breast of eagle.*

5 Dollars 1860 . . . . . . . . . . . . . . . . . . . . . . . . . . . . . . . . . . . . . . . . . . . . . . . . . . . . . . 2,000.00

## NORRIS, GRIEG & NORRIS

### *San Francisco, California*

*Eagle. Rev. Legend.*

5 Dollars 1849. Plain or reeded edge . . . . . . . . . . . . . . . . . . . . . . . . . . . . . . . . . . 950.00

## OREGON EXCHANGE CO.

### *Oregon City, Oregon*

*Beaver and initials. Rev. Legend.*

5 Dollars 1849 . . . . . . . . . . . . . . . . . . . . . . . . . . . . . . . . . . . . . . . . . . . . . . . . . . . . . . 2,500.00
10 Dollars 1849 . . . . . . . . . . . . . . . . . . . . . . . . . . . . . . . . . . . . . . . . . . . . . . . . . . . . 9,000.00

## J. S. ORMSBY

### *San Francisco, California*

*"J. S. O." Rev. Value. Undated but struck in 1849.*

5 Dollars ND . . . . . . . . . . . . . . . . . . . . . . . . . . . . . . . . . . . . . . . . . . . . . . . . . . . . . . —
10 Dollars ND . . . . . . . . . . . . . . . . . . . . . . . . . . . . . . . . . . . . . . . . . . . . . . . . . . . . . —

## PACIFIC CO.

### *San Francisco, California*

*Liberty Cap. Rev. Eagle.*

5 Dollars 1849 . . . . . . . . . . . . . . . . . . . . . . . . . . . . . . . . . . . . . . . . . . . . . . . . . . . . . —
10 Dollars 1849 . . . . . . . . . . . . . . . . . . . . . . . . . . . . . . . . . . . . . . . . . . . . . . . . . . . . —

## JOHN PARSONS & CO.

### *Tarryall Mines, Colorado*

*Stamping machine. Rev. Eagle and "Pikes Peak Gold." Undated
but struck in 1861.*

2½ Dollars ND . . . . . . . . . . . . . . . . . . . . . . . . . . . . . . . . . . . . . . . . . . . . . . . . . . . . . —
5   Dollars ND, . . . . . . . . . . . . . . . . . . . . . . . . . . . . . . . . . . . . . . . . . . . . . . . . . . . . —

### SHULTS & CO.

#### *San Francisco, California*

*"Shults & Co." on head band of Liberty. Rev. Eagle.*

5 Dollars 1851 ............................................................. 4,000.00

### TEMPLETON REID

#### *Lumpkin County, Georgia*

*Legend on each side.*

| | | |
|---|---|---|
| 2½ | Dollars 1830 | —— |
| 5 | Dollars 1830 | —— |
| 10 | Dollars 1830 | —— |
| 10 | Dollars ND | —— |

### TEMPLETON REID

#### *San Francisco, California*

*Legend on each side.*

10 Dollars 1849 ............................................................ ——
25 Dollars 1849 ............................................................ ——

## UNITED STATES ASSAY OFFICE OF GOLD

### San Francisco, California

*Eagle. Rev. Legend in tablet.*

10 Dollars 1852, 53. Two varieties .......................................... 500.00
20 Dollars 1853. Two varieties ............................................. 950.00

*Eagle. Rev. Machine made criss-cross of circular lines. Octagonal shaped.*
50 Dollars 1852. Two varieties .............................................. 2,500.00

## WASS, MOLITOR & CO.

### San Francisco, California

*"W.M. & Co." on head band of Liberty. Rev. Eagle.*

5 Dollars 1852 ........................................................... 1,200.00
10 Dollars 1852, 55. Two varieties ......................................... 1,000.00
20 Dollars. 1855. Two varieties ............................................ 2,750.00

*Liberty head. Rev. Name and value.*
50 Dollars 1855 . . . . . . . . . . . . . . . . . . . . . . . . . . . . . . . . . . . . . . . . . . . . . . . . . . 5,000.00

# United States Proof Sets
## (1936 to date)

A Proof Set contains five coins; the 1c, 5c, 25c, and 50c pieces. From 1936 through 1942, unequal amounts were struck of each denomination; from 1950 to date equal amounts have been struck. In the column under Amount Minted, the figure shows the total number of *complete* sets minted in each year. In 1942, two types of proof 5 Cent pieces were struck, the standard coin and the one with silver content; hence, there are two listings for the 1942 Proof Set. In 1973 and 1974, the dollar was added to the set. In 1975, the Proof Set contained the 1975-S 1c, 5c and 10c pieces plus the 1976-S Bicentennial 25c, 50c and dollar. Because of speculation, the valuations are subject to fluctuation.

| Year | Amount Minted | Value | Year | Amount Minted | Value | Year | Amount Minted | Value |
|---|---|---|---|---|---|---|---|---|
| 1936 | 3,837 | 3,250.00 | 1960 large |  |  | 1974 | 2,617,350 | 4.00 |
| 1937 | 5,542 | 2,500.00 | date |  | 12.50 | 1975 | 2,845,451 | 6.00 |
| 1938 | 8,045 | 1,200.00 | 1961 | 3,028,244 | 11.50 | 1976 |  |  |
| 1939 | 8,795 | 1,100.00 | 1962 | 3,218,039 | 11.50 | 3-pc. set | 3,295,715 | 9.50 |
| 1940 | 11,246 | 800.00 | 1963 | 3,075,645 | 11.50 | 1976 | 4,149,730 | 4.00 |
| 1941 | 15,287 | 700.00 | 1964 | 3,949,634 | 8.00 | 1977 | 3,251,152 | 3.75 |
| 1942 with |  |  | 1965 special |  |  | 1978 | 3,127,781 | 4.00 |
| one nickel | 21,120 |  | mint set | 2,360,000 | 2.50 | 1979 Type I | 3,677,175 | 6.50 |
| 1942 with |  |  | 1966 special |  |  | 1979 | Type II | 60.00 |
| two nickels |  | 700.00 | mint set | 2,261,583 | 2.75 | 1980 | 3,547,030 | 5.00 |
| 1950 | 51,386 | 375.00 | 1967 special |  |  | 1981 Type I | 4,063,083 | 5.00 |
| 1951 | 57,500 | 225.00 | mint set | 1,863,344 | 4.00 | 1981 | Type II | 100.00 |
| 1952 | 81,980 | 130.00 | 1968 |  |  | 1982 | 3,857,479 | 4.00 |
| 1953 | 128,800 | 75.00 | proof set | 3,041,509 | 3.50 | 1983 | 3,183,765 | 8.00 |
| 1954 | 233,300 | 40.00 | 1969 | 2,934,631 | 3.50 | 1984 |  | 12.00 |
| 1955 | 378,200 | 42.50 | 1970 small |  |  | 1985 |  | 12.50 |
| 1956 | 669,384 | 21.00 | date | 2,632,810 | 40.00 | 1986 |  | 12.00 |
| 1957 | 1,247,952 | 13.00 | 1970 large |  |  | 1987 |  | 9.00 |
| 1958 | 875,652 | 20.00 | date |  | 9.00 |  |  |  |
| 1959 | 1,149,291 | 13.50 | 1971 | 3,224,138 | 3.00 |  |  |  |
| 1960 small |  |  | 1972 | 3,267,667 | 3.00 |  |  |  |
| date | 1,691,600 | 16.00 | 1973 | 2,769,624 | 4.00 |  |  |  |

# United States Paper Money
## (1861 to date)
### *Large Size Notes, Small Size Notes, Fractional Currency*
### *1 DOLLAR NOTES*

Torn, frayed or excessively worn notes command little or no premium.

All modern Federal Reserve Notes after 1974 have no premium.

| Type of Issue | Series | Portrait or Main Design | Value |
|---|---|---|---|
| **LARGE SIZE NOTES** | | | **USED CONDITION** |
| U.S. Note (Legal Tender) | 1862 | Chase | 20.00 |
| " | 1869 | Washington | 25.00 |
| " | 1874 | Washington | 15.00 |
| " | 1875 | Washington | 9.00 |
| " | 1878 | Washington | 9.00 |
| " | 1880 | Washington | 10.00 |
| " | 1917 | Washington | 5.00 |
| " | 1923 | Washington (Red Seal) | 7.50 |
| Silver Certificate | 1886 | Martha Washington | 16.00 |
| " | 1891 | Martha Washington | 15.00 |
| " | 1896 | George and Martha Washington (on Rev.) | 20.00 |
| " | 1899 | Lincoln and Grant | 4.50 |
| " | 1923 | Washington (Blue Seal) | 3.00 |
| Treasury or Coin Note | 1890 | Stanton | 20.00 |
| " | 1891 | Stanton | 10.00 |
| National Bank Note | Old (original) | Two maidens standing | 30.00 |
| " | 1875 | Two maidens standing | 30.00 |
| Federal Reserve Bank Note | 1918 | Washington | 4.50 |
| **SMALL SIZE NOTES** | | | **NEW CONDITION** |
| U.S. Note (Red Seal) | 1928 | Washington | 20.00 |
| Silver Certificate (Blue Seal) | 1928 (A-E) | Washington | 3.50 |
| " | 1934 | Washington | 2.50 |
| Silver Certificate (Blue Seal) | 1935 (A-H*) | Washington | 1.20 |
| " | 1957 (A-B) | Washington | 1.10 |
| Hawaiian Issue (Brown Seal) | 1935-A | Washington | 10.00 |
| Armed Forces Issue (Yellow Seal) | 1935-A | Washington | 12.00 |
| Federal Reserve (Green Seal) | 1963 (A-B) | Washington | 1.00 |
| " | 1969 (A-D) | Washington | 1.00 |
| " | 1974 | Washington | Current |

*1935-G with and without motto

### 2 DOLLAR NOTES

Torn, frayed or excessively worn notes command little or no premium.

All modern Federal Reserve Notes after 1974 have no premium.

| LARGE SIZE NOTES | | | USED CONDITION |
|---|---|---|---|
| U.S. Note (Legal Tender) | 1862 | Hamilton | 20.00 |
| " | 1869 | Jefferson | 22.50 |
| " | 1874 | Jefferson | 20.00 |
| " | 1875 | Jefferson | 17.50 |
| " | 1878 | Jefferson | 17.50 |
| " | 1880 | Jefferson | 10.00 |
| " | 1917 | Jefferson | 5.00 |

| Type of Issue | Series | Portrait or Main Design | Value |
|---|---|---|---|
| **LARGE SIZE NOTES** | | | **USED CONDITION** |
| Silver Certificate | 1886 | Gen. Hancock | 24.00 |
| " | 1891 | William Windom | 22.50 |
| " | 1896 | Fulton and Morse (on Rev.) | 32.00 |
| " | 1899 | Washington | 12.00 |
| Treasury or Coin Note | 1890 | Gen. McPherson | 35.00 |
| " | 1891 | Gen. McPherson | 20.00 |
| National Bank Note | Old (original) | Large, horizontal "lazy" 2 | 100.00 |
| " | 1875 | Large, horizontal "lazy" 2 | 100.00 |
| Federal Reserve Bank Note | 1918 | Jefferson | 12.00 |
| **SMALL SIZE NOTES** | | | **NEW CONDITION** |
| U.S. Note | 1928 (A-G) | Jefferson | 4.00 |
| " | 1953 (A-C) | Jefferson | 2.25 |
| " | 1963 (A) | Jefferson | 2.10 |

## 5 DOLLAR NOTES

Torn, frayed or excessively worn notes command little or no premium.
All modern Federal Reserve Notes after 1974 have no premium.

| Type of Issue | Series | Portrait or Main Design | Value |
|---|---|---|---|
| **LARGE SIZE NOTES** | | | **USED CONDITION** |
| Demand Note | 1861 | Hamilton | 150.00 |
| U.S. Note (Legal Tender) | 1862 | Hamilton | 17.00 |
| " | 1863 | Hamilton | 17.00 |
| " | 1869 | Jackson | 22.00 |
| " | 1875 | Jackson | 15.00 |
| " | 1878 | Jackson | 12.00 |
| " | 1880 | Jackson | 10.00 |
| " | 1907 | Jackson | 10.00 |
| Silver Certificate | 1886 | Grant | 70.00 |
| " | 1891 | Grant | 35.00 |
| " | 1896 | Grant and Sheridan (on Rev.) | 65.00 |
| " | 1899 | Indian Chief, Onepapa | 40.00 |
| " | 1923 | Lincoln | 45.00 |
| Treasury or Coin Note | 1890 | Gen. Thomas | 32.00 |
| | | Gen. Thomas | 30.00 |
| National Bank Note | Old (original) | Landing of Columbus (on Rev.) | 25.00 |
| " | 1875 | Landing of Columbus (on Rev.) | 25.00 |
| " | 1882 | Garfield; brown back | 15.00 |
| " | 1882 | Garfield; "1882-1908" on back | 15.00 |
| " | 1882 | Garfield; "Five Dollars" on back | 18.00 |
| " | 1902 | Harrison; red seal | 11.00 |
| " | 1902 | Harrison; blue seal; "1902-1908" on back | 7.00 |
| " | 1902 | Harrison; blue seal only | 7.00 |
| Federal Reserve Bank Note | 1915 | Lincoln | 9.00 |
| " | 1918 | Lincoln | 9.00 |
| Federal Reserve Note | 1914 | Lincoln; red seal | 12.00 |
| " | 1914 | Lincoln; blue seal | 6.00 |
| National Gold Bank Note | 1870-74 | Gold coins on bank | 200.00 |

| Type of Issue | Series | Portrait or Main Design | Value |
|---|---|---|---|
| **SMALL SIZE NOTES** | | | **NEW CONDITION** |
| U.S. Note | 1928 (A-F) | Lincoln | **6.50** |
| " | 1953 (A-C) | Lincoln | **5.50** |
| " | 1963 | Lincoln | **5.10** |
| Silver Certificate | 1934 (A-D) | Lincoln | **6.00** |
| " | 1953 (A-B) | Lincoln | **5.25** |
| National Bank Note | 1929 | Lincoln | **15.00** |
| Federal Reserve Bank Note | 1929 | Lincoln | **10.00** |
| Federal Reserve Note | 1928 (A-D) | Lincoln | **8.00** |
| " | 1934 (A-D) | Lincoln | **5.25** |
| " | 1950 (A-E) | Lincoln | **5.00** |
| " | 1963 (A) | Lincoln | **5.00** |
| " | 1969 (A-C) | Lincoln | **5.00** |
| " | 1974 | Lincoln | **Current** |
| Hawaiian Issue (Brown Seal) | 1934 (A) | Lincoln | **28.00** |
| Armed Forces Issue (Yellow Seal) | 1934-A | Lincoln | **20.00** |

## 10 DOLLAR NOTES

Torn, frayed or excessively worn notes command little or no premium.

All modern Federal Reserve Notes after 1974 have no premium.

| **LARGE SIZE NOTES** | | | **USED CONDITION** |
|---|---|---|---|
| Demand Note | 1861 | Lincoln | **275.00** |
| U.S. Note (Legal Tender) | 1862 | Lincoln | **40.00** |
| " | 1863 | Lincoln | **40.00** |
| " | 1869 | Webster | **45.00** |
| " | 1875 | Webster | **30.00** |
| U.S. Note (Legal Tender) | 1878 | Webster | **30.00** |
| " | 1880 | Webster | **17.00** |
| " | 1901 | Lewis and Clark; bison | **40.00** |
| " | 1923 | Jackson | **70.00** |
| Compound Interest Note | 1863-65 | Chase | **175.00** |
| Interest Bearing Note (one year) | 1864 | Chase | **375.00** |
| Refunding Certificate | 1879 | Franklin | **140.00** |
| Silver Certificate | 1878 | Robert Morris | **500.00** |
| " | 1880 | Robert Morris | **70.00** |
| " | 1886 | Thomas Hendricks | **50.00** |
| " | 1891 | Thomas Hendricks | **22.00** |
| " | 1908 | Thomas Hendricks | **20.00** |
| Treasury or Coin Note | 1890 | Gen. Sheridan | **50.00** |
| " | 1891 | Gen. Sheridan | **30.00** |
| National Bank Note | Old (original) | De Soto at the Mississippi (on Rev.) | **40.00** |
| " | 1875 | De Soto at the Mississippi (on Rev.) | **40.00** |
| " | 1882 | Franklin with kite; brown back | **25.00** |
| " | 1882 | Same with "1882-1908" on back | **25.00** |
| " | 1882 | Same with "Ten Dollars" on back | **28.00** |
| " | 1902 | McKinley; red seal | **20.00** |
| " | 1902 | McKinley; blue seal; "1902-1908" on back | **12.00** |
| " | 1902 | McKinley; blue seal only | **12.00** |

| Type of Issue | Series | Portrait or Main Design | Value |
|---|---|---|---|
| **LARGE SIZE NOTES** | | **USED CONDITION** | |
| Federal Reserve Bank Note | 1915 | Jackson | **22.50** |
| " | 1918 | Jackson | **22.50** |
| Federal Reserve Note | 1914 | Jackson; red seal | **13.00** |
| " | 1914 | Jackson; blue seal | **11.00** |
| National Gold Bank Note | 1870-75 | Gold coins on back | **250.00** |
| Gold Certificate | 1907 | Michael Hillegas | **13.00** |
| " | 1922 | Michael Hillegas | **13.00** |
| | | | |
| **SMALL SIZE NOTES** | | **NEW CONDITION** | |
| Silver Certificate | 1933 | Hamilton | **1,200.00** |
| " | 1934 (A-D) | Hamilton | **12.00** |
| " | 1953 (A-B) | Hamilton | **11.00** |
| National Bank Note | 1929 | Hamilton | **20.00** |
| Federal Reserve Bank Note | 1929 | Hamilton | **12.00** |
| Federal Reserve Note | 1928 (A-C) | Hamilton | **10.50** |
| " | 1934 (A-D) | Hamilton | **10.00** |
| " | 1950 (A-E) | Hamilton | **10.00** |
| " | 1963 (A) | Hamilton | **10.00** |
| " | 1969 (A-C) | Hamilton | **10.00** |
| " | 1974 | Hamilton | **Current** |
| Hawaiian Issue (Brown Seal) | 1934-A | Hamilton | **35.00** |
| Armed Forces Issue (Yellow Seal) | 1934 (A) | Hamilton | **30.00** |
| Gold Certificate | 1928 | Hamilton | **45.00** |

## 20 DOLLAR NOTES

Torn, frayed or excessively worn notes command little or no premium.
All modern Federal Reserve Notes after 1974 have no premium.

| | | | |
|---|---|---|---|
| **LARGE SIZE NOTES** | | **USED CONDITION** | |
| Demand Note | 1861 | Liberty Standing | **1,200.00** |
| U.S. Note (Legal Tender) | 1862 | Liberty Standing | **45.00** |
| " | 1863 | Liberty Standing | **45.00** |
| " | 1869 | Hamilton | **100.00** |
| " | 1875 | Hamilton | **30.00** |
| " | 1878 | Hamilton | **25.00** |
| " | 1880 | Hamilton | **22.50** |
| Compound Interest Note | 1863–65 | Lincoln | **400.00** |
| Interest Bearing Note (one year) | 1864 | Lincoln | **750.00** |
| Silver Certificate | 1878 | Stephen Decatur | **600.00** |
| " | 1880 | Stephen Decatur | **125.00** |
| " | 1886 | Daniel Manning | **100.00** |
| " | 1891 | Daniel Manning | **30.00** |
| Treasury or Coin Note | 1890 | John Marshall | **100.00** |
| " | 1891 | John Marshall | **120.00** |
| National Bank Note | Old (original) | Baptism of Pocahontas (on Rev.) | **60.00** |
| " | 1875 | Baptism of Pocahontas (on Rev.) | **60.00** |
| " | 1882 | Battle of Lexington; brown back | **28.00** |
| " | 1882 | Same with "1882-1908" on back | **28.00** |
| " | 1882 | Same with "Twenty Dollars" on back | **32.00** |
| " | 1902 | Hugh McCulloch; red seal | **25.00** |
| " | 1902 | Hugh McCulloch; blue seal; "1902-1908" on back | **22.00** |

| Type of Issue | Series | Portrait or Main Design | Value |
|---|---|---|---|
| **LARGE SIZE NOTES** | | | **USED CONDITION** |
| National Bank Note | 1902 | Huch McCulloch; blue seal only | 22.00 |
| Federal Reserve Bank Note | 1915 | Cleveland | 40.00 |
| " | 1918 | Cleveland | 40.00 |
| Federal Reserve Note | 1914 | Cleveland; red seal | 25.00 |
| " | 1914 | Cleveland; blue seal | 22.00 |
| National Gold Bank Note | 1870–75 | Gold coins on back | 400.00 |
| Gold Certificate | 1863 | Eagle on shield | —— |
| " | 1882 | Garfield | 32.00 |
| " | 1905 | Washington | 70.00 |
| " | 1906 | Washington | 27.00 |
| " | 1922 | Washington | 27.00 |
| **SMALL SIZE NOTES** | | | **NEW CONDITION** |
| National Bank Note | 1929 | Jackson | 30.00 |
| Federal Reserve Bank Note | 1929 | Jackson | 22.00 |
| Federal Reserve Note | 1928 (A–C) | Jackson | 21.00 |
| " | 1934 (A–D) | Jackson | 20.00 |
| " | 1950 (A–E) | Jackson | 20.00 |
| " | 1963 (A) | Jackson | 20.00 |
| " | 1969 (A–C) | Jackson | 20.00 |
| " | 1974 | Jackson | **Current** |
| Hawaiian Issue (Brown Seal) | 1934 (A) | Jackson | 50.00 |
| Gold Certificate | 1928 | Jackson | 50.00 |

## 50 DOLLAR NOTES

Torn, frayed or excessivley worn notes command little or no premium.
All modern Federal Reserve Notes after 1974 have no premium.

| **LARGE SIZE NOTES** | | | **USED CONDITION** |
|---|---|---|---|
| U.S. Note (Legal Tender) | 1862 | Hamilton | 375.00 |
| " | 1863 | Hamilton | 375.00 |
| " | 1869 | Henry Clay | 700.00 |
| " | 1874 | Franklin | 165.00 |
| " | 1875 | Franklin | 150.00 |
| " | 1878 | Franklin | 150.00 |
| " | 1880 | Franklin | 70.00 |
| Compound Interest Note | 1863–65 | Hamilton | **Rare** |
| Interest Bearing Note (one year) | 1864 | Hamilton | **Rare** |
| Interest Bearing Note (two years) | 1863 | Three females | **Rare** |
| Interest Bearing Note (three years) | 1861 | Large eagle | **Rare** |
| " | 1864 | Large eagle | **Rare** |
| " | 1865 | Large eagle | **Rare** |
| " | 1865 | Large eagle | **Rare** |
| Silver Certificate | 1878 | Edward Everett | 650.00 |
| " | 1880 | Edward Everett | 700.00 |
| " | 1891 | Edward Everett | 85.00 |
| Treasury or Coin Note | 1891 | William Seward | 1,200.00 |
| National Bank Note | Old (original) | Embarkation of the Pilgrims (on Rev.) | 450.00 |
| " | 1875 | Embarkation of the Pilgrims (on Rev.) | 450.00 |
| " | 1882 | Washington Crossing the Delaware and at prayer; brown back | 75.00 |
| " | 1882 | Same with "1882-1908" on back | 75.00 |

| Type of Issues | Series | Portrait or Main Design | Value |
|---|---|---|---|
| **SMALL SIZE NOTES** | | | **USED CONDITION** |
| Federal Reserve Bank Note | 1929 | Grant | 51.00 |
| Federal Reserve Note | 1928(A) | Grant | 50.00 |
| " | 1934(A–D) | Grant | 50.00 |
| " | 1950(A–E) | Grant | 50.00 |
| " | 1963-A | Grant | 50.00 |
| " | 1969(A–C) | Grant | 50.00 |
| " | 1974 | Grant | Current |
| Gold Certificate | 1928 | Grant | 150.00 |

## 100 DOLLAR NOTES

Torn, frayed or excessively worn notes command little or no premium

All modern Federal Reserve Notes after 1974 have no premium.

| | | | |
|---|---|---|---|
| **LARGE SIZE NOTES** | | | **USED CONDITION** |
| U.S. Note (Legal Tender) | 1862 | Large eagle | 600.00 |
| " | 1863 | Large eagle | 600.00 |
| " | 1869 | Lincoln | 1,000.00 |
| " | 1875 | Lincoln | 650.00 |
| " | 1878 | Lincoln | 650.00 |
| " | 1880 | Lincoln | 175.00 |
| Compound Interest Note | 1863–65 | Washington standing | 700.00 |
| Interest Bearing Note (one year) | 1864 | Washington standing | Rare |
| Interest Bearing Note (two years) | 1863 | Agriculture and Industry | Rare |
| Interest Bearing Note (three years) | 1861 | Gen. Scott | Rare |
| " | 1865 | Gen. Scott | Rare |
| Silver Certificate | 1878 | Monroe | 800.00 |
| " | 1880 | Monroe | 700.00 |
| " | 1891 | Monroe | 325.00 |
| Treasury or Coin Note | 1890 | Commodore Farragut | 1,000.00 |
| " | 1891 | Commodore Farragut | 1,000.00 |
| National Bank Note | Old (original) | Signing of the Declaration of Independence (on Rev.) | 400.00 |
| " | 1875 | Signing the Declaration of Independence (on Rev.) | 400.00 |
| " | 1882 | Commodore Perry leaving his flagship; brown back | 125.00 |
| " | 1882 | Same with "1882–1908" on back | 120.00 |
| " | 1882 | Same with "One Hundred Dollars" on back | Rare |
| " | 1902 | John Knox; red seal | 110.00 |
| " | 1902 | John Knox; blue seal; "1902 1908" on back | 100.00 |
| " | 1902 | John Knox; blue seal only | 100.00 |
| Federal Reserve Note | 1914 | Franklin; red seal | 100.00 |
| " | 1914 | Franklin; blue seal | 100.00 |
| National Gold Bank Note | 1870–75 | Gold coins on back | 2,000.00 |
| Gold certificate | 1863 | Eagle on shield | —— |
| " | 1870–71 | Thomas Benton | —— |
| " | 1875 | Thomas Benton | —— |
| " | 1882 | Thomas Benton | 110.00 |
| " | 1922 | Thomas Benton | 125.00 |

| Type of Issues | Series | Portrait or Main Design | Value |
|---|---|---|---|
| **SMALL SIZE NOTES** | | | **NEW CONDITION** |
| National Bank Note | 1929 | Franklin | 100.00 |
| Federal Reserve Bank Note | 1929 | Franklin | 100.00 |
| Federal Reserve Note | 1928 (A) | Franklin | 100.00 |
| " | 1934 (A-D) | Franklin | 100.00 |
| " | 1950 (A-E) | Franklin | 100.00 |
| " | 1963-A | Franklin | 100.00 |
| " | 1969 (A-C) | Franklin | 100.00 |
| | 1974 | Franklin | Current |
| U.S. Note (Legal Tender) | 1966 (A) | Franklin | 100.00 |
| Gold Certificate | 1928 | Franklin | 150.00 |

# Fractional Currency

Torn, frayed or excessively worn notes command little or no premium.

## 3 CENT NOTES

| Years of Issue | Description | Used |
|---|---|---|
| 1864-1869 | Small head of Washington. | 3.00 |

## 5 CENT NOTES

| | | |
|---|---|---|
| 1862-1863 | Facsimile of a 5 Cent postage stamp with head of Jefferson | 2.00 |
| 1862-1863 | Same as above but with perforated edges. | 2.50 |
| 1863-1867 | Head of Washington in bronze oval frame. Brown back. | 1.50 |
| 1864-1869 | Head of Spencer M. Clark. Green back. | 1.50 |
| 1864-1869 | Same as above but with red back. | 2.00 |

## 10 CENT NOTES

| Years of Issue | Description | Used |
|---|---|---|
| 1862-1863 | Facsimile of a 10 Cent postage stamp with head of Washington. | 2.00 |
| 1862-1863 | Same as above but with perforated edges. | 2.50 |
| 1863-1867 | Head of Washington in bronze oval frame. Green back. | 1.50 |
| 1864-1869 | Head of Washington. A bronze "10" in each corner. Green back. | 1.50 |
| 1864-1869 | Same as above but with red back. | 2.50 |
| 1869-1875 | Bust of Liberty. | 1.25 |
| 1874-1876 | Head of William M. Meredith. Green seal. | 1.25 |
| 1874-1876 | Same as above but with red seal. | 1.00 |

## 15 CENT NOTES

| | | |
|---|---|---|
| 1869-1875 | Bust of Columbia. | 3.50 |
| Not Issued | Heads of Grant and Sherman. Separate front and back. Green back. | 20.00 |
| Not Issued | Same as above but with red back. | 20.00 |

## 25 CENT NOTES

| | | |
|---|---|---|
| 1862-1863 | Facsimiles of five 5 Cent postage stamps with head of Jefferson. | 3.00 |
| 1862-1863 | Same as above but with perforated edges. | 4.00 |
| 1863-1807 | Head of Washington in bronze oval frame. Purple back. | 1.75 |
| 1864-1869 | Bust of Fessenden. Green back. | 1.75 |
| 1864-1869 | Same as above but with red back. | 3.00 |
| 1869-1875 | Bust of Washington. | 1.25 |
| 1874-1876 | Bust of Robert V. Walker. | .75 |

## 50 CENT NOTES

| | | |
|---|---|---|
| 1862-1863 | Facsimiles of five 10 Cent postage stamps with head of Washington. | 3.00 |
| 1862-1863 | Same as above but with perforated edges. | 5.00 |
| 1863-1867 | Head of Washington in bronze oval frame. Red back. | 1.75 |
| 1864-1869 | Bust of Gen. Spinner. Green back with a "50" at each end. | 1.75 |
| 1864-1869 | Same as above but with red back. | 2.00 |
| 1864-1869 | Bust of Gen. Spinner. Green back with "50" in center. | 1.75 |
| 1864-1869 | Seated figure of Justice. Green back. | 2.00 |
| 1864-1869 | Same as above but with red back. | 2.00 |
| 1869-1875 | Bust of Lincoln. | 4.00 |
| 1869-1875 | Bust of E. M. Stanton. | 2.00 |
| 1869-1875 | Bust of Samuel Dexter. | 2.50 |
| 1874-1876 | Bust of William Crawford. | 1.50 |

158

# Confederate States of America

Torn, frayed or excessively worn notes command little or no premium.

## PAPER MONEY ISSUES

All notes were issued from Richmond, Virginia, except the few 1861 issues listed as from Montgomery, Alabama.

In recent years, facsimiles have been made of many Confederate notes. Many people mistake them for genuine pieces. They are usually on much heavier paper and are invariably in new condition. In many cases, the word, "Facsimile" may actually be found in quite small letters somewhere on the note.

Confederate notes will sometimes be found cut or slit in a regular pattern, or with holes punched through. These indicate cancellation by the Confederacy, and are worth less than uncancelled specimens.

For further general comment on Confederate currency, please see under "United States Paper Money" in the General Information following the Preface.

## 50 CENT NOTES

| Year | Portrait or Main Design | Used |
|------|------------------------|------|
| 1863 | Jefferson Davis. Blank Rev. | 1.25 |
| 1864 | Similar to above except for date. | 1.00 |

## 1 DOLLAR NOTES

| | | |
|------|------------------------|------|
| 1862 | Steamship with sails; female standing at left; Lucy Pickens at right. Blank Rev. | 3.00 |
| 1862 | Similar to above, but overprinted with a large green "1" and "ONE." Blank Rev. | 5.00 |
| 1862 | C. Clay. Blank Rev. | 4.00 |
| 1863 | Similar to above except for date. | 3.25 |
| 1864 | Similar to above except for date. | 1.00 |

## 2 DOLLAR NOTES

| | | |
|------|------------------------|------|
| 1861 | The "South" attacking the "North" with sword; J. P. Benjamin at left. Blank Rev. | 25.00 |
| 1862 | The "South" attacking the "North" with sword; J. P. Benjamin at left. Blank Rev. | 3.25 |
| 1862 | Similar to above but overprinted with a large green "2" and "TWO." Blank Rev. | 14.50 |
| 1862 | Ornamented "2" in center; J. P. Benjamin at right. Blank Rev. | 2.50 |
| 1863 | Similar to above except for date. | 2.50 |
| 1864 | Similar to above except for date. | 2.00 |

## 5 DOLLAR NOTES

| | | |
|------|------------------------|------|
| 1861 | Liberty seated with shield and eagle, a "5" in front; sailor at left. Blank Rev. | 200.00 |
| 1861 | "V" in upper left; "5" in upper right. Blue Rev. | 200.00 |
| 1861 | Five females seated; standing female at left; Washington at right. Blank Rev. | 22.50 |
| 1861 | Child at left; blacksmith at right. Blank Rev. | 27.50 |
| 1861 | C. Memminger; Minerva at right, "V" below. Blank rev. | 13.00 |
| 1861 | Similar to above except that "FIVE" is below Minerva. Blank Rev. | 5.00 |

| Year | Portrait or Main Design | Used |
|---|---|---|
| 1861 | Blacks loading cotton on ship at left; Indian girl at right. Blank Rev. | 225.00 |
| 1861 | Female seated on cotton bale; sailor at left. Blank Rev. | 3.00 |
| 1861 | Sailor and cotton bales; C. Memminger at left; two females at right. Blank Rev. | 3.00 |
| 1862 | State Capitol at Richmond, Va.; C. Memminger at right. Blue Rev. | 2.00 |
| 1863 | Similar to above except for date. | 2.00 |
| 1864 | Similar to above except for date. | 1.50 |

## 10 DOLLAR NOTES

| | | |
|---|---|---|
| 1861 | Liberty seated with shield and eagle; female at left. Blank Rev. | 3.00 |
| 1861 | Indian family; female with trident at left; female with "X" at right. Blank Rev. | 30.00 |
| 1861 | Cotton wagon; male bust at left; harvester at right. Blank Rev. | 35.00 |
| 1861 | R. Hunter at left; a child at right. Blank Rev. | 12.00 |
| 1861 | Female with anchor; R. Hunter at left; C. Memminger at right. Blank Rev. | 5.00 |
| 1861 | Similar to above except that an "X" is overprinted in red at each side of the female. Blank Rev. | 5.00 |
| 1861 | Liberty with eagle and shield at upper left; small train at right. Blank Rev. | 250.00 |
| 1861 | Two females with urn at upper left; small train at right. Blank Rev. | 2.00 |
| 1861 | Black with cotton; landscape at right. Blank Rev. | 6.00 |
| 1861 | Military figures at dinner; R. Hunter at left; Minerva at right. Blank Rev. | 3.00 |
| 1862 | Female leaning on cotton bales, ships in rear; R. Hunter at right. Blank Rev. | 3.00 |
| 1862 | Female seated with wheat; R. Hunter at right. Blank Rev. | 600.00 |
| 1862 | State Capitol at Columbia, S. C.; R. Hunter at right. Blue Rev. | 1.50 |
| 1863 | Similar to above except for date. | 1.50 |
| 1864 | Horses pulling artillery pieces; R. Hunter at right. Blue Rev. | 1.50 |

## 20 DOLLAR NOTES

| | | |
|---|---|---|
| 1861 | Full masted sailing ship. Blank Rev. | 2.50 |
| 1861 | Three females in center, Liberty standing at left. Blank Rev. | 60.00 |
| 1861 | Full masted sailing ship; sailor at left. Blank Rev. | 2.00 |
| 1861 | Female with globe; female at left; blacksmith at right. Blank Rev. | 200.00 |
| 1861 | Female between Cupid and beehive; Vice President Stephens at left; female with anchor at right. Blank Rev. | 1.75 |
| 1861 | Vice President Stephens. Blank Rev. | 17.50 |
| 1862 | Liberty seated with shield of the Confederacy; R. Hunter at right. Blank Rev. | 400.00 |
| 1862 | State Capitol at Nashville, Tenn.; Stephens at right. Blue Rev. | 4.00 |
| 1863 | Similar to above except for date. | 1.50 |
| 1864 | Similar to above except for date. | 1.25 |

## 50 DOLLAR NOTES

| | | |
|---|---|---|
| 1861 | Three black farm workers. Blank Rev. Montgomery, Ala. | 500.00 |
| 1861 | Two females on cotton bale; Justice at left; Washington at right. Blank Rev. | 60.00 |
| 1861 | Washington in center; seated figure at left. Blank Rev. | 8.00 |
| 1861 | Female and money chests; two sailors at left. Blank Rev. | 3.00 |

| Year | Portrait or Main Design | Used |
|---|---|---|
| 1861 | Railroad train; female with anchor at left; female with scales at right. Blank Rev. | 225.00 |
| 1861 | Jefferson Davis. Blank Rev. | 6.00 |
| 1862 | Jefferson Davis. Green Rev. | 5.00 |
| 1863 | Similar to above except for date. | 5.00 |
| 1864 | Similar to above except for date and a Blue Rev. | 2.00 |

## 100 DOLLAR NOTES

| | | |
|---|---|---|
| 1861 | Railroad train in center; Liberty at left. Blank Rev. Montgomery, Ala. | 700.00 |
| 1861 | Railroad train in center; Justice at left; Minerva at right. Blank Rev. | 65.00 |
| 1861 | Two females in cloud; Washington at left. Blank Rev. | 50.00 |
| 1861 | Blacks loading cotton wagon; sailor at left. Blank Rev. | 3.00 |
| 1862 | Railroad train; milkmaid at left. Blank Rev. | 2.00 |
| 1862 | Blacks in cotton field; J. C. Calhoun at left; Liberty at right. Blank Rev. | 3.00 |
| 1862 | Lucy Pickens; two soldiers at left; Randolph at right. Green Rev. | 17.50 |
| 1863 | Similar to above except for date. | 5.50 |
| 1864 | Similar to above except for date and a Blue Rev. | 1.50 |

## 500 DOLLAR NOTES

| | | |
|---|---|---|
| 1861 | Train on bridge; cattle below. Blank Rev. Montgomery, Ala. | 1,750.00 |
| 1864 | Confederate flag over horseman at left; "Stonewall' Jackson at right. Blank Rev. | 20.00 |

## 1,000 DOLLAR NOTE

| | | |
|---|---|---|
| 1861 | John C. Calhoun and Andrew Jackson. Blank Rev. Montgomery, Ala. | 1,950.00 |

## CONFEDERATE COIN ISSUES

No Confederate coin was ever struck for actual circulation. However, four genuine trial specimens of a half dollar were allegedly struck. The reverse die of this coin was used at a later date to manufacture restrikes and it is these restrikes which appear on the market. Genuine U.S. half dollars of 1861 were used for this purpose, the reverse being planed off and then struck with the Confederate die.

The so-called Confederate Cent of 1861 shows a Liberty Head on the Obv. and the value on the Rev. A few specimens were struck privately in Philadelphia at the instigation of the Confederacy, but no coins were ever delivered. Both restrikes and modern replicas exist of this coin.

| | | | |
|---|---|---|---|
| **CONFEDERATE SILVER HALF DOLLAR.** | 1861 | Fine | 400.00 |
| **CONFEDERATE COPPER CENT.** | 1861 | Proof | 1,250.00 |

# THE COINAGE OF BRITISH NORTH AMERICA

## Canada

## LARGE CENTS

### Head of Queen Victoria

| Date | Amount Minted | Value | Date | Amount Minted | Value |
|---|---|---|---|---|---|
| 1858 | 421,000 | 10.00 | 1892 | 1¼ million | .40 |
| 1859 | 9½ million | .50 | 1893 | 2 million | .30 |
| 1876-H | 4 million | .50 | 1894 | 1 million | 1.00 |
| 1881-H | 2 million | .75 | 1895 | 1¼ million | .60 |
| 1882-H | 4 million | .30 | 1896 | 2 million | .40 |
| 1884 | 2½ million | .30 | 1897 | 1½ million | .40 |
| 1886 | 1½ million | .65 | 1898-H | 1 million | 1.25 |
| 1887 | 1½ million | .65 | 1899 | 2½ million | .40 |
| 1888 | 4 million | .30 | 1900 | 1 million | 1.50 |
| 1890-H | 1 million | 1.50 | 1900-H | 2⅔ million | .30 |
| 1891 Large date | 1½ million | 1.50 | 1901 | 4 million | .30 |
| 1891 Small date | Part of above | 13.00 | | | |

### Head of King Edward VII

| | | | | | |
|---|---|---|---|---|---|
| 1902 | 3 million | .25 | 1907 | 2½ million | .25 |
| 1903 | 4 million | .25 | 1907-H | 800,000 | 3.00 |
| 1904 | 2½ million | .30 | 1908 | 2⅓ million | .25 |
| 1905 | 2 million | .30 | 1909 | 4 million | .20 |
| 1906 | 4 million | .25 | 1910 | 5 million | .20 |

### Head of King George V

| | | | | | |
|---|---|---|---|---|---|
| 1911 | 4⅔ million | .20 | 1916 | 11 million | .11 |
| 1912 | 5 million | .15 | 1917 | 12 million | .11 |
| 1913 | 5¾ million | .15 | 1918 | 13 million | .11 |
| 1914 | 3½ million | .25 | 1919 | 11¼ million | .11 |
| 1915 | 4¾ million | .25 | 1920 | 7 million | .11 |

## SMALL CENTS

### Head of King George V

| | | | | | |
|---|---|---|---|---|---|
| 1920 | 15½ million | .04 | 1929 | 12¼ million | .03 |
| 1921 | 7½ million | .06 | 1930 | 2½ million | .40 |
| 1922 | 1¼ million | 3.00 | 1931 | 3¾ million | .20 |
| 1923 | 1 million | 6.00 | 1932 | 21⅓ million | .02 |
| 1924 | 1½ million | 1.00 | 1933 | 12 million | .02 |
| 1925 | 1 million | 3.50 | 1934 | 7 million | .05 |
| 1926 | 2¼ million | .50 | 1935 | 7½ million | .05 |
| 1927 | 3½ million | .25 | 1936 | 8¾ million | .05 |
| 1928 | 9 million | .03 | | | |

161

### *Head of King George VI*

(The following valuations are for coins in brilliant, new condition, and showing no
signs of wear. Used or circulated Cents from 1937 to date
do not command a premium.)

| | | NEW | | | NEW |
|---|---|---|---|---|---|
| 1937 | 10 million | .50 | 1946 | 56⅔ million | .10 |
| 1938 | 18⅓ million | .50 | 1947 | 31 million | .50 |
| 1939 | 21⅔ million | .50 | 1947 Maple leaf | 43¾ million | .35 |
| 1940 | 85¾ million | .25 | 1948 | 24¾ million | .50 |
| 1941 | 56⅓ million | 2.50 | 1949 | 33⅓ million | .25 |
| 1942 | 76 million | 2.00 | 1950 | 60½ million | .25 |
| 1943 | 89 million | 1.00 | 1951 | 80½ million | .10 |
| 1944 | 44¼ million | 2.00 | 1952 | 67⅔ million | .10 |
| 1945 | 77½ million | .10 | | | |

| Obv. Type | Rev. Type | Obv. Type | Commemorative |
|---|---|---|---|
| 1953-1964 | 1937- | 1965- | Rev. 1967 |

### *Head of Queen Elizabeth II*

(The valuations are for coins in brilliant, new condition)

| | | NEW | | | NEW |
|---|---|---|---|---|---|
| 1953 | 72¼ million | .20 | 1970 | 311¼ million | .01 |
| 1954 | 22 million | .50 | 1971 | 298¼ million | .01 |
| 1955 | 56⅔ million | .10 | 1972 | 451⅓ million | .01 |
| 1956 | 78⅔ million | .10 | 1973 | 457 million | .01 |
| 1957 | 100½ million | .10 | 1974 | 692 million | .01 |
| 1958 | 57¾ million | .10 | 1975 | 642⅓ million | .01 |
| 1959 | 83⅔ million | .05 | 1976 | 701 million | .01 |
| 1960 | 75¾ million | .05 | 1977 | 453 million | .01 |
| 1961 | 139½ million | .05 | 1978 | 911 million | .01 |
| 1962 | 227¼ million | .05 | 1979 | 754 million | .01 |
| 1963 | 279 million | .05 | 1980 | 911¾ million | .01 |
| 1964 | 484⅔ million | .05 | 1982 | 876 million | .01 |
| 1965 | 304½ million | .01 | 1983 | 975½ million | .01 |
| 1966 | 183⅔ million | .01 | 1984 | 838¼ million | .01 |
| 1967 | 345¼ million | .01 | 1985 | | .01 |
| 1968 | 329⅔ million | .01 | 1986 | | .01 |
| 1969 | 335¼ million | .01 | 1987 | | .01 |

## SILVER 5 CENTS

### *Head of Queen Victoria*

(The following valuations are for coins in G-VG condition)

| Date | Amount Minted | Value | Date | Amount Minted | Value |
|------|---------------|-------|------|---------------|-------|
| 1858 Small date | 1½ million | 2.50 | 1887 | 500,000 | 2.50 |
| 1858 Large date | Part of above | 35.00 | 1888 | 1 million | 1.10 |
| 1870 | 2¾ million | 1.50 | 1889 | 1¼ million | 3.50 |
| 1871 | 1½ million | 1.50 | 1890-H | 1 million | 1.00 |
| 1872-H | 2 million | 1.00 | 1891 | 1¾ million | 1.10 |
| 1874-H | 800,000 | 1.75 | 1892 | 860,000 | 1.25 |
| 1875-H | 1 million | 25.00 | 1893 | 1¾ million | 1.00 |
| 1880-H | 3 million | .75 | 1894 | 500,000 | 2.75 |
| 1881-H | 1½ million | 1.00 | 1896 | 1½ million | 1.00 |
| 1882-H | 1 million | 1.00 | 1897 | 1⅓ million | 1.00 |
| 1883-H | 600,000 | 1.50 | 1898 | 580,717 | 2.00 |
| 1884 | 200,000 | 14.00 | 1899 | 3 million | .75 |
| 1885 | 1 million | 1.50 | 1900 | 1¾ million | .75 |
| 1886 | 1¾ million | 1.10 | 1901 | 2 million | .75 |

### *Head of King Edward VII*

| Date | Amount Minted | Value | Date | Amount Minted | Value |
|------|---------------|-------|------|---------------|-------|
| 1902 | 2 million | .50 | 1906 | 3 million | .50 |
| 1902-H | 2¼ million | .50 | 1907 | 5¼ million | .45 |
| 1903 | 1 million | .70 | 1908 | 1¼ million | 1.50 |
| 1903-H | 2⅔ million | .50 | 1909 | 1¾ million | .75 |
| 1904 | 2⅓ million | .50 | 1910 | 6 million | .55 |
| 1905 | 2⅔ million | .50 | | | |

### *Head of King George V*

| Date | Amount Minted | Value | Date | Amount Minted | Value |
|------|---------------|-------|------|---------------|-------|
| 1911 | 3⅔ million | .60 | 1917 | 5⅔ million | .35 |
| 1912 | 5¾ million | .35 | 1918 | 5¾ million | .35 |
| 1913 | 5½ million | .35 | 1919 | 8 milion | .35 |
| 1914 | 4¼ million | .35 | 1920 | 10⅔ million | .35 |
| 1915 | 1¼ million | 1.50 | 1921 | 2½ million | 600.00 |
| 1916 | 2⅓ million | .60 | | | |

## NICKEL 5 CENTS

*Head of King George V*

| | | | | | |
|------|-----------|-------|------|-----------|-----|
| 1922 | 4¾ million | .06 | 1930 | 3⅔ million | .07 |
| 1923 | 2½ million | .07 | 1931 | 5 million | .06 |
| 1924 | 3 million | .06 | 1932 | 3¼ million | .07 |
| 1925 | 200,050 | 10.00 | 1933 | 2½ million | .07 |
| 1926 | 933,577 | 1.00 | 1934 | 3¾ million | .06 |
| 1927 | 5¼ million | .06 | 1935 | 3¾ million | .06 |
| 1928 | 4½ million | .06 | 1936 | 4⅓ million | .06 |
| 1929 | 5½ million | .06 | | | |

Beaver Type
1937-1942 & 1946-1952

V for Victory
1943-1945

Nickel
Bicentennial
1951

*Head of King George VI*

## Beginning with the 1942 Tombac issue, the shape of the nickel is 12-sided, rather than round

| Date | Amount Minted | Value | Date | Amount Minted | Value |
|------|--------------|-------|------|--------------|-------|
| 1937 | 5 million | .05 | 1946 | 7 million | .05 |
| 1938 | 4 million | .05 | 1947 | 7⅔ million | .05 |
| 1939 | 5⅔ million | .05 | 1947 Maple Leaf | 9½ million | .05 |
| 1940 | 14 million | .05 | 1948 | 1¾ million | .15 |
| 1941 | 8⅔ million | .05 | 1949 | 13 million | .05 |
| 1942-Nickel | 6¾ million | .05 | 1950 | 12 million | .05 |
| 1942 Tombac | 3⅓ million | .08 | 1951 Regular | 4⅓ million | .05 |
| 1943 | 24¾ million | .05 | 1951 Commem. | 9 million | .05 |
| 1944 | 11½ million | .05 | 1952 | 10¾ million | .05 |
| 1945 | 18¾ million | .05 | | | |

12-sided 1953-1962            Mature Head Type           Commemorative
Round 1963-1964                1965-               Rev. 1967

## *Head of Queen Elizabeth II*

| Date | Amount Minted | NEW | Date | Amount Minted | NEW |
|------|--------------|-----|------|--------------|-----|
| 1953 | 16⅔ million | .50 | 1971 | 27⅓ million | .05 |
| 1954 | 7 million | .75 | 1972 | 62½ million | .05 |
| 1955 | 5⅓ million | .50 | 1973 | 53½ million | .05 |
| 1956 | 9⅓ million | .25 | 1974 | 94¾ million | .05 |
| 1957 | 7⅓ million | .25 | 1975 | 138.8 million | .05 |
| 1958 | 7½ million | .25 | 1976 | 55 million | .05 |
| 1959 | 11½ million | .10 | 1977 | 89 million | .05 |
| 1960 | 37 million | .07 | 1978 | 137 million | .05 |
| 1961 | 47¾ million | .06 | 1979 | 186¼ million | .05 |
| 1962 | 46¼ million | .06 | 1980 | 134¾ million | .05 |
| 1963 | 44 million | .06 | 1981 | 99 million | .05 |
| 1964 | 78 million | .05 | 1982 | 105½ million | .05 |
| 1965 | 84¾ million | .05 | 1983 | 72½ million | .05 |
| 1966 | 27½ million | .05 | 1984 | 84 million | .05 |
| 1967 | 58¾ million | .05 | 1985 | | .05 |
| 1968 | 99¼ million | .05 | 1986 | | .05 |
| 1969 | 27¾ million | .05 | 1987 | | .05 |
| 1970 | 5¾ million | .05 | | | |

## 10 CENTS

*Head of Queen Victoria*

| Date | Amount Minted | Value | Date | Amount Minted | Value |
|---|---|---|---|---|---|
| 1858 | 1¼ million | 3.00 | 1888 | 500,000 | 2.75 |
| 1870 | 1⅔ million | 2.75 | 1889 | 600,000 | 120.00 |
| 1871 | 800,000 | 3.00 | 1890-H | 450,000 | 2.75 |
| 1871-H | 1¾ million | 4.75 | 1891 | 800,000 | 2.75 |
| 1872-H | 1 million | 20.00 | 1892 | 520,000 | 2.25 |
| 1874-H | 600,000 | 2.25 | 1893 Flat top 3 | 500,000 | 2.25 |
| 1875-H | 1 million | 40.00 | 1893 Round top 3 | Part of above | 175.00 |
| 1880-H | 1½ million | 2.25 | 1894 | 500,000 | 1.75 |
| 1881-H | 950,000 | 3.25 | 1896 | 650,000 | 1.25 |
| 1882-H | 1 million | 1.75 | 1898 | 720,000 | 1.25 |
| 1883-H | 300,000 | 4.50 | 1899 | 1¼ million | .75 |
| 1884 | 150,000 | 20.00 | 1900 | 1 million | .50 |
| 1885 | 400,000 | 3.25 | 1901 | 1¼ million | .50 |
| 1886 | 800,000 | 3.00 | | | |
| 1887 | 350,000 | 2.75 | | | |

## Head of King Edward VII

| Date | Amount Minted | Value | Date | Amount Minted | Value |
|------|--------------|-------|------|--------------|-------|
| 1902 | 720,000 | .35 | 1906 | 1⅔ million | .35 |
| 1902-H | 1 million | .35 | 1907 | 2⅔ million | .35 |
| 1903 | 500,000 | .75 | 1908 | 761,631 | .35 |
| 1903-H | 1⅓ million | .35 | 1909 | 1½ million | .35 |
| 1904 | 1 million | .75 | 1910 | 4⅔ million | .35 |
| 1905 | 1 million | .65 | | | |

## Head of King George V

| Date | Amount Minted | Value | Date | Amount Minted | Value |
|------|--------------|-------|------|--------------|-------|
| 1911 | 2¾ million | 2.75 | 1921 | 2½ million | .30 |
| 1912 | 3¼ million | .30 | 1928 | 2½ million | .30 |
| 1913 Small leaves | 3½ million | .30 | 1929 | 3¼ million | .30 |
| 1913 Large leaves | Part of above | 20.00 | 1930 | 1¾ million | .30 |
| 1914 | 2½ million | .30 | 1931 | 2 million | .30 |
| 1915 | 672,408 | .30 | 1932 | 1¼ million | .30 |
| 1916 | 4¼ million | .30 | 1933 | 672,368 | .30 |
| 1917 | 5 million | .30 | 1934 | 384,056 | .30 |
| 1918 | 5 million | .30 | 1935 | 384,592 | .30 |
| 1919 | 7¾ million | .30 | 1936 | 2¾ million | .30 |
| 1920 | 6¼ million | .30 | | | |

## Head of King George VI

| Date | Amount Minted | Value | Date | Amount Minted | Value |
|------|--------------|-------|------|--------------|-------|
| 1937 | 2½ million | .45 | 1946 | 6⅓ million | .25 |
| 1938 | 4¼ million | .25 | 1947 | 4½ million | .25 |
| 1939 | 5½ million | .25 | 1947 Maple leaf | 9⅔ million | .25 |
| 1940 | 16½ million | .25 | 1948 | 422,741 | 1.25 |
| 1941 | 8¾ million | .25 | 1949 | 11⅓ million | .25 |
| 1942 | 10¼ million | .25 | 1950 | 17¾ million | .25 |
| 1943 | 21¼ million | .25 | 1951 | 15 million | .25 |
| 1944 | 9⅓ million | .25 | 1952 | 10½ million | .25 |
| 1945 | 11 million | .25 | | | |

Obv. Type 1953-1964  Rev. Type 1937-  Obv. Type 1965-  Commemorative Rev. 1967

### *Head of Queen Elizabeth II*

| Date | Amount Minted | Value | Date | Amount Minted | Value |
|---|---|---|---|---|---|
| 1953 | 18½ million | .25 | 1970 | 5¼ million | .10 |
| 1954 | 4½ million | .25 | 1971 | 41 million | .10 |
| 1955 | 12¼ million | .25 | 1972 | 60 million | .10 |
| 1956 | 16¾ million | .25 | 1973 | 167¾ million | .10 |
| 1957 | 15⅔ million | .25 | 1974 | 201½ million | .10 |
| 1958 | 11 million | .25 | 1975 | 207⅔ million | .10 |
| 1959 | 19⅔ million | .25 | 1976 | 95 million | .10 |
| 1960 | 45½ million | .25 | 1977 | 128½ million | .10 |
| 1961 | 26¾ million | .25 | 1978 | 170⅓ million | .10 |
| 1962 | 41¾ million | .25 | 1979 | 237 million | .10 |
| 1963 | 42 million | .25 | 1980 | 169¾ million | .10 |
| 1964 | 49½ million | .25 | 1981 | 124 million | .10 |
| 1965 | 57 million | .25 | 1982 | 94 million | .10 |
| 1966 | 34⅓ million | .25 | 1983 | 111 million | .10 |
| 1967 | 63 million | .25 | 1984 | 119 million | .10 |
| 1968 Silver | 70½ million | .20 | 1985 | | .10 |
| 1968 Nickel | 107 million | .10 | 1986 | | .10 |
| 1969 | 55¾ million | .10 | 1987 | | .10 |

## 20 CENTS

### *Head of Queen Victoria*

| 1858 | 750,000 | 15.00 |
|---|---|---|

## 25 CENTS

### *Head of Queen Victoria*

| Date | Amount Minted | Value | Date | Amount Minted | Value |
|------|---------------|-------|------|---------------|-------|
| 1870 | 900,000 | **3.75** | 1887 | 100,000 | **15.00** |
| 1871 | 400,000 | **4.50** | 1888 | 400,000 | **2.75** |
| 1871-H | 748,000 | **4.50** | 1889 | 66,340 | **17.50** |
| 1872-H | 2¼ million | **3.25** | 1890-H | 200,000 | **3.25** |
| 1874-H | 1⅔ million | **3.25** | 1891 | 120,000 | **7.00** |
| 1875-H | 1 million | **60.00** | 1892 | 510,000 | **2.75** |
| 1880-H | 400,000 | **4.25** | 1893 | 100,000 | **7.00** |
| 1881-H | 820,000 | **3.50** | 1894 | 220,000 | **2.75** |
| 1882-H | 600,000 | **3.75** | 1899 | 415,580 | **2.50** |
| 1883-H | 960,000 | **2.50** | 1900 | 1⅓ million | **2.00** |
| 1885 | 192,000 | **15.00** | 1901 | 640,000 | **2.00** |
| 1886 | 540,000 | **2.75** | | | |

### *Head of King Edward VII*

| Date | Amount Minted | Value | Date | Amount Minted | Value |
|------|---------------|-------|------|---------------|-------|
| 1902 | 464,000 | **1.10** | 1906 | 1¼ million | **1.10** |
| 1902-H | 800,000 | **1.10** | 1907 | 2 million | **1.10** |
| 1903 | 846,150 | **1.10** | 1908 | 466,625 | **1.10** |
| 1904 | 400,000 | **1.10** | 1909 | 1⅓ million | **1.10** |
| 1905 | 800,000 | **1.10** | 1910 | 3½ million | **1.10** |

### *Head of King George V*

| Date | Amount Minted | Value | Date | Amount Minted | Value |
|------|---------------|-------|------|---------------|-------|
| 1911 | 1⅔ million | 3.75 | 1927 | 468,096 | 7.00 |
| 1912 | 2½ million | 1.00 | 1928 | 2 million | .75 |
| 1913 | 2¼ million | 1.00 | 1929 | 2⅔ million | .75 |
| 1914 | 1¼ million | 1.00 | 1930 | 961,174 | 1.00 |
| 1915 | 238,378 | 2.00 | 1931 | 537,815 | 1.00 |
| 1916 | 1½ million | 1.00 | 1932 | 537,994 | 1.00 |
| 1917 | 3¼ million | .75 | 1933 | 421,282 | 1.25 |
| 1918 | 4¼ million | .75 | 1934 | 384,505 | 1.25 |
| 1919 | 5¾ million | .75 | 1935 | 537,997 | 1.25 |
| 1920 | 2 million | .75 | 1936 | 972,094 | .75 |
| 1921 | 575,268 | 2.00 | 1936 Dot below date | 153,685 | 7.00 |

**Head of King George VI**

| Date | Amount Minted | Value | Date | Amount Minted | Value |
|------|---------------|-------|------|---------------|-------|
| 1937 | 2⅔ million | .65 | 1946 | 2¼ million | .65 |
| 1938 | 3¼ million | .65 | 1947 | 1½ million | .65 |
| 1939 | 3½ million | .65 | 1947 Maple leaf | 4⅓ million | .65 |
| 1940 | 9½ million | .65 | 1948 | 2½ million | .65 |
| 1941 | 6⅔ million | .65 | 1949 | 8 million | .65 |
| 1942 | 7 million | .65 | 1950 | 9⅔ million | .65 |
| 1943 | 13½ million | .65 | 1951 | 8¼ million | .65 |
| 1944 | 7¼ million | .65 | 1952 | 8¾ million | .65 |
| 1945 | 5¼ million | .65 | | | |

# Canada (continued)

## 171

| Obv. Type 1953-1964 | Rev. Type 1937- | Obv. Type 1965- | Commemorative Rev. 1967 | Commemorative Rev. 1973 |

### *Head of Queen Elizabeth II*

| Date | Amount Minted | Value | Date | Amount Minted | Value |
|---|---|---|---|---|---|
| 1953 | 11¼ million | .65 | 1970 | 10⅓ million | .25 |
| 1954 | 2⅓ million | .65 | 1971 | 48 million | .25 |
| 1955 | 9½ million | .65 | 1972 | 43¾ million | .25 |
| 1956 | 11¼ million | .65 | 1973 | 135 million | .25 |
| 1957 | 12⅓ million | .65 | 1974 | 192⅓ million | .25 |
| 1958 | 9¾ million | .65 | 1975 | 141 million | .25 |
| 1959 | 13½ million | .65 | 1976 | 86.8 million | .25 |
| 1960 | 22¾ million | .65 | 1977 | 99⅔ million | .25 |
| 1961 | 18¼ million | .65 | 1978 | 176½ million | .25 |
| 1962 | 29½ million | .65 | 1979 | 131 million | .25 |
| 1963 | 21¼ million | .65 | 1980 | 76 million | .25 |
| 1964 | 36½ million | .65 | 1981 | 131½ million | .25 |
| 1965 | 44¾ million | .65 | 1982 | 131 million | .25 |
| 1966 | 25⅓ million | .65 | 1983 | 167 million | .25 |
| 1967 | 48¾ million | .65 | 1984 | 119¼ million | .25 |
| 1968 Silver | 71½ million | .50 | 1985 | | .25 |
| 1968 Nickel | 88⅔ million | .25 | 1986 | | .25 |
| 1969 | 133 million | .25 | 1987 | | .25 |

## 50 CENTS

### *Head of Queen Victoria*

| Date | Amount Minted | Value | Date | Amount Minted | Value |
|------|---------------|-------|------|---------------|-------|
| 1870 | 450,000 | 15.00 | 1892 | 151,000 | 7.50 |
| 1871 | 200,000 | 20.00 | 1894 | 29,036 | 60.00 |
| 1871-H | 45,000 | 30.00 | 1898 | 100,000 | 7.50 |
| 1872-H | 80,000 | 12.50 | 1899 | 50,000 | 22.50 |
| 1881-H | 150,000 | 12.50 | 1900 | 118,000 | 12.50 |
| 1888 | 60,000 | 30.00 | 1901 | 80,000 | 12.50 |
| 1890-H | 20,000 | 200.00 | | | |

### *Head of King Edward VII*

| Date | Amount Minted | Value | Date | Amount Minted | Value |
|------|---------------|-------|------|---------------|-------|
| 1902 | 120,000 | 2.25 | 1907 | 300,000 | 2.50 |
| 1903-H | 140,000 | 3.00 | 1908 | 121,260 | 2.50 |
| 1904 | 60,000 | 25.00 | 1909 | 198,648 | 2.50 |
| 1905 | 40,000 | 25.00 | 1910 | 640,141 | 2.50 |
| 1906 | 350,000 | 2.50 | | | |

The valuations listed in this book closely approximate how much established coin dealers will pay for any material needed in their stock.

*Head of King George V*

| Date | Amount Minted | Value | Date | Amount Minted | Value |
|------|---------------|-------|------|---------------|-------|
| 1911 | 204,475 | **2.50** | 1920 | 559,521 | **2.00** |
| 1912 | 283,248 | **2.00** | 1921 | 176,793 | **2,500.00** |
| 1913 | 263,290 | **2.00** | 1929 | 228,021 | **2.00** |
| 1914 | 157,537 | **10.00** | 1931 | 57,581 | **2.50** |
| 1916 | 454,853 | **2.00** | 1932 | 19,213 | **20.00** |
| 1917 | 739,715 | **2.00** | 1934 | 38,435 | **2.50** |
| 1918 | 832,805 | **2.00** | 1936 | 38,550 | **2.50** |
| 1919 | 1 million | **2.00** | | | |

**Head of King George VI**

| Date | Amount Minted | Value | Date | Amount Minted | Value |
|---|---|---|---|---|---|
| 1937 | 192,016 | 2.00 | 1947 | 424,885 | 2.00 |
| 1938 | 192,018 | 2.00 | 1947 Maple leaf, straight 7. | | |
| 1939 | 287,976 | 2.00 | | 38,433 | 7.00 |
| 1940 | 2 million | 1.50 | 1947 Maple leaf, curved 7. | | |
| 1941 | 1⅔ million | 1.50 | | Part of above. | 400.00 |
| 1942 | 2 million | 1.50 | 1948 | 37,784 | 17.50 |
| 1943 | 3 million | 1.50 | 1949 | 858,991 | 2.00 |
| 1944 | 2½ million | 1.50 | 1950 | 2⅓ million | 2.00 |
| 1945 | 2 million | 1.50 | 1951 | 2½ million | 1.50 |
| 1946 | 950,235 | 1.50 | 1952 | 2½ million | 1.50 |

**(The valuations in this book are based on the coins being in G-VG condition, unless otherwise noted.)**

Obv. Type 1953-1964　First Rev. Type 1953-1958　Second Rev. Type 1959-　Commem. Rev. 1967　Obv. Type 1965-

**Head of Queen Elizabeth II**

## Head of Queen Elizabeth II

| Date | Amount Minted | Value | Date | Amount Minted | Value |
|------|---------------|-------|------|---------------|-------|
| 1953 | 1¾ million | 1.25 | 1971 | 2¼ million | .50 |
| 1954 | 506,305 | 1.25 | 1972 | 2½ million | .50 |
| 1955 | 753,511 | 1.25 | 1973 | 2½ million | .50 |
| 1956 | 1⅓ million | 1.25 | 1974 | 3½ million | .50 |
| 1957 | 2¼ million | 1.25 | 1975 | 3¾ million | .50 |
| 1958 | 3 million | 1.25 | 1976 | 3 million | .50 |
| 1959 | 3 million | 1.25 | 1977 | 709,939 | 1.00 |
| 1960 | 3½ million | 1.25 | 1978 | 3⅓ million | .50 |
| 1961 | 3½ million | 1.25 | 1979 | 3½ million | .50 |
| 1962 | 5¼ million | 1.25 | 1980 | 1½ million | .50 |
| 1963 | 8⅓ million | 1.25 | 1981 | 2¾ million | .50 |
| 1964 | 9⅓ million | 1.25 | 1982 | 2⅓ million | .50 |
| 1965 | 12⅔ million | 1.25 | 1983 | 2¼ million | .50 |
| 1966 | 7⅔ million | 1.25 | 1984 | 1¼ million | .50 |
| 1967 | 4¼ million | 1.25 | 1985 | | .50 |
| 1968 | Nickel, reduced size, 4 mil. | .50 | 1986 | | .50 |
| 1969 | 7⅓ million | .50 | 1987 | | .50 |
| 1970 | 2½ million | .50 | | | |

# SILVER DOLLARS

Commemorative
1935

Regular Issue
1936

Rev. Type
1935-1936

## Head of King George V

| Date | Amount Minted | Used | Unc | Date | Amount Minted | Used | Unc |
|------|---------------|------|-----|------|---------------|------|-----|
| 1935 | 428,120 | 4.00 | 20.00 | 1936 | 306,100 | 3.50 | 20.00 |

Obv. Type
1937-1952

Regular Rev.
1937-1952

Commemorative Rev.
1939

Commemorative Rev.
1949

### *Head of King George VI*

| Date | Amount Minted | Used | Unc | Date | Amount Minted | Used | Unc |
|------|--------------|------|-----|------|--------------|------|-----|
| 1937 | 241,002 | 3.50 | 25.00 | 1947 Maple leaf | | | |
| 1938 | 90,304 | 5.00 | 50.00 | | 21,135 | 70.00 | 200.00 |
| 1939 | 1⅓ million | 3.00 | 12.00 | 1948 | 18,780 | 250.00 | 400.00 |
| 1945 | 38,391 | 40.00 | 150.00 | 1949 | 672,298 | 4.00 | 20.00 |
| 1946 | 93,055 | 7.50 | 70.00 | 1950 | 261,002 | 4.00 | 15.00 |
| 1947 Blunt 7 | 65,595 | 20.00 | 80.00 | 1951 | 420,620 | 3.50 | 12.00 |
| 1947 Pointed 7 | | | | 1952 | 408,835 | 3.50 | 12.00 |
| | Part of above | 50.00 | 350.00 | | | | |

Obv. Type
1953-1964

Regular Rev. Type

Obv. Type
1965-

Commemorative Rev.
1958

Commemorative Rev.
1964

Commemorative Rev.
1967

Commemorative Rev.
1970

Commemorative Rev.
Nickel—1971

Commemorative Rev.
Silver—1971

Commemorative Rev.
Nickel—1973

Commemorative Rev.
Silver—1973

Commemorative Rev.
1974

Commemorative Rev.
Silver—1975

Commemorative Rev.
Silver—1976

Commemorative Rev.
Silver—1977

Note: From 1981 onwards, .500fine silver dollars exist in both proof-like (Unc) and, only as parts of sets, proof.

### Head of Queen Elizabeth II

| Date | Amount Minted | Used | Unc |
|------|---------------|------|-----|
| 1953 | 1 million | 3.00 | 7.00 |
| 1954 | 242,815 | 4.00 | 9.00 |
| 1955 | 274,810 | 4.00 | 9.00 |
| 1956 | 209,092 | 4.50 | 9.00 |
| 1957 | 496,389 | 3.00 | 5.00 |
| 1958 | 3 million | 3.00 | 9.00 |
| 1959 | 1½ million | 3.00 | 5.00 |
| 1960 | 1½ million | 3.00 | 5.00 |
| 1961 | 1¼ million | 3.00 | 5.00 |
| 1962 | 1¾ million | 3.00 | 5.00 |
| 1963 | 4¼ million | 3.00 | 5.00 |
| 1964 | 7¼ million | 3.00 | 5.00 |
| 1965 | 10¾ million | 3.00 | 5.00 |
| 1966 | 10 million | 3.00 | 5.00 |
| 1967 | 7 million | 3.00 | 5.00 |
| 1968 Nickel, reduced size, 6 mil. | | | 1.00 |
| 1969 | 4¾ million | | 1.00 |
| 1970 | 4¼ million | | 1.00 |
| 1971 Nickel 4¼ million | | | 1.00 |
| 1971 Silver, proof-like, cased, 555,564 | | | 5.00 |
| 1972 Nickel 2⅔ million | | | 1.00 |
| 1972 Silver, proof-like, cased, 350,019 | | | 5.00 |
| 1973 Nickel 3¼ million | | | 1.00 |
| 1973 Silver, proof-like, cased, 709,670 | | | 5.00 |
| 1974 Nickel 2¾ million | | | 1.00 |
| 1974 Silver, proof-like, cased, 977,644 | | | 5.00 |
| 1975 Nickel 3¼ million | | | 1.00 |
| 1975 Silver, proof-like, cased 931,000 | | | 5.00 |
| 1976 Nickel 2½ million | | | 1.00 |
| 1976 Silver, proof-like cased, 483,722 | | | 5.00 |
| 1977 Nickel 1⅓ million | | | 1.00 |
| 1977 Silver, proof-like, cased, 744,848 | | | 5.00 |

| Date | Amount Minted | Used | Unc |
|------|---------------|------|-----|
| 1978 Nickel 3 million | | | 1.00 |
| 1978 Silver, proof-like, cased, 709,602 | | | 5.00 |
| 1979 Nickel 2½ million | | | 1.00 |
| 1979 Silver, proof-like, cased, 826,695 | | | 5.00 |
| 1980 Nickel 3⅓ million | | | 1.00 |
| 1980 Silver, proof-like, cased, 539,617 | | | 10.00 |
| 1981 Nickel 2¾ million | | | 1.00 |
| 1981 Silver, proof-like, cased, 699,494 | | | 10.00 |
| 1982 Nickel 1 million | | | 1.00 |
| 1982 Nickel, Constitution 9¾ million | | | 1.00 |
| 1982 Silver, proof-like, cased, 903,888 | | | 7.00 |
| 1983 Nickel 2¼ million | | | 1.00 |
| 1983 Silver, proof-like, cased, 159,400 | | | 5.00 |
| 1984 Nickel, 1¼ million | | | 1.00 |
| 1984 Nickel, Cartier 7 million | | | 1.00 |
| 1984 Silver, proof-like, cased, 133,610 | | | 4.00 |
| 1985 Nickel | | | 1.00 |
| 1985 Silver, proof-like, cased, | | | 4.00 |
| 1986 Nickel | | | 1.00 |
| 1986 Silver, proof-like, cased, | | | 7.00 |
| 1987 Nickel | | | 1.00 |
| 1987 Silver, proof-like, cased, | | | 6.00 |

# Olympic Commemorative Coins

The same obverse, the head of Queen Elizabeth II, appears on all of the coins. The valuations are for coins in brilliant, new condition.

### SERIES I, 1973

| Denomination | Date | Reverse Design | |
|--------------|------|----------------|---|
| 5 Dollars | 1973 | Map of North America | 5.50 |
| 5 Dollars | 1973 | Kingston Skyline | 5.50 |
| 10 Dollars | 1973 | Map of the World | 11.00 |
| 10 Dollars | 1973 | Montreal Skyline | 11.00 |
| 4-piece Uncirculated Set, cased | | | 32.50 |
| 4-piece Proof Set, cased | | | 40.00 |

## SERIES II, 1974

| Denomination | Date | Reverse Design | Value |
|---|---|---|---|
| 5 Dollars | 1974 | Athlete with Olympic Torch | 5.50 |
| 5 Dollars | 1974 | The Laurel Wreath | 5.50 |
| 10 Dollars | 1974 | The Greek God, Zeus | 11.00 |
| 10 Dollars | 1974 | The Temple of Zeus | 11.00 |
| 4-piece Uncirculated Set, cased | | | 32.50 |
| 4-piece Proof Set, cased | | | 40.00 |

## SERIES III, 1974

| 5 Dollars | 1974 | Canoeing | 5.50 |
|---|---|---|---|
| 5 Dollars | 1974 | Rowing | 5.50 |
| 10 Dollars | 1974 | Cyclists | 11.00 |
| 10 Dollars | 1974 | Lacrosse | 11.00 |
| 4-piece Uncirculated Set, cased | | | 32.50 |
| 4-piece Proof Set, cased | | | 40.00 |

## SERIES IV, 1975

| 5 Dollars | 1975 | Marathon | 5.50 |
|---|---|---|---|
| 5 Dollars | 1975 | Javelin | 5.50 |
| 10 Dollars | 1975 | Hurdles | 11.00 |
| 10 Dollars | 1975 | Shotput | 11.00 |
| 4-piece Uncirculated Set, cased | | | 32.50 |
| 4 piece Proof Set, cased | | | 40.00 |

## SERIES V, 1975

| 5 Dollars | 1975 | Swimming | 5.50 |
|---|---|---|---|
| 5 Dollars | 1975 | Diving | 5.50 |
| 10 Dollars | 1975 | Sailing | 11.00 |
| 10 Dollars | 1975 | Kayak | 11.00 |
| 4-piece Uncirculated Set, cased | | | 32.50 |
| 4-piece Proof Set, cased | | | 40.00 |

## SERIES VI, 1976

| 5 Dollars | 1976 | Fencing | 5.50 |
|---|---|---|---|
| 5 Dollars | 1976 | Boxing | 5.50 |
| 10 Dollars | 1976 | Soccer | 11.00 |
| 10 Dollars | 1976 | Field hockey | 11.00 |
| 4-piece Uncirculated Set, cased | | | 32.50 |
| 4-piece Proof Set, cased | | | 40.00 |

## SERIES VII, 1976

| 5 Dollars | 1976 | Olympic Village | 5.50 |
|---|---|---|---|
| 5 Dollars | 1976 | Olympic Flame | 5.50 |
| 10 Dollars | 1976 | Olympic Stadium | 11.00 |
| 10 Dollars | 1976 | Olympic Velodrome | 11.00 |
| 4-piece Uncirculated Set, cased | | | 32.50 |
| 4-piece Proof Set, cased | | | 40.00 |

## CALGARY WINTER OLYMPICS, 1988

| | | | |
|---|---|---|---|
| 20 Dollars | 1985 | Downhill Skier | 17.50 |
| 20 Dollars | 1985 | Speed Skater | 17.50 |
| 20 Dollars | 1986 | Biathlon | 17.50 |
| 20 Dollars | 1986 | Hockey | 17.50 |
| 20 Dollars | 1986 | Cross Country Skier | 17.50 |
| 20 Dollars | 1986 | Free Style Skier | 17.50 |

# GOLD COINS

## Canadian Types

## Head of King George V

### 5 DOLLARS

| Date | Amount Minted | Value |
|---|---|---|
| 1912 | 165,680 | 150.00 |
| 1913 | 98,832 | 150.00 |
| 1914 | 31,122 | 450.00 |

### 10 DOLLARS

| | | |
|---|---|---|
| 1912 | 74,759 | 400.00 |
| 1913 | 149,232 | 400.00 |
| 1914 | 140,068 | 450.00 |

## Head of Queen Elizabeth II

### 5 DOLLARS

| | | |
|---|---|---|
| 1982 | 246,000 | 30.00 |
| 1983 | 198,000 | 30.00 |
| 1984 | 262,000 | 30.00 |
| 1985 | | 30.00 |
| 1986 | | 30.00 |

### 10 DOLLARS

| | | |
|---|---|---|
| 1982 | 184,000 | 85.00 |
| 1983 | 192,000 | 85.00 |
| 1984 | 313,000 | 85.00 |
| 1985 | | 85.00 |
| 1986 | | 85.00 |

### 20 DOLLARS

| | | |
|---|---|---|
| 1967 | 337,512 proofs | 150.00 |

## 50 DOLLARS

Maple Leaf Gold Bullion Coins

| Date | Amount Minted | Value | Date | Amount Minted | Value |
|---|---|---|---|---|---|
| 1979 | 1 million | 375.00 | 1983 | 776,000 | 375.00 |
| 1980 | 1 ¼ million | 375.00 | 1984 | 1,002,000 | 375.00 |
| 1981 | 863,000 | 375.00 | 1985 | | 375.00 |
| 1982 | 883,000 | 375.00 | 1986 | | 375.00 |

## 100 DOLLARS

| | | | | |
|---|---|---|---|---|
| 1976 27 mm. Olympics (.585) | | | 1982 Constitution | |
| 572,387 proofs | **80.00** | | 200,000 proofs | **150.00** |
| 1976 25 mm. Olympics | | | 1983 St. John's 82,000 proofs | **200.00** |
| 335,779 proofs | **125.00** | | 1984 Cartier 67,000 proofs | **170.00** |
| 1977 Jubilee 180,396 proofs | **250.00** | | 1985 National Parks | |
| 1978 Geese 200,000 proofs | **150.00** | | 200,000 proofs | **200.00** |
| 1979 Children 250,000 proofs | **150.00** | | 1986 Peace proofs | **180.00** |
| 1980 Eskimo 300,000 proofs | **150.00** | | 1987 Calgary Olympics | |
| 1981 National Anthem | | | Proofs | **175.00** |
| 102,000 proofs | **150.00** | | | |

# English Type Sovereigns or Pounds

Normal type Gold 1 Pound pieces of English design, struck at the Ottawa Mint and with the "C" mint mark on the ground under the horse. The coins from 1908 through 1910 are with the head of Edward VII and those from 1911 through 1919 are with the head of George V.

| | | | | | |
|---|---|---|---|---|---|
| 1 Pound 1908-C | 636 | **750.00** | 1 Pound 1914-C | 14,891 | **150.00** |
| 1 Pound 1909-C | 16,273 | **150.00** | 1 Pound 1916-C | 6,111 | **Rare** |
| 1 Pound 1910-C | 28,012 | **125.00** | 1 Pound 1917-C | 58,845 | **85.00** |
| 1 Pound 1911-C | 256,946 | **80.00** | 1 Pound 1918-C | 106,516 | **85.00** |
| 1 Pound 1913-C | 3,715 | **250.00** | 1 Pound 1919-C | 135,889 | **85.00** |

# Newfoundland
## (complete from 1865 to 1947)

### LARGE CENTS
#### *Head of Queen Victoria*

| Date | Amount Minted | Value | Date | Amount Minted | Value |
|---|---|---|---|---|---|
| 1865 | 240,000 | .30 | 1885 | 40,000 | 4.50 |
| 1872-H | 200,000 | .30 | 1888 | 50,000 | 3.75 |
| 1873 | 200,025 | .30 | 1890 | 200,000 | .30 |
| 1876-H | 200,000 | .30 | 1894 | 200,000 | .30 |
| 1880 | 400,000 | .30 | 1896 | 200,000 | .30 |

#### *Head of King Edward VII*

| Date | Amount Minted | Value | Date | Amount Minted | Value |
|---|---|---|---|---|---|
| 1904-H | 100,000 | .75 | 1909 | 200,000 | .30 |
| 1907 | 200,000 | .30 | | | |

### Head of King George V

| Date | Amount Minted | Value |
|------|---------------|-------|
| 1913 | 400,000 | .15 |
| 1917-C | 702,350 | .15 |
| 1919-C | 300,000 | .15 |
| 1920-C | 302,184 | .15 |
| 1929 | 300,000 | .15 |
| 1936 | 300,000 | .15 |

## SMALL CENTS

### Head of King George VI

| Date | Amount Minted | Value | Date | Amount Minted | Value |
|------|---------------|-------|------|---------------|-------|
| 1938 | 500,000 | .10 | 1943-C | 1¼ million | .10 |
| 1940 | 300,000 | .40 | 1944-C | 1⅓ million | .10 |
| 1941-C | 827,662 | .10 | 1947-C | 313,772 | .10 |
| 1942 | 2 million | .10 | | | |

## SILVER 5 CENTS

### Head of Queen Victoria

| Date | Amount Minted | Value |
|------|---------------|-------|
| 1865 | 80,000 | 6.00 |
| 1870 | 40,000 | 6.50 |
| 1872-H | 40,000 | 6.00 |
| 1873 | 44,260 | 6.50 |
| 1873-H | Part of above | 100.00 |
| 1876-H | 20,000 | 10.00 |
| 1880 | 40,000 | 6.50 |
| 1881 | 40,000 | 3.75 |
| 1882-H | 60,000 | 3.00 |
| 1885 | 16,000 | 20.00 |
| 1888 | 40,000 | 3.75 |
| 1890 | 160,000 | 2.50 |
| 1894 | 160,000 | 2.50 |
| 1896 | 400,000 | 1.50 |

### Head of King Edward VII

| Date | Amount Minted | Value |
|------|---------------|-------|
| 1903 | 100,00 | .50 |
| 1904-H | 100,000 | .50 |
| 1908 | 400,000 | .50 |

### Head of King George V

| Date | Amount Minted | Value |
|------|---------------|-------|
| 1912 | 300,000 | .50 |
| 1917-C | 300,319 | .50 |
| 1919-C | 100,844 | .50 |
| 1929 | 300,000 | .50 |

### Head of King George VI

| | | |
|------|---------|-------|
| 1936 | 100,000 | .30 |
| 1940-C | 200,000 | .30 |
| 1941-C | 612,641 | .30 |
| 1942-C | 298,348 | .50 |
| 1943-C | 351,666 | .30 |
| 1944-C | 286,504 | .30 |
| 1945-C | 203,828 | .30 |
| 1946-C | 2,041 | 75.00 |
| 1947-C | 38,400 | .50 |

## 10 CENTS

### Head of Queen Victoria

| | | |
|------|---------|-------|
| 1865 | 80,000 | 2.75 |
| 1870 | 30,000 | 25.00 |
| 1872-H | 40,000 | 2.25 |
| 1873 | 23,614 | 3.00 |
| 1876-H | 10,000 | 5.50 |
| 1880 | 10,000 | 5.50 |
| 1882-H | 20,000 | 1.50 |
| 1885 | 8,000 | 11.00 |
| 1888 | 30,000 | 1.75 |
| 1890 | 100,000 | .75 |
| 1894 | 100,000 | .75 |
| 1896 | 230,000 | .60 |

### Head of King Edward VII

| | | |
|--------|---------|-----|
| 1903 | 100,000 | .60 |
| 1904-H | 100,000 | .60 |

### Head of King George V

| | | |
|--------|---------|-----|
| 1912 | 150,000 | .60 |
| 1917-C | 250,805 | .60 |
| 1919-C | 54,342 | .60 |

*Head of King George VI*

| Date | Amount Minted | Value | Date | Amount Minted | Value |
|------|---------------|-------|------|---------------|-------|
| 1938 | 100,000 | .45 | 1944-C | 151,471 | .45 |
| 1940 | 100,000 | .45 | 1945-C | 175,833 | .45 |
| 1941-C | 483,630 | .45 | 1946-C | 38,400 | 50.00 |
| 1942-C | 292,736 | .45 | 1947-C | 61,988 | 1.00 |
| 1943-C | 104,706 | .45 | | | |

## 20 CENTS

*Head of Queen Victoria*

| Date | Amount Minted | Value | Date | Amount Minted | Value |
|------|---------------|-------|------|---------------|-------|
| 1865 | 100,000 | 1.25 | 1885 | 40,000 | 1.25 |
| 1870 | 50,000 | 1.75 | 1888 | 75,000 | 1.25 |
| 1872-H | 90,000 | 1.25 | 1890 | 100,000 | 1.25 |
| 1873 | 45,797 | 1.50 | 1894 | 100,000 | 1.25 |
| 1876-H | 50,000 | 1.50 | 1896 | 125,000 | 1.25 |
| 1880 | 30,000 | 1.50 | 1899 | 125,000 | 1.25 |
| 1881 | 60,000 | 1.25 | 1900 | 125,000 | 1.25 |
| 1882-H | 100,000 | 1.25 | | | |

*Head of King Edward VII*

| Date | Amount Minted | Value |
|------|---------------|-------|
| 1904-H | 75,000 | 1.50 |